THE ILLUSTRATED BOOK OF
POKER
AND POKER PLAYING

THE ILLUSTRATED BOOK OF
POKER
AND POKER PLAYING

TREVOR SIPPETS

HERMES
HOUSE

This edition is published by Hermes House

Hermes House is an imprint of Anness Publishing Ltd
Hermes House, 88–89 Blackfriars Road,
London SE1 8HA
tel. 020 7401 2077; fax 020 7633 9499;
www.annesspublishing.com

Anness Publishing has a new picture agency outlet for
images for publishing, promotions or advertising. Please
visit our website www.practicalpictures.com for more
information.

ETHICAL TRADING POLICY
Because of our ongoing ecological investment programme,
you, as our customer, can have the pleasure and
reassurance of knowing that a tree is being cultivated on
your behalf to naturally replace the materials used to make
the book you are holding. For further information about
this scheme, go to www.annesspublishing.com/trees

A CIP catalogue record for this book is available from the
British Library.

Designed and produced for Anness Publishing by
the bridgewater book company ltd.

Publisher: Joanna Lorenz
Editorial Director: Helen Sudell
Project Manager: Polita Caaveiro
Designer: Simon Goggin
Art Director: Lisa McCormick
Photography: Andrew Perris
Editorial Reader: Jay Thundercliffe
Production Controller: Lee Sargent

10 9 8 7 6 5 4 3 2 1

CONTENTS

INTRODUCTION

In one form or another, poker and its antecedents have been played for over 500 years. The game is such a part of western culture, at least, that many poker-related phrases have found their way into everyday language. The uninitiated may regard it as just a card game, albeit one that particularly engages people who possess an innate desire to gamble. Yet to anyone who has ever played poker, such a basic definition of this challenging and often rewarding pursuit cannot begin to tell the whole story. Indeed, some players regard poker as less of a game and more a way of life. Now, in the early stages of the 21st century, those elements of poker that have contributed to its longevity are being discovered by a new generation of players every day. All over the world, newcomers are learning how to bluff, bet and rake in the chips, as well as experiencing the heartbreak associated with losing a large pot courtesy of a bad beat.

The rapid increase in the popularity of poker and its elevation from card game to cultural phenomenon has been a notable feature of the past decade. Televised poker tournaments have helped generate more interest in the game than ever before, with professional players and tournament winners now frequently acquiring celebrity status on the back of such media exposure.

Magazine articles, books and advertising continue to feed the public's renewed appetite for the game. While poker has often been characterized as glamorous, many stars from the worlds of film, television and sport are keen players whose endorsement helps bolster that image. Poker has simply never been more fashionable.

Helping to keep it that way are the online casinos which, since the launch of PlanetPoker in 1998, have become multimillion-dollar businesses attracting the interest of serious corporate players. ParadisePoker, an early competitor in the market, was bought for US$297.5m by Sportingbet Plc in October 2004 and its share price, quoted on the London Stock Exchange's Alternative Investment Market (AIM), soon increased by 375 per cent. This commercial interest is readily understood given the fact that in April 2005, according to UK bookmakers Ladbrokes, around US$180m was being wagered at online poker tables every day. Interactive gambling online is expected to generate annual turnover of US$100 billion and pre-tax profits of US$11 billion by 2010. There are now hundreds of online sites offering convenient and instant access to a poker game from the comfort of home, allowing hundreds of thousands of players to exercise their skill and judgement simultaneously, around the clock.

PLAYER E

Right: In this book, rules and strategies are clearly explained and regularly illustrated with diagrams that show example poker hands, both on and off the table, for greater understanding. From simple to complex, you will be guided through a wide variety of poker scenarios step-by-step.

Right: Learning poker is a challenging but fulfilling pastime and one that can become a passion for many players.

The one obstacle hampering projected economic growth in online gaming, however, is the legislation enacted in the United States that restricts American financial institutions from processing transactions to Internet gaming operations. The Unlawful Internet Gambling Enforcement Act of October 2006 does not prohibit online poker as such, but it effectively reduces the incentive to play by making it unlawful for home-based Americans to access their online gaming accounts to make or receive payments. Since the United States accounted for just over half of all online poker players when the act became law, the leading companies in the market are expected to consolidate their positions to cope with the inevitable short-term decline in demand for their product. As more companies chase fewer customers, so mergers and acquisitions are also predicted to occur while attention turns to expanding the market in Europe and the rest of the world.

Despite the legal situation in the United States, the impact of televised poker and online gaming has been to revive interest in playing poker socially, whether in clubs or at home, as the game continues to shed its sometimes dubious reputation in favour of growing respectability. More women are playing, taking advantage of the wealth of online opportunities to practise their skills before tackling opponents away from the virtual poker environment. Live poker may still be dominated by men in numerical terms but latest estimates suggest that women represent 40 per cent of the online market. It seems likely that this interest will soon be reflected at the poker tables in casinos and clubs; the ability to play skilful poker is not uniquely a masculine trait.

Having located poker in a contemporary context, the aim of this book is to explain the many aspects of the game that have helped to establish it as one of the more enduring of human pastimes. The opening chapters will focus on the essential knowledge required to enable anyone to play poker with a degree of confidence, on the assumption that the reader has little or no actual playing experience. From the deal to the showdown, there will be explanations of how to play, how to bet, and how to distinguish a potential winning hand from a likely loser. Other important facets to be covered are simple tactical play, betting strategies and the elements involved in bluffing opponents. Since poker is clearly replete with a colourful vocabulary all its own, the terminology will also be explained.

Later chapters will develop some of the basic concepts and highlight more sophisticated elements of poker play with a view to helping regular players improve their game. The difference between playing in tournaments and playing cash games will be considered, along with the contrasting features of fixed-limit, pot-limit and no-limit poker. These stylistic differences present any serious poker player with a wealth of options when it comes to choosing which game to play and for how much. An appreciation of their impact on any poker game is especially important now that the boom in online poker has extended its reach into so many homes.

Illustrations, diagrams and comments throughout are intended to supplement the text and underline key points regarding play. Finally, a comprehensive glossary of poker terms, odds tables and a guide to other published work worthy of consideration is included for reference.

THE HISTORY OF POKER

As the first decade of the new millennium gathers pace, the status of poker as the game of choice among card players worldwide remains intact. Crucially, poker's image has also undergone a transformation. Television schedules are liberally sprinkled with poker programming offering viewers a chance to see the world's best players, many of whom are young and precociously talented, demonstrating their skills at the table. The result of this recent development is that big-screen representations of the game have also been updated. Poker-playing scenes set in Wild West saloon bars are now rivalled by luxurious settings for the game in which even James Bond, as depicted in *Casino Royale* (2006), does his bit to bolster the popularity of Texas Hold 'em. That poker should feature in such a high-profile cinema release underlines the enduring appeal of a game that has a rich and colourful history like no other.

Right: In the early years of the 21st century, poker has emerged as the world's most popular card game following a massive boost in interest stimulated by television and the Internet. After 200 years of evolution, it now enjoys a much more positive image as the game's association with the lawlessness of the Wild West and the Mafia-run Las Vegas casinos finally begins to wane. Today, poker is big business and has an air of legitimacy that should ensure that the stigma previously associated with playing the game remains a thing of the past.

ORIGINS OF POKER

Determining the exact origins of poker has proved an elusive task for those researching the history of the game. It is widely accepted that poker as it is played today developed rapidly in the United States during the 18th and 19th centuries, following the influx of immigrants seeking work and fresh opportunities in the New World. In his book *An Exposure of the Arts and Miseries of Gambling*, published in 1834, author Jonathan H. Green describes the rules of poker, the so-called 'cheating game'. This refers to a game involving a deck of just 20 cards that had overtaken three-card monte in terms of popularity as a betting medium, ironically because it was considered less prone to manipulation by 'card sharps'. Although he did not identify it as poker, this same game was also described by English actor Joseph Cowell in 1829. He had witnessed it being played in New Orleans and was aware of its popularity on the Mississippi riverboats, which effectively transported it through Louisiana and into the rest of the country.

The European influence

Card games had been growing in popularity throughout France since the 15th century, while in Germany a similar game named pochen or pochspiel held sway. However, the French connection is thought to provide the most tangible link in the evolution of poker, as the colonials who settled in Canada and New Orleans imported a gambling and bluffing game named poque. Both games were played with a deck of either 32 or 36 cards, and winning hands were limited to pairs, three of a kind and four of a kind. Elsewhere in Europe, the Spanish game primero, dating back to 1526, is thought to have been an influence on poque and pochen, although, like France's brelan and the English game of brag, players only received three cards with which to make a hand. Italy played host to il frusso, which incorporated much the same elements as the other European games.

However, though it is impossible to prove beyond doubt, all may owe their origins to a Persian game called Âs Nas. Similar to five-card stud poker, Âs Nas was played with either 20 or 25 cards, depending on

Above: The French connection is thought to be the most tangible link in the evolution of poker. French colonials who settled in Canada and New Orleans imported a gambling and bluffing game called poque. However, some people believe the game may be descended from the German game of pochen, the English game of brag or even the Persian game of Âs Nas.

Left: When gambling fell out of favour in frontier towns such as New Orleans, poker was forced onto the paddle-steamers that chugged along the Mississippi river. Gaming on the paddle steamers travelling the Mississippi effectively transported games such as poker through Louisiana and the rest of America.

the number of players. Yet, although the cards for playing this game were known to exist in the 16th century, no mention is made of the game until 1890, some years after poker itself was already established. Whatever the provenance of poker, it is the impact of post-18th-century American culture on the game that has accelerated its development into the phenomenally popular diversion known today.

Playing cards

The first playing cards were introduced into Europe in the 14th century by the Saracens and Moors, their origins being traced back to 10th-century China and, latterly, Egypt. These early cards were made of thin slices of ivory or wood and frequently featured colourful, hand-painted designs. As such, they were generally the preserve of the wealthy and it was only with the development of printing from woodcuts and the subsequent invention of the printing press that cheaper decks could be produced. The French influence in North America popularized card games, leading to further evolution in card design as Americans began to make their own modifications in around 1800. These included the addition of indices in the corners (the identifying marks placed in the cards' borders or corners) and double-headed court cards for easier recognition, patterned rather than plain backs as well as rounded corners and varnished surfaces to help reduce wear and tear.

Below: A selection of historic cards showing that the basic design of the court cards and the suits has remained unchanged for centuries. From the left: 16th-century French king of spades, 17th-century queen of hearts, German double-headed king of clubs from 1860, a jack of diamonds from Belgium, 1811.

THE SUITS
♦ ♣ ♥ ♠

The suits of clubs, diamonds, hearts and spades are believed to have been standardized by the French, who also introduced the representations of royal court figures for the higher-value cards. Although refined in detail, owing to improvements in printing methods, the basic design of the court cards has remained unchanged for at least 200 years. Traditional Latin and German playing cards feature variations on the theme of the suits. Spanish and Italian playing cards, for example, feature coins, cups, swords and batons while Germanic designs incorporate hearts, leaves, bells and acorns.

Above: A set of three cards showing the modern double-headed court cards of the king, queen and jack. Modern playing cards carry index labels on opposite corners to facilitate identifying the cards when they overlap. Round corners were introduced to eliminate the problem of wear and tear resulting from traditional square corners.

THE AMERICAN GAME

It was not until after the end of the American Civil War in 1865 that poker could be said to have shrugged off the European influences that shaped its development. By 1875, with the 52-card deck widely used and jokers introduced, the game had become a prominent facet of American culture. The 50 years leading up to that point had seen the game move from its original base in the Mississippi delta to the frontier towns of the Wild West and then on to California as a gold rush took hold in 1849. However, five-card draw and five-card stud poker were not as popular with some prospectors as games such as roulette, which offered a quicker route to riches compared to a card game that required patience and a little application in order to earn any reward. Despite the game not proving to everyone's taste as well as meeting opposition from various prohibitionist movements of the 19th century, poker continued to be played by those Americans who accepted risk and speculation as as a natural feature of everyday life.

New Orleans

The first casino to open in the United States was owned by John Davis, whose establishment in New Orleans fed the public desire for gambling by remaining open 24 hours a day. Food, alcohol, dancing girls and popular games like faro and roulette were all part of the casino experience for Davis's clients. Such was the success of his venture that more casinos soon followed, creating a reputation for the 'Big Easy' as the country's gambling capital. This cultural shift made New Orleans attractive to various full-time card players and professional cheats, both groups seeking to exploit the naive and the gullible. The waterfront area, known as 'the swamp', became a virtual no-go area for the law as the gamblers and cheats policed themselves. Those who either won more than seemed polite or who were otherwise exposed as frauds knew that they ran the risk of instant summary justice from their victims, sympathy for their plight being in short supply.

Above: A woman driving a wagon in New Orleans in 1900. The city became the first in America to host a casino when owner John Davis opened a 24-hour gambling venue in 1922. Very soon the 'Big Easy' as it was nicknamed, became renowned for attracting gamblers. An attempt was made to outlaw gambling in Louisiana in 1911 but this was never seriously enforced and New Orleans continued to benefit economically from the tourists who came to try their luck at the gaming tables.

Right: John Doyle hosts a poker party at his Arizona ranch with Judge Brown and Professor Burrison in 1887, illustrating how the popularity of the game had spread north and west from the Mississippi delta area where it initially developed.

Riverboat gambling

The casinos of New Orleans drew many more visitors to the city, boosting its economy and that of the surrounding area. As the riverboats of the Mississippi, the Missouri and the Ohio contributed to the commercial growth of the region, so they provided the means for the professional gamblers to ply their trade and seek fresh markets of their own. This was no easy task since an increasing number of towns were already passing legislation to outlaw various gambling practices in a bid to drive them away. Vicksburg in Mississippi took such action as early as 1835, but the thousands of multi-decked paddle-steamers remained a haven for the poker players and card sharps, who often dressed in fine, fashionable clothes to offset their negative image.

By this time poker had distanced itself from its precursors with players having to negotiate just one round of betting based upon the strength of their five-card hand. Initially, with decks consisting of only 20 cards, the game was limited to four players and there was no draw, the mechanism which enables players to exchange a card in their hand with a fresh

card from the deck. Ever mindful of an opportunity to tip the odds in their favour, card professionals gradually started to implement the use of 52-card decks to play poker and, within a couple of decades, this game had almost completely eclipsed the 20-card version. A bigger deck meant that more players could be accommodated during a game and the introduction of the draw gave them a chance to improve their hand. The price to be paid was an extra betting round, the impact of which was to increase the levels of skill and judgement required to win.

POKER IN THE WILD WEST

The global success of the Western as a Hollywood film genre, albeit one which conveyed a slightly romanticized view of America's past, is obviously the major reason why poker is so often associated with the Wild West. Although sometimes peripheral to the action, the game features in countless saloon-bar scenes, accurately representing its popularity in the staging posts, mining towns and cattle-transit stations of the time. Less accurate are the portrayals of the West's legendary characters whose heroic deeds were exaggerated, if not entirely fabricated, for the entertainment of avid newspaper readers on the East Coast. Writers such as E.Z.C. Judson, publisher of a weekly sensationalist magazine called *Ned Buntline's Own*, helped create the enduring myths about the West and its adventurers. As a result, towns such as Deadwood and Tombstone became more famous for the fatal resolution of betting disputes than for the mineral riches that led to their existence.

Life as a professional gambler was fraught with danger since so many potential sore losers possessed impulsive natures and firearms. Indeed, the invention of the small Derringer pistol, inaccurate beyond six feet, stemmed from the need for gamblers to keep an ace up their sleeve, figuratively speaking. To offset the danger, those with a penchant for a gamble often ran saloons or brothels in order to provide a regular income and, given the prevailing morality of the times, to legitimize their lifestyle. In 1849 the fabled Gold Rush diverted attention further west as prospectors headed for California. Such was the influx of people to the area that San Francisco very soon overtook New Orleans as the nation's biggest gambling centre.

Legality and morality

The call for gambling to be outlawed has been heard regularly throughout history, with gamblers viewed as both morally bankrupt and in need of protection from their perceived weakness. Certainly, bearing in mind that poker was originally called 'the cheating game', it is understandable why those who insisted on playing were so often cautioned by others of a more temperate nature. The sharp practices of the so-called professional gamblers were targeted in western frontier towns towards the end of the 19th century, with certain games either made illegal or strictly controlled. Although few of these laws were ever enforced, a total ban was introduced in the early 20th century in several states.

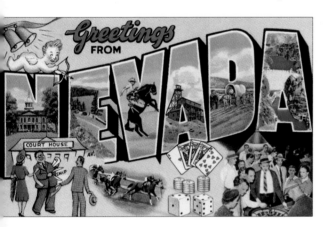

Above: Picture postcard from Nevada, 1941. Along with many other states, Nevada's legislators had sought to ban gambling. In 1931, a ruling from California's attorney general that draw poker was a game of skill and should not be subject to anti-gambling law allowed Nevada to relax its prohibitive stance. In turn, Las Vegas developed into the gambling capital of the world.

Right: Robert Mitchum in *Blood on the Moon*, 1948, looking on as a game of five-card stud develops in a scene that typifies poker's representation in the Western. In 1968, Mitchum starred with Dean Martin in *Five Card Stud*, another Western which, as the title implies, centred on events at the poker table.

Above: Prospectors in a gold mining town in Nevada. Gold was discovered at Goldfield, Nevada, in 1902 and six months later there was a bustling frontier town on the site. Note that there are a hotel, theatre, bank, jewellery store, and a horse market already established. Goldfield was one of the last mining boom towns.

Left: James Butler 'Wild Bill' Hickok, pictured in 1873 as he appeared when performing in one of William 'Buffalo Bill' Cody's Wild West shows. The frontiersman and famed marksman also spent time enforcing the law as a US marshal before being killed in a Deadwood saloon bar by Jack McCall while playing poker in 1876. The cards he was holding at the time – black aces and eights – have since been known as the 'Dead Man's Hand'.

By 1988, Nevada and New Jersey were the only states where gambling was permitted, though the situation has changed radically to the extent that only two, Utah and Hawaii, now actively prohibit gambling.

Apart from the practice being restricted to adults, opportunities to gamble legally are now available to most in the developed world. Yet the varied legislation applicable across different American states, primarily aimed at prohibiting organized gambling, has created a confusing picture that currently renders a friendly game of poker at home potentially illegal. More dramatically, though Americans constitute the majority of online poker players, this activity has effectively been rendered illegal in the US following the successful passage of the Unlawful Internet Gaming Act in October 2006. Various interpretations of the 1961 American Wire Act, originally introduced to prevent racketeers betting by telegraph, have often been made to suggest that online gambling is illegal. Under the terms of the new law, it is now illegal for American banks, credit card companies and other financial institutions to engage in transactions with online gaming companies. As a consequence, online poker players based in the US are now prevented from depositing and withdrawing sums from their online poker accounts.

EARLY RANKING OF HANDS
♦ ♣ ♥ ♠

Throughout poker's evolution the ranking of hands was not as clearly defined as it is today. The introduction of the straight – five cards of differing suits in a numerical sequence, for example 6, 7, 8, 9, 10 – and the flush – five non-sequential cards of the same suit – created problems for poker philosophers of the time. Confusion reigned regarding the validity of these hands and, even when accepted, their value in relation to other hands did not always reflect their true merit in terms of probability. Traditionalists who had grown used to the concept of four aces representing the premium hand found it difficult to acknowledge that the odds against securing a sequence of five cards in the same suit – a straight flush (see below) – were greater, rendering the hand more valuable.

20TH-CENTURY POKER

Draw poker and five-card stud remained the predominant variations well into the 20th century, but to these staples of the genre was added the communal card game, of which Texas Hold 'em is currently the most popular example. Games such as wild widow and spit in the ocean embodied the idea of a common card being dealt and were popular during the 1920s. Another development was the concept of high-low poker in which the pot, the term for the total stakes bet during the playing of each hand, was divided equally between the highest and lowest hands still standing at the time of the showdown, which is the point in the game when the betting has concluded and players reveal their cards to determine the winner. A further development was lowball, which was simply a draw poker game in which the lowest hand, not the highest, took the pot.

By the 1930s, a variation on the theme of stud poker had emerged, with players being dealt seven cards rather than five, a development which, once again, increased the number of betting rounds to be withstood before the conclusion of each hand. The possibility of players securing stronger poker hands using five of the seven cards available to them, working in tandem with more betting opportunities, led to its growth in popularity. It soon eclipsed five-card stud which, by comparison with this relative newcomer, was perceived as a sterile and much less dynamic game. A lowball version of seven-card stud, usually referred to as razz, inevitably evolved and the seven-card game, whether played high or low, became the poker variation of choice for many players. As recently as the 1980s, another popular game emerged in the shape of Omaha Hold 'em, often referred to as simply Omaha. A community card game, the format of Omaha is based on the game that is currently the most popular of all poker variations – Texas Hold 'em.

Cataloguing the game

A sense of how poker had captured the imagination of the American public is gleaned from the efforts to catalogue all that was known of the game in the early 20th century. The fruits of this research materialized in 1905 with the publication of R.F. Foster's book *Practical*

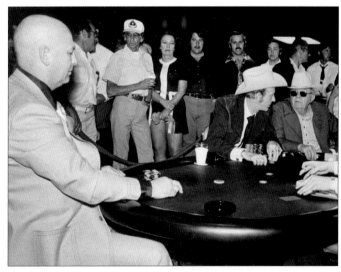

Above: 'Amarillo Slim' Preston (centre) chats with casino owner Benny Binion while playing Bill Lee (far left) in a US$10,000 challenge match at the Hotel Sahara in Las Vegas, 1975. Preston had been eliminated from the World Series of Poker (WSOP) world championship game but quickly found another poker challenge. In this case, Lee emerged victorious when Preston's pair of sixes proved insufficient to beat Lee's pair of queens in the final hand.

Left: Thomas Austin 'Amarillo Slim' Preston, winner of the 1972 WSOP championship, is arguably the first true poker celebrity of the modern era. Regular appearances on American TV chat shows following his WSOP triumph drew attention to the previously obscure world of the professional poker player.

Poker. At around the same time, references to 'dealer's choice' appeared, suggesting that several variations of poker were already widely played, with the nominated dealer deciding which would apply for each individual hand. Over the years, additional publications of Hoyle's famous guide to card games, which originated in 1742, have included numerous poker variations and serve as a record of the latter-day development of the game. More recently, poker literature has expanded to include many books on the theories behind successful poker play, a trend established by Frank R. Wallace in 1968 with his *Advanced Concepts of Poker.* This was the first of many books to analyse the game sufficiently to identify the ruthless and aggressive betting strategies typically adopted by profitable players.

Poker professionals

The poker professionals of the 19th century were an itinerant breed who favoured card games over other forms of gambling since a minimal amount of equipment was required compared to other games like faro and roulette. Armed with a deck of cards, the professional could establish a game almost anywhere and at any time, although the need for some means of self-defence was taken as read. But those who gambled for a living, generally being regarded as crooks themselves, frequently encountered keen poker players among the criminal fraternity. This, of course, presented additional risks. Similarly, the professionals and hustlers of the mid-20th century regularly operated on the edges of legality and often faced opponents with a marked aversion to losing.

NATIVE INDIAN RESERVATIONS
♦ ♣ ♥ ♠

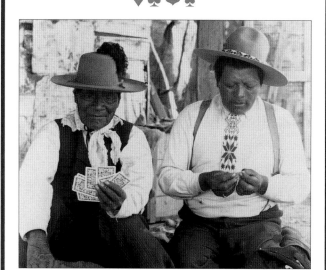

Above: As a pastime, playing cards was not confined to the colonists emanating from Europe since it also proved popular with the indigenous peoples of America.

One of the driving forces behind the expansion of gambling in America has been the Indian Gaming Regulatory Act of 1988, allowing the various Native American tribes to run casinos on their land as a concession to exercising some autonomy over their affairs. Commercially successful, and well run, these operations have fed the appetite for the nation's gamblers and helped generate employment opportunities and better economic prospects for the many local people who work in them.

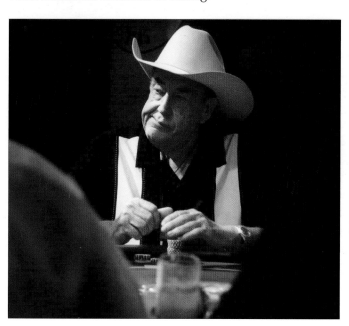

Right: Poker chips, or poker tokens, are used to keep track during gambling to replace money being handled at the table during a game.

Left: Doyle 'Texas Dolly' Brunson, a contemporary of 'Amarillo Slim', at the launch party of the World Poker Exchange London Open in August 2005. Brunson won the WSOP world championship in 1976 and 1977, following which he collaborated on *Doyle Brunson's Super System: A Course in Power Poker,* a book still regarded as essential reading for the discerning player.

For legendary players such as Johnny Moss, Doyle 'Texas Dolly' Brunson and Thomas 'Amarillo Slim' Preston, being hijacked at gunpoint and forced to hand over the money they had just won was one of the hazards of their chosen profession. Anecdotes about their adventures from the 1950s onwards highlight how many parts of post-war America still resembled the Wild West in terms of their apparent lawlessness.

LAS VEGAS

Though the Wild West imagery associated with poker is familiar to us all, the game has also become inexorably linked with a city that is arguably the gambling capital of the world – Las Vegas. The reasons for its dramatic development from a small crossroads watering hole in the Nevada Desert to the glittering tourist destination of legend are threefold. The relaxation of Nevada's state laws prohibiting gambling in 1931 coincided with the construction of the Hoover Dam 30 miles away, a project that attracted many thousands of labourers, and potential gamblers, in Depression-era America. Organized criminals who had prospered during Prohibition by meeting the public demand for alcohol, gambling and other vices, exploited this attractive opportunity. As a means of laundering their profits, the Mafia gangs

of New York, Detroit, St Louis and Chicago knew that running a casino had proven merit, and money was soon poured into the construction of these pleasure palaces designed to meet the needs of a new market.

Within 20 years, Las Vegas had become a hugely popular destination for people seeking the pleasures offered by legal gambling. Gradually, increasing numbers of professional poker players moved to the city to take advantage of the constant stream of tourists, until the World Series of Poker (WSOP) was established, promoting both the game and the city as a whole. In truth, most casino operators view poker ambivalently since tables take up a substantial amount of room that might otherwise be devoted to games that earn them higher profits. However, the resurgence in poker's popularity means that casinos are again content to welcome players in the knowledge that, once inside, they are likely to spend their money on other diversions.

The Mafia

Benjamin 'Bugsy' Siegel, a Brooklyn-born bookmaker, is the man credited with first visualizing the possibilities offered by Nevada's relaxation of its gambling laws. In league with New York crime boss Meyer Lansky, he set about construction of the

Above: The Fremont Street Experience in Las Vegas boasts 10 casinos and over 60 restaurants, all contained in an area that is covered by a permanent canopy and illuminated by two million lights.

Right: Charles 'Lucky' Luciano, the New York vice king, was deported from America during the war years. Here he is shown in his car after a special government commission had placed him under police surveillance. Under the 'admonitory' sentence, Luciano had to spend every night at his home in Naples from 9pm to 7am for the next two years, and was barred from public entertainment places and individuals 'suspected of socially dangerous activities' or who had criminal records. The commission ruled there was a reasonable suspicion that Luciano had contacts in the underworld and also was involved in narcotics traffic and horse-race fixing.

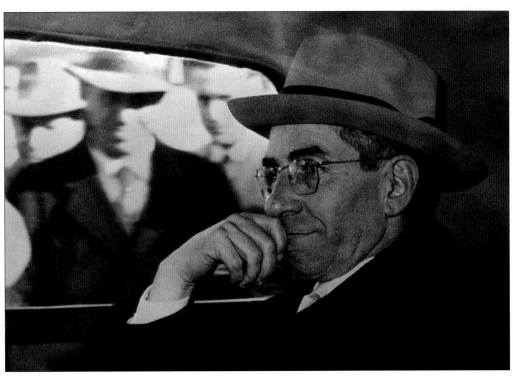

Flamingo Hotel and Casino but wound up making an enemy of gangster Charles 'Lucky' Luciano and was murdered in 1947. On the Las Vegas Strip, other hotel-casinos were built using money from the Teamsters Union Pension Fund, under the control of the Mafia. The criminal gangs were soon happily taking a cut from casino profits behind the scenes, despite maintaining a respectable image in public. This was bolstered by the regular presence in Las Vegas of Hollywood's elite, including the legendary Rat Pack, led by Frank Sinatra.

The Mafia's controlling influence in Las Vegas, however, was under attack from two sides, as law enforcement agencies and big business sought to drive them out and take back control of the city. Efforts to prosecute some of the leading crime bosses finally proved successful in the 1980s but, long before then, billionaire recluse Howard Hughes had influenced the Nevada State Government to permit public corporations to own casinos. This led to greater interest from the giants of Wall Street before the speculative commercial boom of the 1980s saw further acquisitions by, among others, Mirage Resorts Inc, owners of the Golden Nugget, the Mirage and Treasure Island. The major leisure corporations have since marketed Las Vegas to tourists previously disturbed by its sleazy image, although, for many, the historic undercurrent of criminality remains part of its appeal.

The Rat Pack

Apart from the gambling on offer, the other great draw in Las Vegas during the early 1960s was the entertainment provided by the top stars of the day. The leading light was Frank Sinatra, who regularly teamed up with Dean Martin, Sammy Davis Jr and comedian Joey Bishop for shows at the Sands Hotel and Casino. Along with actor Peter Lawford, brother-in-law to President John F. Kennedy, they became known as the Rat Pack, a group of entertainers whose talent was matched by their prodigious appetite for drinking, gambling and consorting with a string of attractive and equally famous women. They were the epitome of 'cool' and their association with Las Vegas helped the city maintain its allure.

Above: Howard Hughes, famous aviator and film producer (pictured in 1940), whose efforts indirectly led to the Mafia's grip on Las Vegas being loosened. His persistent lobbying of the Nevada State Government led to a change in state law allowing public corporations, as well as private individuals, to own casinos. One by one, the Mafia casino owners sold their interests to powerful leisure and entertainment companies. In 1967, Hughes himself bought the Desert Inn having tired of the owners' insistence that their reclusive guest should leave.

Left: Dean Martin and his friends, Joey Bishop and Frank Sinatra, opened a three-week engagement at the Sands Hotel in Las Vegas, April 1966, determined that their songs, patter and assorted hijinks qualify them as 'The Men from SPREE', (Society for the Prevention of Routine Entertainment Events).

POKER IN THE 21ST CENTURY

Left: Players at Binion's Horseshoe casino Las Vegas during the 2001 World Series of Poker (WSOP) championship – an annual event initiated by the casino's original owner Benny Binion in 1970. In that inaugural competition, 35 players competed for the unofficial accolade of world champion. By 2001, the WSOP had grown to 26 tournaments spread over a five-week period. In May 2001, the US$10,000 no-limit Texas Hold 'em world championship was won by Carlos Mortensen who beat 612 other entrants to claim the US$1,500,000 first prize.

Below: An aerial shot of Casino Barrière de Deauville in France during the French Open tournament in 2005, a televised event – the fifth of seven tournaments in the inaugural European Poker Tour (EPT). Coverage of the WSOP and World Poker Tour (WPT) on cable television had prompted TV director and player John Duthie to instigate a similar operation in Europe. Brandon Schaefer carried away the €144,000 (US$186,500) prize.

The advent of online poker over the last decade has, of course, been a massive boost to the game's popularity and the establishment of businesses with multimillion-dollar turnover has helped to improve its image. PlanetPoker began the online trend in 1998 but it is PartyPoker that currently heads the rankings as the busiest and most popular poker website, accommodating almost half of all online poker traffic. Analysts expect the industry's annual turnover to exceed US$100 billion by 2010 as interest in poker builds upon the convenience of playing from home. The changing face of the game is underlined by the WSOP championship successes of Chris Moneymaker in 2003 and Greg Raymer in 2004, as both of these players qualified for the main event via online satellite tournaments. Their victories provided a boost for the credibility of online poker and its supporters, as well as keeping alive the dream that anyone, given the requisite amount of skill and luck, can become a world champion.

Poker on television

While online poker offers a convenient means of playing the game, it is television that has boosted poker's profile and helped create a market served by the virtual casinos and gaming rooms of the Internet. Initial attempts to cover the WSOP on television were very limited, there being no way of discovering what cards each player held until or unless there was a showdown. Roving reporters and camera operators from American channel ESPN tried to capture the excitement of the event but it was difficult to retain the interest of viewers other than diehard poker fans. Coverage of the game changed with the introduction of miniature cameras positioned beneath specially designed tables featuring glass panels, pioneered on the UK's *Late Night Poker* in 1999. Now viewers could

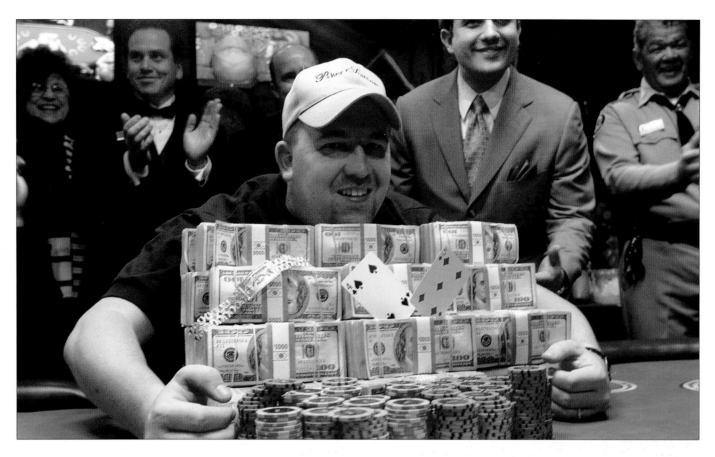

see the players' cards and understand the dynamics of the game – invariably no-limit Texas Hold 'em – and the strategies employed by the professionals.

This innovation led to improvements in ESPN's coverage of the WSOP, which is now more extensive than ever and features many of the supporting events as well as the main championship game itself. Encouraging ratings for what was considered a minority interest led to a commission from the Travel Channel, owned by the American company Discovery Communications Inc., to establish the World Poker Tour (WPT) in 2003. The tour comprises several tournaments contested at various locations, primarily in America, highlights of which are then shown on any one of up to 100 channels globally. Crucially, anyone able to pay the entry fee is welcome to participate and several hundred players, both amateur and professional, normally compete in each event. Within a year, the European Poker Tour (EPT) was instigated along similar lines while TV production companies, often sponsored by online poker sites, now stage an increasing number of tournaments specifically for the small screen. Finally, proof that televised poker was a ratings winner came with the launch in March 2005 of the Poker Channel, the first of its kind to broadcast nothing but poker-related programming.

Above: American Chris Moneymaker, pictured with his US$2,500,000 prize for winning the 2003 WSOP championship US$10,000 no-limit Texas Hold 'em tournament. His success helped boost the profile of online poker since it was via the PokerStars website that he entered a US$40 satellite tournament that ultimately led to a seat at the world championship game itself. In beating over 800 other entrants to the title, he confounded the experts because he arrived in Las Vegas with no experience of live tournament poker. His skills had been honed in the online poker rooms instead.

TOURNAMENT POKER
♦ ♣ ♥ ♠

Prior to the inception of the WSOP, tournament poker played on a knockout basis was rarely, if ever, contemplated by regular cash game players. The success of the self-styled world championship of poker, however, stimulated interest in this form of the game throughout Las Vegas, extending later to the rest of the world. By its very nature, tournament poker generates confrontations that are ultimately resolved by one player amassing all the chips. Consequently, the inherent drama of proceedings that conclude with a definitive winner satisfies the requirements of television which now features a great deal of poker programming.

WORLD SERIES OF POKER

The World Series of Poker (WSOP) held annually in Las Vegas is undoubtedly the major event on the poker tournament calendar. Over a period of eight weeks, more than 20,000 players can be expected to take part in around 40 different tournaments encompassing several popular poker variations. Entry to these events comes at a cost, ranging from US$500 for the casino employees' tournament to US$10,000 for the no-limit Texas Hold 'em world championship. The prize pools provide a substantial incentive to play, and each winner also receives a gold bracelet as a memento of their victory. If the entry fees seem prohibitively expensive, then numerous satellite tournaments are also held during the year, offering players the chance to win a place in the main event itself for a much smaller sum. Both Chris Moneymaker and Greg Raymer battled through a series of online poker tournaments for a modest outlay before scooping the top prize in the 2003 and 2004 WSOP tournaments respectively.

The early days

Inspired by the heads-up match between Johnny Moss and Nicholas 'Nick the Greek' Dandolos that he staged in 1949, casino owner Benny Binion revived the idea of a contest to determine poker's world champion in 1970.

He had seen the potential for such an event at the Texas Gamblers' Reunion the year before in Reno. This invitation-only festival at Tom Morehead's Riverside Casino saw a handful of leading professionals play poker against each other and garnered a fair degree of publicity. When Morehead sold his casino, Binion acquired the rights to his tournament and replicated

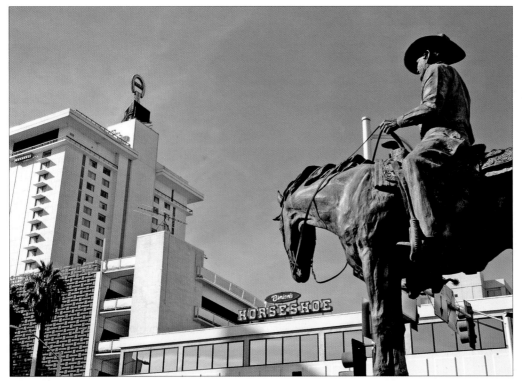

Above: Joe Hachem proudly displays his WSOP gold bracelet after becoming world champion in July 2005. Born in Lebanon, Hachem moved to Australia in 1972 and settled in Melbourne where he lives with his wife and family. He often played poker at a local casino, but began to take the game more seriously as a source of income when a debilitating physical condition left him unable to continue working as a chiropractor.

Left: The statue of Benny Binion outside Binion's Horseshoe Casino, created following the purchase of the Eldorado Club and Apache Hotel in 1951. Always operated as a family concern, Binion ensured his casino directly appealed to serious gamblers by allowing games with higher betting limits than could be found among the resort casinos and hotels on the Strip. This created friction with some of the Mafia-controlled concerns but Binion was not easily intimidated.

the concept at his Horseshoe Casino the following year. Thus, the WSOP was established, with 35 players competing at five poker variations for the accolade of world champion. For the only time in its history, the winner was decided by a vote among the players and Johnny Moss, the doyen of the professional game, was judged the best all-round poker player in the world.

The following year, Binion established the decisive world championship game as a freeze-out tournament with players contributing a US$5,000 fee to buy in to the competition. Significantly, the poker variation he selected for this knockout event was no-limit Texas Hold 'em. Moss won again, beating just five

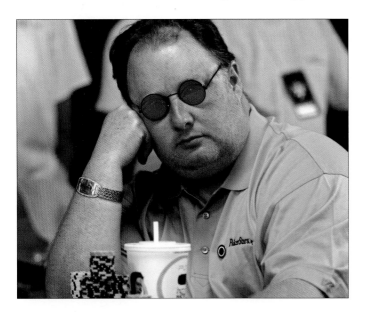

opponents to take the US$30,000 prize and confirm his status as champion. In 1972, the buy-in was raised to its current level of US$10,000 and on this occasion Thomas 'Amarillo Slim' Preston emerged victorious before starting a series of promotional television appearances that firmly planted the WSOP in the public domain.

The present

From an initial entry of 35 players in 1970, the number competing in the world championship game grew to over 5,000 in 2005. As a result, the prize pool exceeded US$50 million with the winner alone, Australian Joseph Hachem, collecting US$7.5 million. The status of being acknowledged world champion, along with the life-changing prize money on offer is now proving so attractive that a limit of 8,000 entrants has been placed on the 2006 renewal. Sadly, the phenomenal success of the WSOP means that it is no longer staged entirely at Binion's Horseshoe Casino. Harrah's Entertainment acquired the casino in 2004, along with the rights to the WSOP, and moved the tournament to Harrah's Rio Casino, although the final two days of the 2005 event were staged back at Binion's. This proved the swansong for the WSOP's association with its original home which was sold on to the MTR Gaming Group in 2005 and now bears the name of Binion's Gambling Hall and Hotel.

Left: Greg 'Fossilman' Raymer, WSOP world champion in 2004, pictured defending his title during the following year's US$10,000 no-limit Texas Hold 'em world championship.

Above: The legendary Benny Binion, the man who devised poker's unofficial world championship, the WSOP. Though he established the Horseshoe in 1951, he had to sell his share of the family business to pay for legal costs incurred defending a charge of tax evasion, for which he was convicted in 1953 and spent four years in jail. This barred him from ever holding a gaming licence but, once his family had regained control of the business, Benny was officially employed as a consultant.

BENNY BINION
♦ ♣ ♥ ♠

Though he lacked a formal education, Benny Binion learned much about human nature while riding the range in Texas as a boy and put these lessons to good use when he arrived in Las Vegas to run his first casino. As a bootlegger and numbers runner, he knew how to survive on the wrong side of the law, somehow even avoiding prison when convicted of first-degree murder. His place in the annals of poker is secure because of the WSOP, of course, but Binion was primarily a gambler who used his insight to provide his fellow gamblers with what they really wanted. Eschewing the glamorous trappings of the hotels and casinos on the Strip, Binion's philosophy for success was simple: "Good food, good whiskey and good gamble. That's all there is to it." He died on Christmas Day, 1989.

Johnny Moss and Nick Dandolos

Earning a living from poker has historically been regarded as a dubious activity. Yet there is no doubt that many famed players retain a sometimes romantic or even heroic status because of their perceived rebelliousness in the face of accepted wisdom. The willingness to back one's judgement with hard cash, relying on one's own wit and resourcefulness in order to prosper, is generally admired. Such qualities have always been found in professional poker players, while exploits on the edges of legality have generated a host of legendary anecdotes. As a result, some of poker's characters have emerged as successful exponents of the game, along with several notable confrontations.

Johnny Moss

Often referred to as the 'Grand Old Man' of poker, Johnny Moss (1907–97) learned how to play the game as a boy when a group of card sharps taught him all the tricks of their trade. As a teenager in Odessa, Texas, his ability to identify foul play saw him employed at a saloon to monitor the card games, giving him the chance to learn about poker strategy. Within a couple of years, he took to the road and led a sometimes hazardous existence as an itinerant gambler – a rounder – travelling the country in order to earn a living from gambling.

As an expert on cheating, Moss took exception to those who lacked respect for the game, always carrying a gun to enforce his stance. On several occasions he ordered opponents to strip at gunpoint to determine whether they were wearing 'holdout machines', devices explicitly designed to conceal cards. Famously, during one particular game he noticed a hole in the ceiling, suggesting that someone on the floor above was looking at his cards. When his suspicions were flatly denied, he shot at the ceiling and wounded the spy, exercising a particularly forceful strategy that confirmed his palpable contempt for poker cheats. Up until his death in 1997, Moss was a regular participant at the WSOP, winning eight gold bracelets and over US$680,000 in tournament prize money. He also won three of the first five world championship events, including the inaugural competition in 1970 when the title was decided by a vote among the contestants.

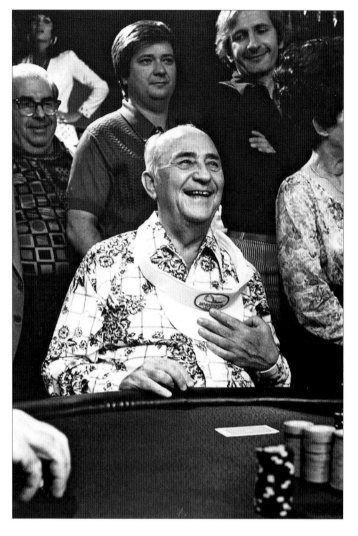

Above: Johnny Moss, acknowledged as the best poker player in the world by his peers at the first WSOP in 1970 after a series of games encompassing the most popular variations at the time. The following year he won again, though the decisive championship event on that occasion was a knockout Texas Hold 'em tournament, a change that ultimately led to the upsurge in this particular poker game's global popularity.

Moss v Dandolos

This legendary poker confrontation took place in 1949, when America's most notable gambler Nicholas 'Nick the Greek' Dandolos approached casino owner Benny Binion with a proposition. He wanted to play poker for exceptionally high stakes against just one opponent, in what is known as a heads-up confrontation, with a no-limit betting structure in operation. This allows players to bet their entire chip stack at any moment during the play of a hand, there being no upper limit on the size of any bet. Seeing an opportunity to publicize his business, Binion agreed to stage it, provided he could choose the opponent and have the pair play in public. He contacted his old friend Johnny Moss, regarded as the best poker player alive, and invited him to the game, which began almost immediately upon his arrival. Dandolos, flush with a reputed US$10 million in stake money accrued during a successful run in New York, held the upper hand for the first few weeks, but Moss fought back. Apart from breaks for sleep, the marathon contest lasted for five months and regularly drew crowds of interested spectators eager to witness the action. Eventually, it was Dandolos who conceded defeat with the famous words: "Mr Moss, I have to let you go", by by which time his losses were at least US$2 million.

Nicholas 'Nick the Greek' Dandolos

One of the most fearless gamblers of all time, Dandolos was born in Crete in 1883 and moved to North America as a teenager to find his fortune. While based in Montreal, he quickly made his mark as a gambler, striking up a lucrative friendship with jockey Phil Musgrave, whose insight helped him accumulate US$500,000 in a single horse-racing season. From there, he moved to Chicago, where he turned his attentions to cards and dice, having already lost his first fortune. Such was his skill and mathematical acumen that casinos frequently offered him jobs, which he always declined because of a reluctance to accept the likely cut in pay. Although he conceded defeat in the marathon poker confrontation with Johnny Moss, Dandolos remained a keen competitor, whose lifetime's betting turnover is thought to have touched US$500 million dollars. When he died on Christmas Day 1966, this legendary big-time gambler was penniless.

Above: Nicholas 'Nick the Greek' Dandolos (right), outside the Federal Court in Los Angeles with his attorney, P. Basil Lambros. Dandolos had been testifying during a case in which three men were accused of plotting to extort money in 1964 from a hotelier named Ray Ryan, a man Dandolos himself had previously pursued in connection with a gambling debt. Though his gambling exploits were legendary, Dandolos died a pauper.

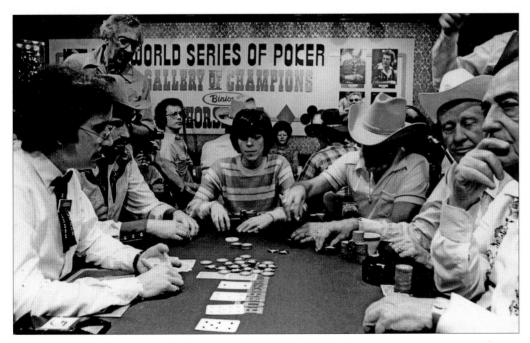

Left: Action from the WSOP with Stu 'The Kid' Ungar (centre), 'Amarillo Slim' Preston (second right) and Johnny Moss (far right) all involved at the same table. Moss claimed the title of world champion on three occasions, in 1970, 1971 and 1974 while Ungar achieved the same feat with victories in 1980, 1981 and 1997. Preston's world championship bracelet was earned in 1972 when the tournament was played as a 'winner takes all' event.

Brunson, Hellmuth, Smith and Hooks

Doyle 'Texas Dolly' Brunson

Without a doubt, many of the legendary players of contemporary poker history have enjoyed dramatic lives, and Doyle 'Texas Dolly' Brunson is no exception. Born in Longworth, Texas, in 1933, the physically imposing Brunson was an accomplished athlete as a teenager, but his dreams of a career in professional basketball were ended by an industrial accident that broke his leg in two places. After recovering his fitness, he found that regular jobs paid far less than he was consistently able to win at the poker table. So, in partnership with Thomas 'Amarillo Slim' Preston and Brian 'Sailor' Roberts, Brunson set about earning a living in the card rooms of Texas. Six years of hustling together ended ignominiously on their first trip to Las Vegas, when they lost their entire six-figure bankroll, this being the cash players set aside strictly for poker. Later, after miraculously overcoming cancer in the early 1960s, Brunson made his way back to Las Vegas, moving there permanently in 1973. The newly established WSOP attracted his attention and Brunson became world champion in both 1976 and 1977. Famously, he won the final pot in both tournaments

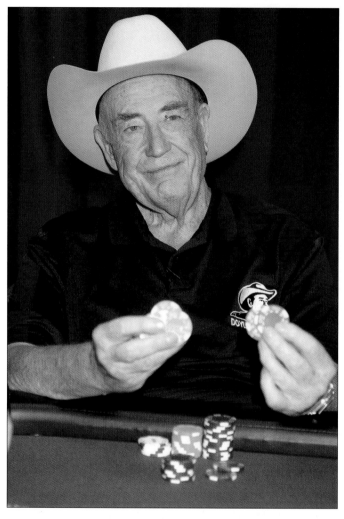

with the same hand – a full house of tens over twos. His book, *Doyle Brunson's Super System: A Course in Power Poker*, was first published in 1978 and is still regarded as a classic treatise on how to play the game. Now into his seventies, Brunson is still competing and winning on the tournament circuit, with today's top players acknowledging that he has probably done more to popularize poker than anyone else.

Above: Veteran Doyle 'Texas Dolly' Brunson promotes a televised tournament in London in 2005. A career in basketball was a possibility for the man from Longworth, Texas, but a serious leg injury curtailed any ambitions Brunson had to become a professional sportsman. He concentrated his efforts on poker and took to the road with 'Amarillo Slim' Preston and Brian 'Sailor' Roberts, the three of them seeking out high-stakes games wherever they could find them. Still a regular participant in tournaments around the world, Brunson is one of the most recognizable and respected characters in the game.

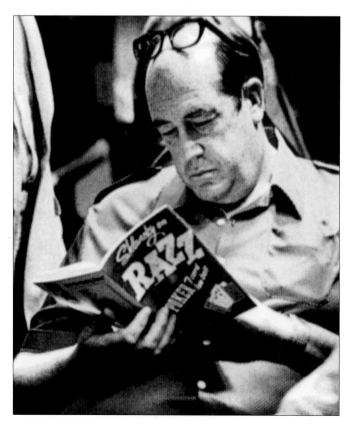

Left: A younger Doyle Brunson takes time out to read *Sklansky on Razz*, one of several poker books by mathematician and professional gambler David Sklansky, a contributor to Brunson's own book *Super System: A Course in Power Poker*.

Above: Poker professional Phil Hellmuth, the self-styled 'poker brat' who holds the record for the greatest number of prize-money finishes at the WSOP and is the joint record holder for the most WSOP tournament wins, having secured his tenth title in 2006. All ten have been in Texas Hold 'em events although he is an adept stud poker player too.

Above: Chess champion Bobby Fischer prepares for his famous 1972 duel with Russian chess grandmaster Boris Spassky in Reykjavik, Iceland. Among the chess experts assisting Fischer during his successful bid for the world championship was Kenny 'What a Player' Smith who later turned to professional poker.

Phil Hellmuth

Born in Madison, Wisconsin, Phil Hellmuth is arguably the biggest name in poker today. He shot to prominence when he won the ultimate prize at the WSOP in 1989, aged 24. Within seven years, his peers were talking about him as the best tournament poker player in the world. Yet, despite this respect for his ability, Hellmuth has not always endeared himself to opponents. The title of his forthcoming autobiography, *Poker Brat*, highlights his tendency in the past to show plenty of emotion during a game, even churlishly berating other players for their style of play.

Although experience has mellowed him a little, Hellmuth is calculating enough to realize that maintaining this feisty, combative image keeps his profile high at a time when poker is subject to widespread media interest. Since his 1989 triumph, Hellmuth has amassed 50 tournament wins and is currently the second most successful player at the WSOP in terms of prize money accrued. In March 2005, he won the National Heads-Up Poker Championship in Las Vegas, earning US$500,000 in the process, and he also triumphed in series three of *Late Night Poker*, a televised tournament shown on UK television's Channel 4. Married with two sons, Hellmuth is the author of three books on poker and has also produced an instructional video on the game.

Smith versus Hooks

The novelty value of a hand contested by these two players is sufficient for it to have entered poker folklore. Kenny Smith, famed for always wearing a silk top hat and shouting "what a player" each time he won a hand, was also a respected chess master who had assisted Bobby Fischer during his 1972 world championship campaign. His opponent in this heads-up situation, which emerged during a game of Texas Hold 'em, was Bob Hooks, runner-up in the 1975 WSOP world championship. Hooks called for the amount of the 'blind', the compulsory bet made by the two players to the dealer's left, but Smith made a substantial raise before the 'flop', this being the moment when the first three community cards are revealed. Smith's pre-flop raise prompted Hooks, whose two cards comprised a pair of kings, to bet 'all-in', meaning that he pushed all his remaining chips into the pot. Smith now faced a massive call, but he simply stared at Hooks, showing no apparent intention of ever making a decision. After several minutes, with everyone beginning to wonder how to resolve the situation, Hooks broke one of the defining rules of the game by calmly looking at Smith's cards himself. Seeing a pair of aces, the only hand that could possibly be ahead of him at this point, he moved Smith's chips into the pot, played out the hand and duly lost.

ULLIOTT, PEARSON AND PRESTON

Dave 'Devilfish' Ulliott

Probably the most famous British poker player currently in action is Dave 'Devilfish' Ulliott, a jeweller from Hull in northern England, His success in the inaugural series of *Late Night Poker* on Channel 4 renewed interest in the game in Britain and brought his talents to a much wider audience. However, his wisecracking style and dry sense of humour disguise a cool and calculatedly aggressive approach to poker. In fact, some observers consider that his self-confident comments, if taken at face value, border on arrogance. But with over US$3 million in tournament prize money to his name, Ulliott is entitled to consider himself one of the premier players in the world.

On the other side of the Atlantic, Ulliott earned respect at the WSOP in 1997 when winning the US$2,000 pot-limit Texas Hold 'em event made him one of very few non-Americans to claim a WSOP title. Earlier that year, a friend had coined the nickname 'Devilfish'

while Ulliott was playing heads-up in a pot-limit Omaha event against multiple-tournament winner Men 'The Master' Nguyen, the pair of them being the only players left in the competition. If not cooked properly, eating the devilfish can prove fatal and evidently 'The Master' experienced a night of poker indigestion. Since 1997, Ulliott has regularly made the final tables at tournaments and enjoyed a fine run at the 2005 WSOP when he secured three prize-money finishes. Ulliott now appears in televised tournaments regularly.

Walter 'Puggy' Pearson

A colourful character of the Las Vegas poker scene in the 1960s and 1970s, Walter 'Puggy' Pearson, who died in April 2006, was renowned as one of the great hustlers of his day. Apart from playing professional poker, Pearson also learned how to play golf once he discovered the opportunities for betting on various aspects of the game as the round progressed. On the

Left: Men 'The Master' Nguyen in action at the poker table. Feared and respected in equal measure by his peers, Nguyen fled his native Vietnam in 1978 and was granted asylum by the United States later that year, eventually settling in Los Angeles. His first experience of poker came on a trip to Las Vegas in 1984 and yet by 1987 he had already won his first tournament. Married with eight children, Nguyen has won *Card Player Magazine*'s Player of the Year award on four occasions, most recently in 2005.

Below: Dave 'Devilfish' Ulliott, probably Britain's most famous poker player and currently the most successful in terms of tournament prize money won. A pawnbroker and jeweller by trade, Ulliott began to take poker seriously during the early 1990s, travelling throughout the UK in search of high-stakes cash games. His first visit to the WSOP in 1997 resulted in victory in the US$2,000 pot-limit Texas Hold 'em tournament.

Above: Walter 'Puggy' Pearson (left), talking about bluffs and aces with 'Amarillo Slim' Preston before the final game that made Pearson world champion in 1973. Pearson grew up in Tennessee in a large family with nine siblings. His nickname 'Puggy' arose from a childhood accident that left him with a disfigured nose at the age of 12.

Left: 'Amarillo Slim' in relaxed mood while at the Poker Million tournament held at the Hilton Hotel Casino on the Isle of Man in November 2000. His four WSOP victories include the world championship in 1972, after which his regular television appearances made him something of a minor celebrity outside the poker world.

putting green he was especially accurate, managing to win money from many of the professional golfers that he challenged to a round. He triumphed in the WSOP no-limit Texas Hold 'em poker world championship in 1973, the first time the tournament was televised, having been runner-up the year before to 'Amarillo Slim' Preston. Perhaps his greatest legacy is the concept of the 'freeze-out' tournament, an idea that he is credited with introducing into Las Vegas and which has been adopted in virtually all major poker tournaments throughout the world. In these events, players start with the same number of chips but they are not allowed to purchase any more during play. Those who lose all their chips are eliminated from the competition.

Thomas 'Amarillo Slim' Preston

If there is one name synonymous with poker in the eyes of the world, that name is undoubtedly 'Amarillo Slim', the pseudonym employed by one Thomas Austin Preston Jr. A renowned storyteller, as shown in his biography *Amarillo Slim in a World Full of Fat People*, Preston has been at ease in the spotlight since 1972, when he won the third WSOP championship

game and immediately embarked on a tour of television chat shows and personal appearances. This had the effect of putting professional poker in the public eye, but also served to introduce one of the game's most colourful characters to the rest of the world.

Always sporting his trademark Stetson, Preston looks every inch the Texan cowboy, although he was actually born in Arkansas, moving to Amarillo with his family when he was a child. He took up poker in his twenties, unusually late in life compared to contemporaries such as Johnny Moss and Doyle Brunson, and has the distinction of having played against presidents Lyndon Johnson and Richard Nixon in his time. Remarkably, in a case of mistaken identity, he was kidnapped while in Colombia to help promote the opening of a new casino. The kidnap resulted, rather bizzarely, in Preston playing poker against drug lord Pablo Escobar. Preston is less of a feature on the tournament circuit these days. As he nears his 80th year, he has declared himself "pokered out" after 50 years of sometimes intense competition that has brought him fame, riches and no less than four WSOP bracelets.

JOHNNY CHAN AND STU UNGAR

Johnny 'Orient Express' Chan

After dropping out of university in Houston, where he was studying hotel and restaurant management, Johnny Chan took up professional gambling in the late 1970s. Originally from Canton in China, he had been brought to the United States by his family in 1968 after spending a few years in Hong Kong, but it was in Las Vegas that he made his reputation as a consummate poker player. Initially, his opponents underestimated his skill, although Chan himself admits that his early successes were counterbalanced by too many occasions when he would chase his losses. Once he addressed this, his game moved to another level and enabled him to win the WSOP world championship in both 1987 and 1988, replicating Doyle Brunson's feat of successive titles a decade earlier. A remarkable hat-trick of titles was denied him by Phil Hellmuth in 1989, when the self-styled poker brat beat Johnny Chan into

second place. By then, his place in poker folklore was assured, courtesy of a cameo appearance in the film *Rounders*, which reinforced his status as the best player in the world.

Outside poker, Chan has invested his money in a fast-food franchise and acts as a consultant to several casinos, harbouring ambitions that he may one day open his own establishment. But it is high-stakes poker that brings out the best in him, a point proven when he claimed his tenth WSOP bracelet in 2005 by winning the US$2,500 pot-limit Texas Hold 'em championship, equalling another of Doyle Brunson's career achievements.

Stu 'The Kid' Ungar

Winner of the WSOP championship event on three occasions, Stu Ungar is regarded by many as the best poker player of all time, although his reputation as an

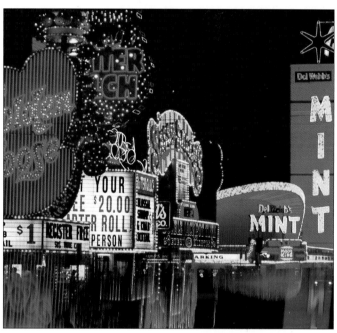

Above: The Las Vegas Strip, more formally known as Las Vegas Boulevard South, is the four-mile-long stretch of road running from McCarran Airport in the south to the Stratosphere Hotel Casino in the north. The majority of the city's largest resort hotels and casinos are located there.

Left: Johnny 'Orient Express' Chan, pictured at the WSOP in 2002. Originally from Canton in China, Johnny Chan arrived in the United States with his family in 1968 and looked set for a career in the family restaurant business. A trip to Las Vegas changed that and by 1987 Chan had become WSOP world champion, a title he successfully defended in 1988. A remarkable hat-trick of victories was denied him in 1989 when Chan finished second to Phil Hellmuth.

Left: Stu Ungar, at the final table of the 1997 WSOP world championship, a tournament he won to claim the US$1 million top prize. After his previous triumphs in 1980 and 1981, his performance in 1997 surprised many people since his hedonistic lifestyle had taken its toll and diminished his skills.

Below: Pictured at the 1980 WSOP are, from left to right, Doyle Brunson, Stu Ungar and Benny Binion's son, Jack, the tournament organizer. Ungar had just won the world championship event and is seen with his US$365,000 winnings having finally beaten Brunson into second place when his 5-high straight – known as a 'wheel' – proved too good for Texas Dolly's two pairs of aces and sevens.

obsessive gambler is equally legendary. As a child, the New Yorker quickly acquired a head for figures and a skill for playing gin rummy, winning his first tournament at the age of ten. He turned professional at 14, by which time he was regularly beating the best players in New York, and left school soon afterwards when a bookmaker paid his entry fee into a gin rummy tournament, which Ungar won without losing a hand. The US$10,000 first prize, however, was lost in one week at the Aqueduct racetrack, setting a pattern for the rest of his life.

Stu sought the big-money gin games of Miami, although his weakness for betting on the horses and other sports ensured that he was frequently broke. He moved to Las Vegas in 1976, where his uncanny ability to memorize cards during a game of blackjack led to the single-deck shoes, from which the cards were dealt during a game, being dropped by casinos. A successful run at Caesar's Palace was halted by a suspicious manager, at which point, in a fit of pique, Ungar correctly forecast the last 18 cards remaining in the deck. He was simply too good and found himself barred from every casino in Las Vegas, although his card-counting ability did win him US$100,000 from casino owner and designer Bob Stupak in 1977. Stupak

had privately challenged Ungar to forecast the rank of each card from the last three decks held in a six-deck shoe, a feat Ungar duly managed.

In 1980, he entered his first WSOP championship and won the main event aged just 24, repeating the feat the next year to seal his reputation and his nickname of 'The Kid'. However, Ungar's self-destructive appetite for cocaine and amphetamines ultimately led to his demise and contributed to his regular bouts of poverty. By 1997, he was considered a spent force, but entered the WSOP after fellow professional, Billy Baxter, paid his US$10,000 entry fee. Ungar's third victory saw him split the US$1 million prize equally with his sponsor.

Just over a year later, Ungar was found dead in a Las Vegas motel room, having suffered heart failure directly attributable to his lifetime of drug abuse. Reputed to have won and lost over US$30 million in all, Ungar's attitude to life is summed up by his remark on winning the 1980 WSOP world championship. Asked what he would do with the money, Ungar giggled as he replied: "Gamble it!" Ungar played 30 major no-limit Hold 'em tournaments in which the buy-in or entry fee was at least US$5,000, managing to win ten, a remarkable strike rate unmatched by any other tournament player.

THE HENDON MOB

Four of the best poker players in the UK, who have been friends since the early 1990s are otherwise known as the 'Hendon Mob'. Brothers Barny and Ross Boatman took part in a regular game organized by Joe Beevers in Hendon where they met Ram Vaswani. The four soon decided to pool their collective resources and tackle the best in the world. Bright, articulate and with a reputation for honourable conduct, they regularly featured on UK television's *Late Night Poker*, raising their profile and prompting them to set up their own poker website, www.thehendonmob.com, which provides news of their exploits. Like Dave Ulliott, the members of the Hendon Mob are heavily involved in promoting the game and regularly participate in televised tournaments specifically devised to exploit the current widespread interest in poker.

Barny 'The Humour' Boatman

The elder of the two brothers, Barny Boatman spent time in various occupations prior to becoming a full-time poker professional, working as a teacher, computer programmer and legal advisor away from the table.

Early success in tournament poker came at London's Grosvenor Victoria Casino, when he won a small seven-card stud event before graduating at the highest level by finishing 16th of 512 entrants at the 2000 WSOP championship event. Since then, he has regularly reached the final table in tournament events and is frequently called upon as an expert pundit to help commentate on televised poker. He also contributes to various articles in poker magazines.

Ross Boatman

Unlike his colleagues in the Hendon Mob, whose celebrity status is entirely attributable to their poker skills, Ross Boatman is also an actor who has worked his way up from fringe theatre productions to appearances in film and on television. Most notably, he played the character of Kevin Medhurst in the popular UK drama series *London's Burning* during the 1990s. His best performance in *Late Night Poker* saw him finish as runner-up in the second series, but he, too, has since enjoyed success elsewhere by finishing among the prizes on the European and World Poker

Above: Actor Ross Boatman, younger of the two brothers in the 'Hendon Mob'. Familiar on British television for his role in the popular series *London's Burning*, he also featured in the films *Bring Me the Head of Mavis Davis* (1997) and *Hard Men* (1996).

Right: Three members of the 'Hendon Mob' pose with poker commentator Jesse May (far right) for a publicity shot in 2003. Barny Boatman (left), Ram Vaswani (second left) and Joe Beevers have, together with Ross Boatman, been at the forefront of efforts to popularize the game in the UK since the late 1990s.

Tours, as well as reaching 34th spot in the 2002 WSOP world championship game. Boatman's first love remains acting, but he admits that his poker is definitely more profitable, with over US$1 million so far accrued in tournament prize money.

Joe 'The Elegance' Beevers

Beevers was introduced to cards by his father who educated him sufficiently to ensure that his prowess at blackjack led to a ban from several London casinos. After completing a degree in finance and accounting, he worked in London for Citibank before turning his attentions to full-time poker, enabling him to become the first of the Hendon Mob to win money at the WSOP in 1996. While that win was in a pot-limit Texas Hold 'em event, he later improved upon that by finishing among the prizes at the 2005 championship event itself. One of his more memorable performances in the UK occurred when finishing second to snooker professional Jimmy White in the 2003 renewal of the Poker Million tournament. In 2006, Beevers managed to finish among the prize money in three WSOP tournaments, matching his achievement of the previous year. At the conclusion of the 2005 WSOP he married his wife, Claire, at the Bellagio in Las Vegas, and they became parents in February 2006 following the birth of twin daughters.

Above left: Simon 'Aces' Trumper (left), John Duthie (centre) and Barny Boatman at the Hilton London Metropole Hotel for a promotional shot. Trumper is a familiar face on UK television having won Channel 4's *Late Night Poker* in series two, while John Duthie won the first Poker Million in 2000. Boatman has twice been the top-placed British finisher in the WSOP world championship.

Above top right: Ram 'Crazy Horse' Vaswani, so called because of his tendency to employ both controlled and erratic styles of play, is the youngest in the Hendon Mob. He could have pursued a professional snooker career but opted to earn a living through poker, a decision that has led to earnings of over US$2 million from tournament play.

Above bottom right: Joe 'The Elegance' Beevers, poised to begin play. He competed in all six *Late Night Poker* tournaments on UK television and reached the final on three occasions, making ten appearances on the programme in all.

Ram 'Crazy Horse' Vaswani

The youngest of the four, Ram Vaswani turned his back on a budding professional snooker career when it became apparent that playing professional poker was likely to prove more lucrative. Like the others in the Hendon Mob, Vaswani performed consistently well on *Late Night Poker* without managing to win a series, but he has regularly reached the final table of many tournaments on the European circuit. Over in Las Vegas, he has managed to obtain ten prize-money finishes, with his best effort being runner-up in a combined Texas Hold 'em and seven-card stud competition. Vaswani remains a confident player and he is likely to be extremely successful – he has over US$2 million in tournament prize money to his name already.

MONEYMAKER, STRAUS AND TOMKO

Chris Moneymaker

An accountant by trade, Moneymaker hit the headlines when he won the world championship at the World Series of Poker in 2003, having entered the competition via an online satellite tournament. An initial US$40 stake to enter one of these preliminary competitions set him on course to working his way through a series of further satellite tournaments until he emerged with the US$10,000 entry fee for the world championship game itself. After outlasting 838 other players, he finally walked away with the US$2.5 million first prize. Although his victory advertised the ability of online poker players and justified their dreams of similar success, Moneymaker stresses that skill as a card player and not luck is still of the utmost importance. Indeed, his advice to budding professionals is to "have a day job", as even the best players must endure losing streaks. Moneymaker currently runs his own company producing poker paraphernalia and continues to feature on the tournament circuit.

Jack 'Treetops' Straus

Often referred to as 'Treetops' on account of his being 6ft 6in tall, Jack Straus enjoyed a reputation as an accomplished cash game player with a distinctively creative style. Like Doyle Brunson, Straus had played basketball at university but it was at poker that he excelled, winning the WSOP world championship in 1982, six years before dying of a heart attack while contesting yet another high-stakes game. Well respected and regarded as something of a gentle giant, he had a reputation for telling hugely entertaining poker tales, some of them a little taller than others.

Yet one of his most striking tales in poker lore, which happened in a high-stakes, no-limit Texas Hold 'em game, provides evidence of Straus's creativity at the table. Playing well and feeling confident, he decided to raise with any two cards before the flop, the moment when the first three community cards are revealed. Unfortunately his hand of 7, 2 'offsuit', meaning simply that he had two cards of differing suits, is recognized as

Above: Jack 'Treetops' Straus wins the 1982 WSOP world championship having famously recovered from holding just a single US$500 chip at one stage of the tournament. The Texan was renowned as a fearless gambler on horse racing and other sports, while at poker he was widely respected for his cash game skills. He died of a heart attack at the Bicycle Club in 1988 while playing poker.

Left: Chris Moneymaker plays the final hand of the WSOP world championship tournament at Binion's Horseshoe in May, 2003. The US$2.5 million prize in the foreground was his a few moments later when he secured a full house of fours over fives to beat Sam Farha. Rather than pay the US$10,000 fee for guaranteed entry to the tournament, Moneymaker won his way through several rounds of preliminary satellite tournaments to earn a shot at the title.

the worst starting hand in the game and did not justify the move. One player was willing to call the raise but Straus's situation seemed to improve when the flop came 7, 3, 3, giving him two pairs, albeit of low rank. Straus bet again but his opponent raised US$5,000, suggesting that he held a higher pair than sevens in his hand already. Straus decided to call anyway. The fourth community card – the 'turn' – was another 2 and Straus immediately bet US$18,000, despite the fact that it had not improved his hand at all and still left him trailing. His opponent hesitated, giving Straus the chance to make him a proposition. In exchange for a single US$25 chip, Straus offered to reveal either one of his personal 'hole cards', those held face down on the table and obscured from view, after which his opponent could decide whether to continue in the hand or fold his cards and concede defeat over the fate of the pot. After a moment's contemplation, his opponent tossed him a chip and pointed to one of Straus's cards, revealed to be the 2. At this, his opponent considered the implications of Straus's unorthodox move and concluded that the other card, logically, also must have been a 2, making a full house. He thought long enough to convince himself he was now behind, with a very poor chance of winning the hand, and duly folded in the face of the psychological pressure applied by Straus's incredibly subtle bluff.

Left: "The guy who invented poker was bright, but the guy who invented the chip was a genius", is a quote attributed to Jules Weintraub, who organized trips to Las Vegas for wealthy gamblers in the 1960s. It is an apt maxim highlighting how gambling for chips often detaches players from the cash sums involved.

Straus versus Tomko

As tournament play was not considered Jack Straus's forte, his win in the 1982 WSOP world championship was a surprise, not least to Straus himself judging by his amazed look when he won the final hand. Dewey Tomko's pair of fours led after the turn card, but a 10 on the river – the fifth and final community card – gave Straus the better pair and he claimed the title along with US$520,000 in prize money.

What makes the triumph stand out is that Straus had been reduced to a solitary US$500 chip earlier in the tournament, inadvertently leaving it under a napkin when he pushed his chips into the pot to call a bet. Thinking he had gone all-in by betting all his remaining chips, but without yet announcing it, he lost the hand and noticed the lucky chip as he rose to leave the table. He was permitted to continue and a few days later emerged as a most remarkable winner.

Above: Dewey Tomko is a proven poker all-rounder having won WSOP titles at no-limit Texas Hold 'em, pot-limit Omaha, and deuce-to-seven draw, one of the popular lowball poker variations at which Tomko is considered a specialist.

DEWEY TOMKO
♦ ♣ ♥ ♠

After finishing second to Jack 'Treetops' Straus in the 1982 WSOP world championship game, Dewey Tomko repeated the achievement when runner-up to Spain's Carlos Mortensen in 2001. Despite just missing out on the most prestigious title, Tomko possesses three WSOP bracelets in recognition of his tournament wins which began in 1979 with victory in the US$1,000 no-limit Texas Hold 'em event. Prior to that, Tomko had been a kindergarten teacher who discovered that regular participation in all-night poker sessions was financially more rewarding than holding down a job. The move to professional poker was a natural progression for someone who had been making money at the game since the age of 16. The pool halls of Pittsburgh, in Tomko's native Pennsylvania, offered sufficient poker action for him to pay for his college education and laid the foundations for his highly successful career in the game. Married with three children, Tomko's overall tournament winnings amount to over US$3 million which, given that tournament victories have been a rare occurrence for him since 1985, is a testament to his ability to reach the prize-money places on a regular basis.

WOMEN POKER PLAYERS

Although the majority of tales from the poker tables of the world invariably concern the exploits of men, the last two decades have seen women making a significant impact on the professional game as they dispel a few myths regarding their innate ability to play at the highest level. Sexism is still encountered, even by some of the more famous players, but this is giving way to respect, as tournament results speak for themselves.

Names from American history such as Belle Siddons, Annie Oakley, Calamity Jane and 'Poker Alice' Iver, all of them respected players, underline the fact that women's historical relationship with poker extends well beyond dealing the cards and acting as promo girls. Professionals such as Cyndy Violette, Jennifer Harman and Melissa Hayden are just a few of the women who have quickly worked their way to the top of the money lists, while Hollywood actress Jennifer Tilly's victory in the 2005 WSOP ladies-only US$1,000 no-limit Texas Hold 'em tournament can only have helped broaden poker's appeal.

Annie Duke

One woman who has earned a reputation as one of the best poker players in the world over the past decade is Annie Duke. She entered the World Series of Poker (WSOP) for the first time in 1994 and finished thirteenth in her maiden tournament, knocking out her brother, Howard Lederer, along the way. He had been playing tournament poker for a couple of years when he introduced Duke to the game in 1992. She tried her hand in Las Vegas and, on the back of her initial success, returned home to her husband armed with the means to supplement their household income. She gained experience playing in some of the tougher clubs and bars of Billings, Montana, but, after winning US$70,000 from her first tournament in Las Vegas, she accepted her brother's advice to capitalize on her ability and play professionally. That Duke made the right decision was apparent when, in 2004, she eliminated several poker legends on her way to victory in the WSOP no-limit Hold 'em Tournament of Champions, where she claimed the US$2 million

Above: Annie Oakley (1860–1926), a respected poker player, became an American celebrity courtesy of her shooting ability with a rifle, a skill that brought her widespread fame as part of 'Buffalo Bill' Cody's touring show.

Right: Annie Duke seen competing at the WSOP world championship in 2005. Duke's most notable success to date came in the 2004 WSOP Tournament of Champions, an event in which she beat Hellmuth, Chan, Brunson and a host of other legendary poker players to win the US$2 million first prize.

prize. Currently acting as a consultant for an online poker site, she is in demand among Hollywood's glitterati as a poker coach and stars in her own television series. Her autobiography, *Annie Duke: How I Raised, Folded, Bluffed, Flirted, Cursed and Won Millions at the World Series of Poker*, was published in 2005.

Kathy Liebert

Currently the top female earner on the tournament circuit, with over US$3 million in prize money won, Kathy Liebert needs little guidance on the intricacies of managing financial risk. Born in 1967, Liebert grew up in New York and obtained a degree in business and finance before working as an analyst for a company in New Jersey. Boredom soon set in and she decided to travel, financing her trip across country with the returns from her successful stock investments. Initially, she indulged her interest in poker by playing low-limit games in Colorado, but eventually Liebert arrived in Las Vegas and, upon the recommendation of a friend, started to take the game seriously.

Since then, she has developed a growing reputation as one of the most ruthless players on tour and someone who enjoys all aspects of tournament play.

Above: Betty Carey, described by 'Amarillo Slim' Preston as the best woman poker player he had ever seen. Preston discovered how good she was when a heads-up challenge between the two ended inside ten minutes as Carey emerged victorious.

Yet, despite her obvious talent, Liebert is content to enter satellite tournaments rather than pay the full entry fee to the bigger events, simply because it helps to keep costs down. Equally, she demonstrated a winner's mentality touched with business acumen when she triumphed in the first PartyPoker Million event in 2002, beating Beri Kecherian and Phil Hellmuth. She cut a deal with them, which saw her first prize reduced, but improved her place money prospects at a time when victory was far from certain.

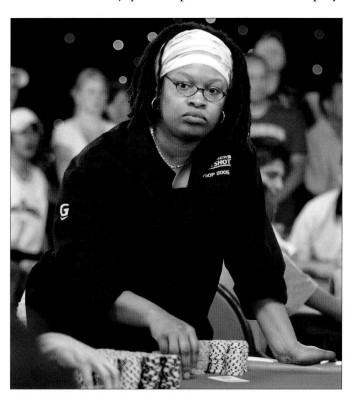

Above: Tiffany Williamson, on her way to 15th place in the 2005 WSOP world championship and a prize of US$400,000. The corporate lawyer from South Carolina had only been playing poker for a year having learned the game while working in London. Her performance in the main event was the best by a woman since Annie Duke's 10th-place finish in 2000.

KATHY LIEBERT
♦ ♣ ♥ ♠

Above: Kathy Liebert, now a resident of Las Vegas, achieved five prize-money finishes at the 2006 WSOP, her best showing yet at poker's annual showpiece event.

Born in Tennessee though raised on Long Island, New York, Kathy Liebert made her mark on the professional poker scene with victory in the PartyPoker Million tournament in 2002. Two years later she won a fixed-limit Texas Hold 'em event at the WSOP to claim her first gold bracelet. Her career earnings from poker to date amount to over US$3 million.

MYTHS AND LEGENDS

Given the confrontational nature of poker and the stakes for which players sometimes compete, many stories have emerged over the years reflecting the best, and the worst, of human nature. Every ambassador for the game proclaims the virtues of coolness under pressure, grace in defeat and modesty in victory, and many of poker's legendary tales feature exhibitions of these qualities. Yet there are others that tell of drastic and unorthodox strategies employed at the poker table in the face of extreme intimidation. In 19th-century America, playing poker could be a serious and potentially deadly pursuit.

Jim Bowie

Poker on the Mississippi riverboats was notorious for attracting hustlers who viewed it as a means of earning a living amid America's harsh, speculative culture. Indeed, being a successful professional card player was synonymous with being a cheat, although not all prospered. One group of players had cause to reconsider their profession in 1832 when inviting a wealthy but evidently naive young man to join them in a poker game during one particular steamboat journey. After predictably losing his entire fortune, the man was sufficiently distraught to be contemplating suicide when he was encountered by Jim Bowie, later

to die at the Alamo, a famous battle between the Republic of Mexico and rebel Texan forces fighting for independence. Suspecting that the man had been duped in an unfair game, Bowie watched the remaining poker players in action for a while until he was confident that someone was cheating. His surveillance paid off and, after pulling a knife on the suspect to force him into revealing his deception, Bowie collected the cash from the table and split the proceeds with the young man.

'Buffalo Bill' and 'Wild Bill' Hickok

Many of the myths surrounding the Wild West stem from the activities of one of its most famous figures, William 'Buffalo Bill' Cody, whose travelling stage show entertained the public for 30 years with fanciful tales of an era that was coming to an end. One story about Cody concerns the occasion when he was challenged to a game of poker by a man who freely proclaimed his contempt for the famous 'Buffalo Bill'. Cody agreed, but insisted that the game should end in a duel, the winner having the first opportunity to shoot his opponent from ten yards. Cody won the game, but his adversary immediately tried to draw his pistol, at which point a certain 'Wild Bill' Hickok pressed a gun to the man's head, judged him a cheat,

Right: James Bowie (1796–1836), aka Jim Bowie, who was a 19th-century pioneer and soldier, and is now immortalized as one of the most colourful folk heroes of Texas history. Born in Kentucky, he spent most of his youth in Louisiana, where he first acquired a reputation for his bold and fearless disposition. Bowie took a prominent part in the Texas Revolution and was killed in the seige of the Alamo. He is also known for the style of knife he carried, which came to be known as the 'Bowie knife'.

Below: 'Buffalo Bill' Cody and Annie Oakley perform a quadrille during the 'Wild West Show'. Though hugely popular at the time, these shows were also responsible for peddling many enduring myths concerning life on the frontier.

THE DEAD MAN'S HAND

Above and right: When 'Wild Bill' Hickok was shot dead, his hand comprised two pairs, black aces and eights, though the identity of the odd remaining card – the 'kicker' – is subject to debate. His killer, Jack McCall, testified that the card was the J diamonds, but Deadwood's museum has a 5 diamonds which it claims is Hickok's real kicker.

and consequently hanged him. The legendary pair, friends for some years, were keen poker players and 'Buffalo Bill' Cody is even reputed to have played one last game when told he had just hours to live.

The Dead Man's Hand

Although he arguably saved 'Buffalo Bill' Cody's life in the interests of fair play, James Butler Hickok was not averse to threatening opponents in a similar fashion when losing a game himself. He worked as a stagecoach driver and scout before his reputation for marksmanship and his uncompromising nature led to him becoming a US marshal. As befits a man nicknamed 'Wild Bill', he is credited with taking part in the first recognized Wild West gunfight when he shot dead Davis J. Tutt in July 1865. Hickok also played professional poker, but in one drunken game he ruthlessly cheated an opponent named McDonald out of a large pot. He claimed a full house to beat McDonald's three jacks but, just as his hand was

revealed to include merely a pair of aces with a six, Hickok drew his pistol and his knife. Faced by the additional six, in the shape of the six-shot revolver, and an ace in the hole – the knife – McDonald wisely chose to concede the hand.

Most famously, 'Wild Bill' Hickok was playing poker when he was shot dead in a saloon bar in Deadwood, South Dakota, in August 1876. A cattle herder named Jack McCall, who was drinking at the bar with his gun concealed, slowly approached the table and shot Hickok in the back of the head. The cards held by 'Wild Bill' at the time showed two pairs – aces and eights, all black – which have been known ever since as the 'Dead Man's Hand'.

The buck stops here

Poker is considered such a quintessentially American game it is hardly surprising that several presidents are known to have enjoyed playing it. 'Amarillo Slim' revealed that he played with Lyndon B. Johnson on occasion, as well as with the Texan's successor, Richard M. Nixon, a man who diligently applied himself to learning everything about the game while serving in the US Navy. Reluctant to risk any money until he felt confident in his ability, Nixon played poker continuously for months with a friend who was prepared to teach him the strategies required to win. Only then was Nixon prepared to gamble for real, and the education stood him in good stead – his winnings from poker partially financed the early stages of his political career. Perhaps the most famous of all poker-playing presidents, however, is Harry S. Truman, the man credited with coining the phrase "the buck stops here" – 'the buck' being another term for the dealer button – while in office. This president, who took the decision to deploy atomic weapons against Japan in 1945, often sought refuge in poker's familiar rhythms when under pressure. Indeed, while considering whether or not to use the bomb, Truman spent many hours relaxing at sea playing poker with members of the press, all the while contemplating one of the most significant decisions in history.

ERROL FLYNN LOSES AN ISLAND
♦ ♣ ♥ ♠

A film star of the 1930s and 40s, Flynn was a renowned drinker, womanizer and gambler, who once lost an entire island in a game of poker. A journey to Jamaica aboard his yacht in 1947 led to Flynn purchasing Navy Island, a haven lying just off Port Antonio that he planned to develop into a holiday resort. But, as he partied away the declining years of his career, Flynn's love of poker meant this ambition would remain unfulfilled, when he gambled away ownership of the island during what he described as "a bad poker night".

Poker and the stars

The film industry, responsible in many ways for popularizing poker, has also been a rich source of stories concerning the stars and their poker exploits. Steve McQueen's familiarity with the game made him a natural for the role of poker hustler Eric Stoner in *The Cincinnati Kid*. As such an integral part of American culture, poker has traditionally been a popular diversion for crews during filming, with McQueen and his co-stars in *The Magnificent Seven*, for instance, famously pictured playing the game. Charles Bronson, another to appear in the classic Western, often sat in

Above: President Harry S. Truman's poker table, complete with cards and a poker chip carousel, is one of the exhibits at the Little White House Museum. Truman played poker while deliberating over whether or not he should order the dropping of an atomic bomb on Japan in 1945.

Right: Errol Flynn in relaxed mood. The film star found more time for poker as his career declined, although this cost him his dream of developing an exclusive holiday resort in Jamaica – the island he bought was gambled away in a poker game.

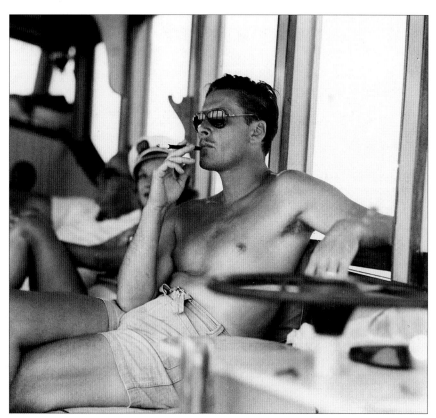

on 24-hour sessions with the likes of Lee Marvin and Telly Savalas while filming *The Dirty Dozen* in London. They were regularly joined by comedian and Oscar-winning director Woody Allen, who was in London filming *Casino Royale* at the time. Such was the reported disorganization behind the scenes of that production that Allen was content to play marathon poker sessions instead.

In fact, Telly Savalas was well respected as a player by the professionals in Los Angeles and Las Vegas, regularly participating in the WSOP and once finishing 21st in the no-limit world championship game. Of the current crop of Hollywood actors famed for their poker skills, Tobey Maguire and Ben Affleck have both won major tournament prizes, with Affleck victorious in the prestigious California State Poker Championship of 2004. This achievement came after Affleck had sought poker lessons from professional player Annie Duke. His next project is reportedly a comedy concerning the poker scene that will feature David Schwimmer, another keen player. Other stars currently making an impact in high-profile poker tournaments are James Woods and Jennifer Tilly, both of whom have managed to win money at the WSOP.

JOHN WAYNE WINS A DOG
♦ ♣ ♥ ♠

American icon John Wayne was typical of many film stars in that he often indulged his fondness for poker with the rest of the crew during breaks in filming, although one game in 1953 saw him win a remarkable pot, even by Hollywood standards. During production of the Western adventure *Hondo*, a drunken poker session resulted in Rudd Weatherwax, owner of Hollywood's canine legend Lassie, losing his faithful collie to the man known as 'Duke'. However, on sobering up the next day, noted dog lover Wayne duly returned the animal to its owner. This is perhaps not surprising – his nickname derived from that given to a pet dog he once owned some years earlier.

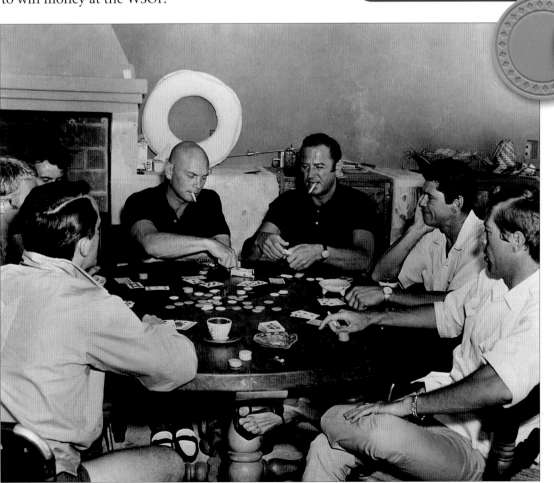

Left: The Magnificent Seven enjoy a game of poker while filming in 1960. Robert Vaughn (left) looks on as Yul Brynner (centre left) makes a move. To Brynner's left are Brad Dexter, Charles Bronson and James Coburn. Playing poker during a break in filming remains almost traditional in Hollywood.

POKER ON FILM

Images of American culture and society have been a fixture of film throughout the history of the moving picture and, naturally, poker has featured in many scenes during that time. Usually, the game provides a context for developing characters and furthering the plot, whether in Westerns, gangster films or more contemporary dramas. For example, in the 1965 Sergio Leone Western *For a Few Dollars More*, Clint Eastwood's first scene as the poncho-wearing bounty hunter sees him interrupt a saloon-bar poker game in pursuit of his quarry. He wins the hand, shoots four bandits and pockets a US$2,000 reward, neatly summarizing the qualities of the so-called 'man with no name'.

In a more contemporary setting, the 1968 comedy *The Odd Couple*, starring Walter Matthau and Jack Lemmon, centres on the relationship between two friends who play in a regular poker game. Developed from a Neil Simon stage play, the story unfolds during a number of scenes in which poker is revealed as the bond tying the characters together.

Similarly, *A Streetcar Named Desire*, made in 1951, was adapted from a Tennessee Williams play originally visualized as a single act with a poker game at its core. In the event, the brooding menace present in Marlon Brando's portrayal of Stanley Kowalski is revealed during a couple of games with his friends, poker being exhibited as a typical medium for very masculine expressions of anger and frustration.

Gangsters and casinos

Many portrayals of poker as a man's game emanate from the gangster genre of films, which is often tied in with the exploits of the Mafia in Las Vegas. Martin Scorsese's 1990 film *Goodfellas* featured the leading characters in a poker scene, while in *Casino*, made in 1995, the emphasis was on the criminal activity in one of the larger Las Vegas gambling joints. The Rat Pack's association with Las Vegas prompted the production of *Ocean's Eleven* in 1960, a popular caper movie that saw Frank Sinatra, Dean Martin, Sammy Davis Jr and the rest attempting to rob five casinos simultaneously. Later, of course, the film was remade with George Clooney cast in the lead role, supported by a few keen poker players and crooks in Matt Damon, Brad Pitt, Don Cheadle and Elliott Gould. For Gould, this represented familiar territory – in 1974 he had teamed up with George Segal to play a couple of gamblers heading for a make-or-break poker game in *California Split*, directed by the acclaimed director Robert Altman. The film also featured a cameo appearance by 1972 WSOP world champion 'Amarillo Slim', which served to heighten his own profile and that of poker as well. In addition to these occasions when poker has been portrayed on film, however, there are a handful of productions that stand out for the manner in which the game itself, and the people who play it, are central to proceedings.

Above: Robert De Niro as Sam 'Ace' Rothstein, the gangster who runs a casino for the Mafia in 1970s Las Vegas, as depicted in Martin Scorsese's *Casino* (1995).

Left: While Henry Hill (Ray Liotta, left) looks on, Tommy DeVito (Joe Pesci) holds all the aces at the poker table in this scene from *Goodfellas* (1990).

A Big Hand for the Little Lady

This light-hearted Western, directed by Fielder Cook in 1966 and starring Henry Fonda and Joanne Woodward, turns on the poker game that Fonda's character, Meredith, simply cannot resist. The pair of them are on the way to California to start a new life with their son but, while stopping in Laredo, Meredith discovers that a big game featuring some of the wealthiest players around is about to start. His wife is appalled at the prospect of seeing their life savings disappear, knowing her husband to be a dreadful player, but she sits in on the game anyway. Things go from bad to worse until, with a winning hand finally in his grasp, Meredith dies of a heart attack, leaving his widow to take his place. At this point she faces a big bet and, in an unlikely twist, dashes to the bank to negotiate a loan using the cards as collateral. This enables her to call the bet and produce the required happy ending.

Although satisfying the need for drama, this type of situation is highly unlikely to arise in reality since the majority of games are played for table stakes. This rule ensures that only the chips on the table may be bet during the play of any hand. Players who do not possess enough to call a bet may still commit their remaining chips to the pot and retain interest in the outcome. Should their hand prove best, they can claim from their opponents an amount equal to the total number of chips they have invested in the pot.

TABLE STAKES
♦ ♣ ♥ ♠

The table stakes ruling prohibits players from introducing additional funds to the game during the play of a hand. A player who does not have enough chips to match the current level of betting may still contest the hand by going all-in, the term used when committing all one's remaining chips to the pot. If the player loses, then it may be possible to buy more chips to continue in the game, but this must be done in a break between hands, not during play itself.

The Cincinnati Kid

Probably the most iconic of all poker films, *The Cincinnati Kid*, directed by Norman Jewison in 1965, features Steve McQueen as Eric Stoner, a young and ambitious poker player in 1930s New Orleans. Confident that he has the ability to be the best, Stoner seeks a confrontation with the acknowledged master of the game – Lancey Howard, or 'The Man' – memorably played by Edward G. Robinson. The stakes are high, though it is not just the money that drives the young pretender, but the status that comes from beating the man regarded as the best poker player around in order to be acknowledged as the new champion. The final scene sees the two men playing a no-limit game of five-card stud which, though it fulfils the need for dramatic tension, stretches credibility in the eyes of experienced players. Stoner bets his way, round by round, towards a hand of three aces and two tens. Yet, despite visibly trailing at every stage, Howard continues to pour cash into the pot and capitalizes on some outrageous fortune to win with a queen-high straight flush (8, 9, 10, J, Q) in diamonds. At this point he utters the immortal line: "Gets down to what it's all about, doesn't it? Making the wrong move at the right time."

Kaleidoscope

An easygoing romantic drama, directed by Jack Smight, made at the height of the 'Swinging Sixties', in 1966. This stylish film features Warren Beatty as the suave Barney Lincoln, a card-playing jetsetter with a secret – he cheats. In an elaborate scheme, Lincoln breaks into the Kaleidoscope factory and etches marks into the metal plates that are used for printing the playing cards used in continental Europe's casinos. Now able to identify the cards face down from the patterns he has doctored, Lincoln embarks on a lucrative gambling

Above: The defining scene from *The Cincinnati Kid* (1965) as Steve McQueen (left) and Edward G. Robinson (right) confront each other in the game that will determine which of them emerges with the reputation for being the best poker player in the country. Shelley Winters (centre) is the dealer.

Left: The iconic Steve McQueen as Eric Stoner in *The Cincinnati Kid*, contemplating his strategy as he engages in another big-money poker game. The film involves him testing his skills at the table as well as having to cope with a complicated love life involving his girlfriend (Tuesday Weld) and his mentor's wife (Ann-Margret).

spree, with nobody suspecting the reason for his success. Unfortunately, his girlfriend is the daughter of a Scotland Yard inspector and, when his ruse is eventually uncovered, he is blackmailed by police into challenging a poker-playing gangster to a game. All he has to do is win to keep up the financial pressure on the crook, a suspected drug smuggler. Predictably, Lincoln's true poker skills are then tested to the full when the cards of another manufacturer are used rather than his preferred Kaleidoscope decks. The undercover cheat must therefore hold his nerve in a quest for redemption.

Above: Teddy KGB (John Malkovich) looking menacingly confident at the poker table in *Rounders* (1998). The film helped rejuvenate interest in the game and inspired a new generation of players, including 2003 WSOP world champion Chris Moneymaker, to take poker seriously.

Rounders

This is the film, directed by John Dahl in 1998, credited with putting poker back on the map and inspiring a new generation of players. The 2003 WSOP world champion Chris Moneymaker is among those claiming to have become much more interested in the game after watching this film. Matt Damon plays a law student, Mike McDermott, who turns his back on poker after losing all his money to the notorious 'Teddy KGB', portrayed with customary relish by John Malkovich. However, when his friend is released from jail and needs help repaying a loan of US$15,000 from Teddy, McDermott comes to the rescue. He returns to the card rooms to put his skills to the test, jeopardizing his relationship with his girlfriend in the process.

As with so many other poker-related films, some of the scenes are a little too contrived to retain credibility, even with a respected card player like Matt Damon heading the cast and a cameo appearance by twice world champion Johnny Chan. Nevertheless, it sheds light on the world of the low-level poker professional and is notable for this essential piece of advice from the main character. "Listen, here's the thing. If you can't spot the sucker in the first half hour at the table, then you are the sucker."

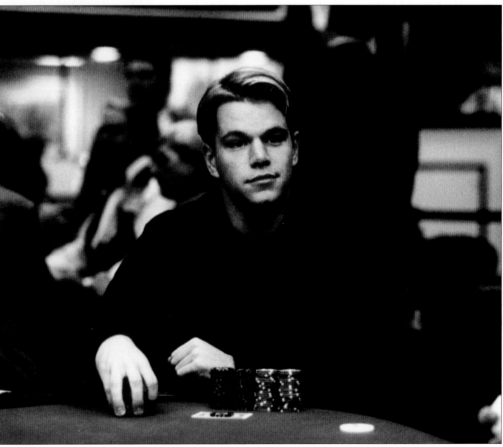

Right: Matt Damon as law student Mike McDermott in *Rounders* (1998). Having quit poker following a defeat to Teddy KGB (John Malkovich), McDermott returns to the tables in order to help a friend repay a loan. The film featured a cameo appearance by Johnny Chan, at the time the WSOP world champion, though the story mainly concerns the low-level professional game.

POKER ON TELEVISION

As already noted, the combined power of television and the Internet over the past decade has helped poker attain a higher profile than at any time in its history. More people then ever before are playing the game and television has been quick to capitalize on this interest, providing poker programming to cater for an expanding audience. This development in televised poker has helped many of the most successful tournament players become household names. Promoted by supermodels and played by film stars, poker is now perceived as a respectable and even glamorous gambling medium that offers the chance, albeit a slim one, for anyone to win a fortune.

Morality tales

Dramatic representations of poker games on the small screen have, naturally, been a staple of numerous television series set in the Wild West, though the game is generally less visible in contemporary settings. Popular Western shows such as *Bonanza*, *Rawhide*, *The Virginian* and, of course, *Maverick* have all employed poker as a means of imparting a few moral concepts, particularly the idea that cheats should never prosper. Westerns apart, one latter-day character certainly identified with poker is the iconic US Army schemer Sergeant Bilko, played by Phil Silvers, who preferred fleecing his men in a game to supervising their duties in the motor pool. More recently, an episode of the long-running comedy series *Friends* was devoted to a poker game, while suggestions that poker may well remain popular in the future are present in various episodes of *Star Trek: The Next Generation*. Additionally, in the original *Star Trek* series, Captain James T. Kirk is confronted by a stubborn and powerful opponent in an episode entitled 'The Corbomite Maneuver', and has to deploy a poker-inspired bluff to save the USS *Enterprise* from destruction. On the back of the game's current popularity, however, the potential for a drama series centred entirely on poker has finally been realized with *Tilt*, written by the team responsible for the film *Rounders*. Michael Madsen plays Don 'The Matador' Everest, whose status is under threat from a group of young poker tyros intent on taking him down as the WSOP approaches. But Las Vegas has a

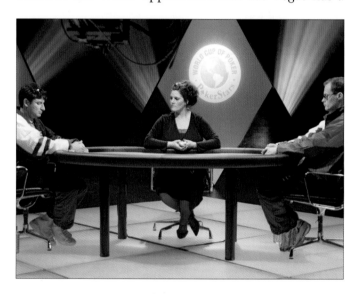

Above: Alex Brenes (left) from Costa Rica, playing in the televised World Cup Poker Tournament in 2005. This team competition features heads-up poker as players duel against each other, one on one, as shown here. Costa Rica went on to win this event to retain the title secured in the inaugural competition the previous year.

Left: John Duthie, winner of the first Poker Million event on the Isle of Man in 2000, is the driving force behind the European Poker Tour (EPT) established in 2004. Inspired by the World Poker Tour (WPT) on American television, the EPT featured six events during the 2006/07 season, concluding with the grand final in Monte Carlo.

few surprises in store for the budding champions. It remains to be seen whether the series will inspire others of a similar nature, but the audience for poker is currently well served by the prolific amount of real tournament play on offer via television.

Above left: Mike Sexton, the WPT's expert presenter and commentator, underlined his knowledge of the game with victory in the 2006 no-limit Texas Hold 'em Tournament of Champions in Las Vegas. His prize for winning was US$1 million.

Above: Andrew Rogers sits calmly with a monitor checking his heart rate, lower right, as he waits for his opponent to make the next move at the Mansionpoker.net Poker Dome Challenge at the Tropicana Resort and Casino in Las Vegas in June 2006.

World Poker Tour

Now an established part of the cable television scene, the World Poker Tour (WPT) was instigated in 2002 by attorney and television producer Stephen Lipscomb. Interest from the Travel Channel saw the establishment of several tournaments under the WPT brand, with highlights of the various games shown during 2003. By February 2004, American network television was sufficiently interested in the viewing figures for NBC to broadcast a special WPT 'Battle of Champions' event. It performed surprisingly well in direct competition with the CBS network's pre-Superbowl coverage and confirmed poker as a truly legitimate televised spectacle. After four successful seasons, the WPT continues to grow in popularity, its programmes currently being presented by WSOP winner Mike Sexton and former newscaster Courtney Friel, who replaced Shana Hiatt in 2005.

European Poker Tour

In the UK, the surprise success of Channel 4's *Late Night Poker*, first broadcast in 1999, has generated many variations on the theme of tournament poker, with an audience for the game existing throughout Europe. Following the example of the WPT, television director John Duthie, a competitor on *Late Night Poker* himself, sought support from online site PokerStars.com and instigated the European Poker Tour (EPT) in 2004. The opening season featured six tournaments, but the EPT has quickly grown to become the most prestigious poker circuit in Europe and is now broadcast in over 40 countries. Apart from being the EPT's chief executive, Duthie also acts as a pundit during the series, a role for which he is eminently suited since he won the Poker Million event in 2000. Interestingly, Duthie came second to the WPT's Mike Sexton in the 2003 European Heads-Up Championship held in Paris.

POKER IN PRINT

Those currently interested in poker and its culture have a wealth of literature from which to glean knowledge of the game. R.F. Foster's *Practical Poker*, published in 1905, was the first serious attempt to record all that was known about poker at the time, but the last 40 years have seen the publication of many more books on the subject. The majority are concerned with teaching readers how to play poker and develop their skills in order to win consistently. Many contemporary professionals have written or endorsed such books, building on the work of some influential poker theorists of the past. For those who wish to know about the poker players themselves, 'Amarillo Slim' and Annie Duke are just two of the big names to have autobiographies currently on the bookshelves. In addition, poker-playing writers Al Alvarez, Anthony Holden and James McManus have all written critically acclaimed accounts of their experiences in the world of professional poker.

Literary references

Perhaps the most famous writer to have included poker tales within his literary work is Mark Twain, a keen advocate of the game he encountered while working on the Mississippi as a steamboat pilot. Indeed, the creator of Tom Sawyer and Huckleberry Finn once stated: "There are few things so unpardonably neglected in our country as poker … It is enough to make you blush." In *The Professor's Yarn*, Twain tells the story of a poker player who manages to even the score against some cheats, a familiar plotline in many gambling tales. Following Twain's example, other writers such as Damon Runyon and Dashiel Hammett incorporated poker in their work, either as a feature of their characters' lives or as a useful plot device. More recently, ubiquitous poker commentator and pundit Jesse May has also written *Shut Up and Deal*, a fictional tale set in American poker rooms of the 1990s.

Above: Damon Runyon, the celebrated journalist and author whose short stories set in Prohibition-era New York vividly describe a world populated by gangsters, actors and gamblers. The famous musical *Guys and Dolls* was inspired by two of his stories.

Right: *Friend in Need* (aka *Passing the Ace Under the Table*) by Cassius Marcellus Coolidge, one of nine depictions of dogs playing poker for which the artist was commissioned in 1903. Two of the original oil paintings from the much-imitated series were sold at auction in 2005 for US$590,000.

Left: Annie Duke secured her reputation as one of the foremost professional poker players in the world with victory in the 2004 WSOP Tournament of Champions, and with it a US$2 million prize.

Below: Mark Twain, born Samuel Langhorne Clemens in 1835, is famed for his portrayals of life on the Mississippi river, the route by which poker spread throughout America. Of the game itself, Twain wrote: "There are few things so unpardonably neglected in our country as poker."

A life in poker

Given the sometimes colourful nature of their exploits, it is hardly surprising that a number of professionals are cashing in on their fame while trying to broaden the game's appeal. For example Phil Hellmuth, arguably the best tournament player in the world, is planning an autobiography, entitled *Poker Brat*, while *Amarillo Slim in a World Full of Fat People*, published in 2003, recounts Thomas Preston's eventful gambling career. Unsurprisingly, given his nihilistic approach to life, the late Stu Ungar is also the subject of a biography by Nolan Dalla and Peter Alson, entitled *One of a Kind: The Rise and Fall of Stuey 'The Kid' Ungar, the World's Greatest Poker Player*. Offering a different perspective on the game is literary critic Al Alvarez's account of the 1981 WSOP, *The Biggest Game in Town*. His analysis of the tournament, linked to the stories behind the players, makes it almost essential reading for anyone interested in the game. In a similar vein, Andy Bellin's *Poker Nation* and Anthony Holden's *Big Deal: One Year as a Professional Poker Player* offer two more interpretations of time spent playing cards for a living.

Poker tuition

Following the success of Frank R. Wallace's 1968 book *Advanced Concepts of Poker*, the 1970s saw a steady growth in the number of publications containing advice on how to play the game. The authoritative musings of top players and theorists revealed the analytical and mathematical skills employed at the poker table by the game's most successful exponents. One of the most influential is David Sklansky's *Hold 'Em Poker*, first published in 1976. He has subsequently written several other books on the game and also contributed to *Doyle Brunson's Super System: A Course in Power Poker*, another 1970s classic that covers a selection of the most popular variations. A guide to WSOP tournament strategy emerged in 1995, written by 1983 WSOP world champion Tom McEvoy while, from the next generation, Phil Hellmuth's *Play Poker Like the Pros*, published in 2003, explains the principles behind successful play. Some focus on one variation, others highlight the ploys to be adopted in a range of poker scenarios, but they represent a mere fraction of the literature available to those seeking to improve their understanding of the game.

HOW TO PLAY

Evidence concerning the origins of poker may be limited but what is certainly clear is that the game possesses qualities that make it immensely enjoyable to play. Most commentators regard poker as being a simple game to learn but one which may take a lifetime to master. For the newcomer, poker's lexicon of terms, added to the wide variety of poker games in existence, can make the journey of discovery seem a daunting prospect. The aim of this chapter, therefore, is to guide beginners through the practical aspects of play while also noting other considerations to be taken into account when sitting at the poker table.

Right: Another hand commences as the dealer distributes the cards to those involved in the game. The number of cards received by each player will depend on the poker variation being played since the first thing to understand about the game is that poker is really a term that applies to a huge family of vying games. Though each variation has its own basic rules and betting structure, this chapter covers those facets common to all poker games which a newcomer needs to understand before settling down to play.

POKER RULES AND REGULATIONS

Poker encompasses a range of hugely popular vying card games in which players bet against each other regarding the relative merits of the cards in their hand. All poker hands must consist of five cards only, although, in most forms of poker, players may be permitted to select these five from several more cards available to them during play. The term hand also applies to each game, typically of a few minutes duration, extending from the deal to the showdown.

Rankings, suits and aces

Binding the hundreds of poker variations together is the ranking of poker hands, a hierarchical list of the 2,598,960 different five-card combinations it is possible to draw from a standard 52-card deck. These rankings are based on the likelihood of being dealt any particular hand, with the most valuable – the royal flush (or royal straight flush) – being that regarded as the least likely to occur. Two other key components of poker are that the suits are of equal value and aces may count as both the highest or lowest card in any suit during the course of play.

One anomaly is that, beyond universal acceptance of the ranking of hands, there are no official rules of play in existence for any of poker's many variations. This situation gives rise to confusion among players new to the game. Unlike most organized professional sports, poker has no established international federation or governing body to ratify the rules, resolve disputes and generally protect the integrity of the game. In tournament poker, however, this may change over time. The World Poker Association was launched in March 2006, and is an organization that aims to establish uniform codes of conduct governing playing rules and etiquette on the global tournament circuit.

Right: The dealer button, sometimes referred to as 'the buck', is used to show which player is acting as the dealer for each particular hand. Buttons are most commonly used in commercial card rooms which employ dealers to control the action. The button provides a simple visual reminder of who is acting as the nominal dealer for each hand.

Royal flush (or royal straight flush). The highest-ranked hand in poker, consisting of an ace-high straight in any one of the four suits. All suits are ranked equally.

Straight flush. The second-best hand in poker, consisting of five cards of the same suit in sequential order. If two or more players hold a straight flush, the high card determines the winner.

Four of a kind. Four cards of one rank supplemented by any additional card. If two or more players hold four of a kind, the highest rank wins.

Full house. Three cards of one rank plus two of another. The value of the hand is determined by the three cards of the same rank meaning, for example, that K, K, K, J, J beats Q, Q, Q, A, A.

Flush. Five cards of the same suit not in sequential order. Competing flushes are determined by the high card, then the second highest and so on. An ace-high flush in diamonds comprising A, J, 10, 5, 2, beats an ace-high flush in spades consisting of A, J, 9, 8, 7, for example.

Object of the game

Poker is a gambling game, of course, and the objective is to win money, usually represented by gaming chips, from the other players at the table. The chips staked during each hand of play constitute the pot and this is claimed by the winner at the conclusion of the hand. The winner is determined by either one of two methods: a player who makes a bet that is unmatched by any opponent can win the pot without having to reveal his cards; alternatively, if two or more players match bets to the conclusion of the hand, they then reveal their cards at the showdown and the holder of the best poker hand claims the spoils.

The gambling element

For any poker session to be meaningful and fulfilling, it must involve gambling for stakes that are of value to the players. Whether that means playing for pennies around the kitchen table or paying the US$10,000 entry fee for the World Series of Poker championship tournament is entirely dependent on a player's resources and motivation. Both experienced players and novices are sensibly advised to select a game at which the stake levels are not so high as to create hardship in the event of a heavy loss. Since one of the key factors required to play good poker is discipline, recognizing one's own skill level and the stakes for which one can afford to play is an important step in the right direction. For the beginner this is crucial advice given that the majority of players will inevitably lose money as they effectively pay for their education during their early games.

Straight. Five cards of differing suits in sequential order. Again, when there are competing straights, the high card determines the winner.

Three of a kind. Three cards of one rank plus two other unmatched cards.

Two pairs. A hand comprising two cards of one rank, two cards of another rank and one odd card, known as the 'kicker'. If two or more players possess two pairs, the high pair dictates the value of the hand, followed by the second pair and ultimately the kicker. So A, A, 2, 2, Q beats K, K, Q, Q, 5 and A, A, 10, 10, Q beats A, A, 10, 10, J.

One pair. Two cards of the same rank plus three unmatched cards. The rank of the pair determines the value of the hand but, should two players both show a pair of the same rank, then the remaining cards come into play. So, 5, 5, A, K, 2, beats 5, 5, A, 10, 8.

High card. A hand comprising five assorted cards, all of differing ranks and suits. Its value is dictated by the highest card.

A DECK OF CARDS

♦ ♣ ♥ ♠

Any standard deck of 52 cards will suffice for an informal game of poker, but it is recommended that a fresh deck is used to underline the integrity of the game, this being common practice in casinos and clubs. In home games, having two easily distinguishable decks in operation is a good idea since this helps to maintain a steady rhythm to proceedings. The spare deck can be shuffled and cut during the play of a hand so that it is immediately ready for dealing the next. Players may request that the deck be changed at any time, perhaps because cards have become inadvertently marked or spoiled during play.

CHIPS, STAKES AND BUY-INS

Before learning the standard playing procedure for any of poker's many variations, prospective players should consider why they wish to engage in a game. This means contemplating whether playing poker is to be purely a social pleasure or a serious pursuit. Poker, by design, generates competition, so it is important for players to be aware of their own attitudes towards winning and losing, since both are inevitable consequences of play. Being fully engaged in a game can provide a player with a vast range of mental and emotional challenges. For those serious enough to consider earning a living from poker, controlling one's emotions and staying focused on the task in hand is an essential skill.

Stakes

Most poker is played socially for modest stakes, enabling players to appreciate the aesthetics of the game without fearing imminent financial ruin. The essence of poker is in the gambling, which is why it is important for players to compete at stake levels within their means. This is crucial, for the cash sums at stake should not distract players from their primary

task, which is to assess opponents, absorb the nuances of play and decide when to make a move. Understanding the character as well as the betting habits of an opponent is crucial to becoming a successful poker player.

The buy-in

Every venue staging a game possesses a set of house rules governing play. These cover the technical issues concerning the betting structures of the poker variations dealt in the establishment, as well as points of etiquette on acceptable behaviour at the table. For example, the minimum amount of money required to sit in on a game – the 'buy-in' – will be stipulated, and there may also be a rule forbidding players from discussing the play of a hand in progress. These rules vary from one card room to the next, and players should take individual responsibility for checking them prior to sitting in on a game. Anybody planning to host a poker game should also devise a basic set of rules governing issues such as the length of each session, the poker variations to be played and any restrictions to be observed regarding the minimum or

Above: Modern-day poker, often played in casinos, can have a very different etiquette to a private game, but is equally exciting.

Right: During the 19th century, poker was largely a private, social pursuit, although high-stake games were liable to turn ugly.

Left: Cards are kept close to the chest and sneaky pocketing of early winnings is strictly off-limits – chips must remain on show and in circulation throughout a game. All casinos have their own unique colourful designs or at least a logo on their poker chip sets.

Below: Betting with chips rather than money helps players lose their gambling inhibitions, and keeps the game running smoothly.

maximum bet. This helps to prevent unnecessary disputes and creates the proper context for poker so that a session balances the social and competitive demands of the participants.

Chips

Poker chips are special tokens representing a fixed amount of money. Especially in card rooms and casinos, poker chips are also known as checks. Each casino has a unique set of chips, even if the casino is part of a larger company. This distinguishes a casino's chips from others, since each chip and token on the gaming floor has to be backed up with the appropriate amount of cash. Durable gaming chips enhance any poker session, since they are cleaner and easier to use than cash, thus quickening proceedings and adding credibility to the game. Using chips does separate players, conceptually at least, from the notion of betting for real cash sums. Novices need to take this effect into account when learning the game, but it can prove beneficial during play. Detaching oneself from the monetary value of the chips at the table helps to reduce inhibitions when betting, which, within the context of the game, is considered essential in enabling a player to make calculated and rational decisions.

CHIP MANAGEMENT
♦ ♣ ♥ ♠

One of the key conventions in poker is that players must ensure that their chips are clearly visible to all at the table during play. Purposely trying to obscure them, by perhaps stacking high-denomination chips behind rows of lower-value chips, is a breach of etiquette. Chips in play at the table must remain in circulation for the duration of the game, with players not permitted to pocket any substantial winnings to protect themselves against a losing session. Also, any player may ask an opponent how many chips they have left when considering a betting decision, often seen in tournament play when one player may consider betting a sufficient amount to force an opponent to bet all-in, if calling.

Left: The colour of plain chips is determined by the denomination. For example 1s are white, 50s are orange, 100s are black, 500s are purple and 1000s are burgundy. The number is embedded so it does not rub off during normal play.

WHERE TO PLAY

The upsurge in poker's popularity has provided experienced players and newcomers alike with an increased range of opportunities to indulge their passion. Online poker leads the way in offering players ready access to a game from the comfort of their own homes. The benefit of this is that newcomers can learn quickly, and in private, before venturing out to test their skills in public. However, poker in the virtual environment denies players the chance to read anything into their opponents' play that may be conveyed through body language, so maintaining a 'poker face' – a face that reveals no thoughts or emotions – is of less importance. For those who relish the face-to-face battles inherent in play, this lack of social interaction at the table reduces the appeal of the game considerably.

Home games

The culture of the home game as a means of entertaining friends or colleagues is an established part of poker. Popularly regarded as an excuse for men to gather on a regular basis, away from the distractions of work and family, the numbers of women who similarly engage in home games renders this image somewhat anachronistic. Overall, the home game is considered the preserve of the amateur player for whom money won or lost is of secondary importance to the social act of participating.

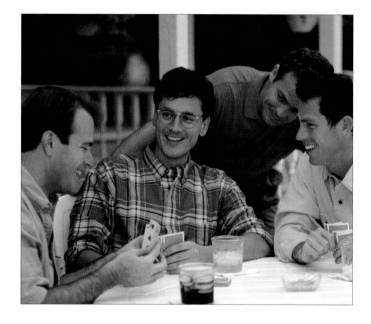

Instigating a regular game requires planning in order to address the potentially contentious issues that may arise during play. Declaring what variation of poker to play, how the betting is to be structured and how much is required to buy in to the game is essential. Also, it is advisable to set a time limit on participation so that everyone who is playing is immediately aware of when play will finish. Players who intend to leave the game before the agreed conclusion are usually expected to make this clear, as a matter of courtesy. Anyone who habitually sits in for a few hands before departing hastily with a quick profit is soon likely to prove an unwelcome participant in a primarily social game. Practical concerns such as the seating available, the decks of cards to be used and

Above: A home poker game in progress, perhaps typically conveying the image of poker as primarily a masculine pursuit. Owing to the explosion in media coverage of poker, the popularity of the game is such that many more people are once again enjoying the social benefits that come with sitting at a table to play cards with a few friends.

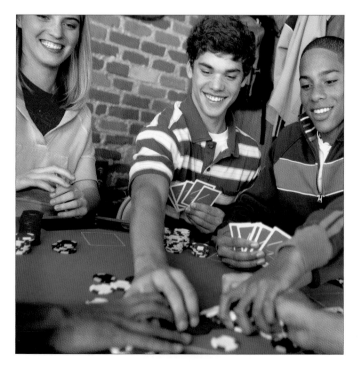

Left: Teenagers having fun playing poker, demonstrating that the game has aspects that make it appealing to people of all ages and doesn't need to involve money changing hands. Card games have long been a source of amusement for friends and family, of course, with many of today's professionals acquiring a taste for poker long before leaving school.

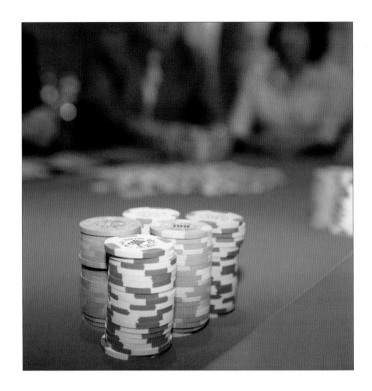

sufficient chips to accommodate all players must be considered. Also, having clear house rules covering acceptable poker play and etiquette will maintain the integrity of the game, making it more enjoyable for all.

Casinos and clubs

Home games may be the natural medium for occasional poker players, but, for those who take the game a little more seriously, playing poker in a casino or at a club will undoubtedly prove appealing. Obviously, with staff on hand to organize the games,

Above: The scene at a casino poker table in Las Vegas, popularly regarded as the poker capital of the world. Anyone who takes their game seriously will gravitate towards a club or casino in order to gain experience, learn from others and perhaps even make a regular income from their favoured pastime.

enforce the rules and even provide refreshments, this pleasure comes at a cost. Poker has never been considered an especially profitable game for casinos because, unlike in blackjack and roulette, players compete against each other and not the house. Instead, a fee, known as the 'rake', is levied in one of two ways. In small-stakes cash games, the house dealer may take a cut from each pot, this being anything from two to ten per cent of the amount staked. Alternatively, there may be a set hourly charge for the facilities, this being more likely in games contested by so-called 'high-rollers' – gamblers who play for large stakes.

Online poker

The proliferation of online poker sites over the last ten years has undoubtedly provided a boost to the game's popularity. Anyone possessing a computer and access to the Internet is now able to sit in at a game within minutes, and millions of people worldwide have been seduced into doing just that. The major sites such as PartyPoker, PokerStars and PokerRoom offer several different poker variations at stake levels ranging from a few cents to hundreds of dollars, the US dollar being the common currency in operation at most sites. It is also possible to play poker online at no cost, since 'play money' games are provided, primarily to encourage newcomers to learn the game inexpensively before trying their luck at the real money tables.

Right: Online poker is one of the success stories of the 21st century with millions of players taking advantage of the Internet to participate in a game from the comfort of home. However, not everybody views such convenient access to gambling opportunities as being personally or socially beneficial.

CHOOSING A GAME

The many variations of poker are testament to the curiosity and resourcefulness exhibited by players in the past as they sought fresh ways to make the game ever more satisfying. Some developments were introduced by sharp players with a keen mathematical knowledge and a desire to make their poker playing more lucrative. Others sprung from a need to include more players in proceedings. The number of cards available to each player, the scale of the betting, and the frequency of betting rounds must all be considered, but the degree of flexibility offered by poker means that one can formulate a game for every occasion.

The number of players

In amateur games, assessing which variation to play is most likely to be influenced by the number of players wishing to participate as well as their individual tastes. On the assumption that one deck of cards must suffice and that discarded cards are not to be recycled during play, choosing the right game can prove challenging. Texas Hold 'em may be appealing for several reasons, but furnishing players with only two cards at the deal makes it a more inclusive game than some others. Between two and twenty players could play, although casinos, both real and online, limit participation to a maximum of ten players as this is much more manageable. As a general guide, draw poker suits up to six players, stud poker should be limited to no more than eight players, and Omaha, like Texas Hold 'em, may accommodate up to ten players at a sitting.

The stakes

Choosing the correct stake level for a game should be governed by two factors: the minimum amount of the buy-in and the betting structure involved. Players are advised to begin with at least one hundred times the value of the minimum bet and this is commonly the upper limit placed on the buy-in for online cash games. To voluntarily buy in for fewer chips than

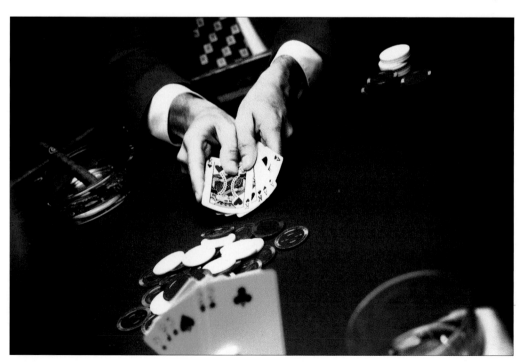

Above: The basic equipment required for a poker game remains a table, a deck of cards and some chips. Depending on the variation played, poker can accommodate from two to twenty players although something between six and ten players is generally the norm. Fewer than six players can make a game uncompetitive while more than ten players at a table can make it almost unmanageable.

Left: A hand of draw poker comes to a conclusion with the 'showdown' as the players in contention for the chips in the centre of the table – the pot – reveal their cards to determine the winner. The game remains the oldest recognized form of poker and is usually the first variation that anyone learns to play.

one's opponents is immediately disadvantageous since a player doing so will soon be pressurized by those in a superior chip position. Equally important is the betting structure of the game. 'Fixed-limit' poker is probably the most popular since it provides players with a means of estimating potential gains and losses during the progress of a hand. This is because, as the term implies, the maximum bet permitted is set at a fixed amount. It therefore represents a less risky prospect than playing 'pot-limit' or 'no-limit' poker, betting structures that permit players to bet all their chips on a single hand. These structures favour the experienced player whereas the style of poker that is most popular among casual players is one incorporating low stakes, strict limits on the maximum bet permitted, and several betting rounds to help build a substantial pot.

Table stakes

A 'table stakes' game is one in which players can only bet with the chips in front of them during the play of a hand. This prevents them from buying more chips during a prolonged betting confrontation. Any player wanting to 'call' – or match – a bet made by an opponent when lacking sufficient chips may still invest in the pot by betting 'all-in' with the remainder. Subsequent bets from other players are kept apart from the original, or main, pot and constitute what is termed a 'side pot', upon which the all-in player has no claim. The rule is applied universally in formal poker and safeguards players from being frozen out of a game in the face of deliberately heavy or intimidating betting by opponents.

DEALER'S CHOICE

♦ ♣ ♥ ♠

A popular means of deciding which poker variation to play is to adopt a policy of 'dealer's choice', whereby the dealer for each hand specifies the game, the procedure and any special rules that may apply. Prevalent in home games where having fun may be more important than winning money, this is the likeliest source of poker variations involving wild cards – nominated cards, twos (deuces) for example, or the joker perhaps, that can be counted as a card of any other value in order to improve the quality of a hand.

Above right: The deck of cards should be shuffled prior to the deal of each hand with care being taken not to expose any cards to players. Ordinarily, the dealer for the next hand will shuffle the cards first before asking the player to the immediate right to cut the deck. Knowing how to shuffle the cards quickly and efficiently is a skill in itself, but it does help to keep the rhythm of the game flowing.

Right: The situation after the 'flop' in Texas Hold 'em for one lucky player who has made a royal flush. Players are dealt two personal cards – hole cards – to start the game. The flop is the moment when the first three of a maximum five community cards are revealed. Here, the player is in the enviable position of already holding an unbeatable hand, known as a 'lock hand' or 'the nuts'.

GENERAL SEQUENCE OF PLAY

Although every poker variation possesses its own specific pattern of play, there are practical elements common to all. Each hand begins with the deal, progresses through a series of betting rounds and ends with the winner claiming the pot, either by making a bet unmatched by any opponent, or by revealing the best poker hand at the end of the final betting round, known as the 'showdown'. The betting itself is usually initiated before the deal, when some or all players, depending on the variation played, make a nominal compulsory bet to ensure that there is a pot to be contested at every deal.

The deal

To begin the game, the nominated dealer must thoroughly shuffle the deck, taking care not to inadvertently expose any card in the process. Usually, the player to the dealer's right then cuts the cards by lifting the top portion of the deck and placing it on the table, at which point the dealer places the remaining cards on top. The dealer then distributes the cards from the top of the deck with each player

receiving one card each, in turn, beginning with the player on the dealer's immediate left. A clockwise distribution around the table follows until each player has the requisite number of cards for the poker variation being played. In draw poker, for example, each player receives a starting hand of five cards all dealt face down. Yet in five-card stud, players receive just two cards with which to begin play, the first dealt face down and the second, face up. This second card, the first exposed, or 'up' card in a player's hand, is known as the 'door card'.

Betting rounds

The betting rounds, or betting intervals as they are sometimes called, are those occasions when players must make a decision as to whether they continue in the hand or not. Depending on the poker variation being played, making a bet may be optional or obligatory. In seven-card stud, for example, the player showing the lowest door card after the deal is obliged to make a nominal bet known as the 'bring-in'. Anyone else wishing to continue in the hand must

Above: A player makes a bet in a game of five-card stud. This poker variation begins with each player receiving two cards, one face down and one face up, prior to the opening betting round.

Left: A casino poker game in progress in which a professional dealer is dealing the cards, clockwise around the table. The game itself is Texas Hold 'em with the players each receiving two cards from the dealer before the first betting round begins.

Left: When betting, players are advised to make their aims clear by announcing 'call' or 'raise', for example, since their betting actions alone may not be obvious to opponents at the table. Also, the chips that constitute a bet should be placed on the table immediately in front of the player, making it clear to everybody how the betting is progressing.

Below: To the victor, the spoils as the showdown reveals who has the best poker hand. The showdown occurs when two or more players have matched bets in the final betting round, after which they display their cards to determine the winner. The only other way in which a player can win the pot during the game is by making a bet that nobody else calls. In this event, the bettor claims the chips without having to show the winning hand.

then put chips into the pot. Yet in Texas Hold 'em, after the 'flop' (the dealing of the first three cards to the board), has been revealed, all players remaining in the hand may opt not to bet. This is known as checking and at this point, the next card, known as the 'turn card', is dealt to the table. In general, the evolution of poker has seen players receiving more cards and having to negotiate more betting rounds for three key reasons. First, to increase the potential size of the pot on offer and thus encourage more players to remain involved in each hand; second, to counteract the caution exhibited by extremely conservative players averse to risk; and third, to increase the levels of skill, deception and subterfuge required to win.

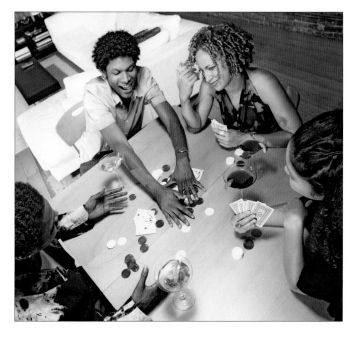

DEALER'S ROLE
♦ ♣ ♥ ♠

During the play of each hand, the dealer is responsible for distributing the cards and ensuring the game is played in accordance with the rules. This involves monitoring play to ensure that everyone acts in turn, bets when required and conducts themselves with appropriate regard for poker etiquette. In casinos and clubs, dealers are often provided as part of the service and can be expected to manage the game smoothly and efficiently. In home games, although proceedings may be more informal, the dealer should be similarly managing the progress of the hand in play, even when no longer competing for the pot.

Determining the winner

In poker there are two methods for determining the winner of each hand. If, at the conclusion of all betting rounds, there are two or more players who have matched stakes, they are required to reveal their cards and the best poker hand on display wins the pot. This is called the showdown. In the event of a tie, the pot is divided equally between those players possessing winning hands of the same value. The other method of winning the pot involves making a bet that no opponent matches. Should this be the case, then the player making the bet can take the pot without revealing the winning hand.

BETTING TERMS EXPLAINED

To obtain the most from poker it is important to understand the meanings of the betting terms used during play. The phrases will be familiar to anyone who has seen poker on television, but for those completely new to the game, the key terms regarding the betting or action at the table are explained here.

Antes and blinds

Compulsory bets called 'antes' are made before the deal of each hand, to guarantee that there is something in the pot to generate competition. Ordinarily, the sums involved are small, relative to the stake levels in operation during the game, and the number of players compelled to pay the ante, or 'ante-up' as it is known, varies depending on the form of poker played. Generally speaking, the more betting rounds there are to be negotiated to the showdown, the smaller the antes required. In Texas Hold 'em and its close poker relative Omaha, the compulsory bets before the deal are known as the 'blinds'. Almost invariably, the two

players to the dealer's immediate left are required to make these bets which, as the term suggests, should be made before they see any cards.

Calling and folding

In order to 'call' a bet, also referred to as 'seeing' a bet, a player must simply match the amount bet by the previous player to have acted in the betting round. For example if the first player to act puts 50 chips in the pot, then all other players have the option of calling that bet of 50 chips to retain their interest. Should they not wish to match the bet, then they must 'fold' – or 'pass' – by discarding their cards. In doing so, they relinquish any claim on the pot and any chips they may have already committed to it.

Bets and raises

Two of the key elements of poker are 'bets' and 'raises' because they increase the cost to opponents of staying in a hand and suggest strength on the part of the

Right: Draw and stud poker variations require all players to pay a nominal sum – the ante – into the pot before the deal. Here, player A is the dealer, as indicated by the dealer button (D), and everybody has 'anted-up' by contributing 10 chips each to the pot. The size of the ante varies depending on the stake levels, but it is usually less than the minimum bet permitted once the cards have been dealt. In this instance, the minimum bet in the first round may be set at 25 chips, for example.

player making them. The term bet specifically refers to the action made by the first player to put chips in the pot during each betting round. Subsequent bets during the round are then referred to as calls or raises. To make a raise involves a player matching the previous bet and then, in most cases, making a bet of at least equal value. For example, if the bet stands at 50 chips, anyone wishing to raise can ordinarily expect to bet at least 100 chips – 50 chips to call the outstanding bet and a further 50 chips to increase the betting level.

The check

Provided no betting – compulsory or voluntary – has yet taken place during a betting round, players may 'check' rather than bet when it is their turn to act. By checking, a player defers a decision to bet but remains in the hand. If an opponent subsequently makes a bet then, of course, players who previously checked must, when the action returns to them, choose whether to fold, call or raise; checking at this stage is no longer an option. Games played for small stakes will often feature informal rules to restrict or prohibit checking, since it is a tactic favoured by conservative players.

Betting statements

When making a betting decision, all players are encouraged to be clear and precise about their intentions. In this regard, verbally announcing "fold", "call" or "raise" keeps everyone informed as the action moves around the table. Most importantly, the intention to call or raise should be stated before a player commits chips to the pot. This is to discourage 'string bets', which occur when a player, while slowly adding chips to the pot, deliberately delays announcing the scale of the bet in order to study the reactions of opponents.

MUCKING A HAND
♦ ♣ ♥ ♠

The 'muck' is the pile of discarded cards that accrue during the play of each hand. As players fold, they 'muck their hand' by placing their cards face down with the other discards. Responsibility for ensuring folded hands are properly mucked falls upon the dealer; only players still contesting the pot should have cards in front of them on the table.

Left: In Texas Hold 'em and Omaha, the two players to the dealer's left make compulsory bets before the deal, these being known as the blinds. Here, the dealer is again player A meaning that player B must pay the small blind – 10 chips – while player C is forced to bet the big blind, typically double the small blind, of 20 chips. After the deal, player D will be the first to make an active decision on whether to contest the hand.

BIG BLIND 20 SMALL BLIND 10

BETTING STRUCTURES

Understanding the betting structure in place and how that affects the style of the game is absolutely imperative when opting to play poker. As with the number of poker variations, several betting structures have been developed over the years to suit the tastes, temperaments and financial means of different players. Cautious players tend to favour the small-stakes, fixed- and spread-limit games in which profits are not so lucrative, but losses can be more easily controlled. Those who prefer a more volatile game are inexorably drawn to pot-limit and no-limit poker where the rewards are potentially high, but the risk of heavy losses is also greater.

Fixed-limit

This betting structure applies traditionally to home or social games and its popularity has ensured that it is widely available in casinos and online. In fixed-limit games, all bets are fixed at a level constituting both the maximum and the minimum permissible. Ordinarily, this level may be doubled in the latter betting rounds of a hand. In a game of five-card stud, for example, bets and raises may be restricted to 100 chips in the first two betting rounds, and to 200 chips in the final two rounds. This would be indicated as a 100/200 fixed-limit game.

Spread-limit

This style of betting differs slightly from fixed-limit poker in that bets may be made for any amount between the specified upper and lower limits. In a 100/300 spread-limit game, therefore, a player may bet any sum from 100 to 300 chips. Any subsequent raises are capped at a maximum of 300 chips. Games with several betting rounds may have an increase in the limit applying for the later rounds. A 100/300/500/1,000 Texas Hold 'em game, for instance, might have maximum bets and raises limited to 300 chips for the first two betting rounds while on the 'turn' and the 'river' – respectively the fourth and fifth community cards dealt to the board – the upper limit would rise to 500 and 1,000 chips respectively.

Above: Chips lined up prior to a tournament. Poker tournaments continue to increase in popularity and, in these, each player is credited with the same number of chips before play commences.

Right: A close-up shot of the moment when the winner rakes in the chips from a big pot. Though inexperienced players tend to think that profitable poker is linked to winning plenty of pots, the key to success is in regularly winning the few really big pots that might be contested during a session. Players who achieve this are generally much more selective in the quality of hands they play.

Pot-limit

This betting structure is most popular among experienced players, but it can be difficult to follow and potentially very expensive for beginners. In pot-limit poker, minimum bets are structured as they are in fixed-limit poker, but the maximum bet is limited only by the size of the pot. For example, assuming the antes total 100 chips, in the opening betting round of a 100/200 game, player A as the first player to act might make the minimum bet of 100 chips, making the pot total 200. Player B must then call for 100 to stay in the game, but, if considering a pot-size raise, that player can raise by a further 300 chips, matching the antes of 100, player A's bet of 100 and player B's own call of 100. With the pot now at 600, player C is faced with a minimum call of 400 chips to match player B's bet and boost the pot to 1,000 chips. If choosing to raise the maximum allowed, player C may bet an additional 1,000 chips, making a bet of 1,400 in total and increasing the pot to

2,000 chips. This illustrates just how rapidly pots can grow in an aggressive pot-limit game and emphasizes the need for cool judgement under pressure.

No-limit

This betting style is applicable in many tournaments, has a minimum betting structure in place in common with fixed-limit poker, but the maximum bet permitted is limited only by the number of chips at a player's disposal. Pushing one's entire chip stack into the pot and betting all-in is a powerful play when in a dominant position during the game, and exudes desperation when short stacked. But this facet of no-limit poker helps create serious opportunities to bluff and intimidate opponents. For that reason, it is generally not recommended for inexperienced players, who may understandably baulk at the idea of having to risk all their chips on the very first hand.

Left: In no-limit poker players have the option to bet 'all-in' by committing all their chips to the pot when it is their turn to act, but they do run the risk of losing all their chips on a single hand if called.

Left: This shows how volatile the betting can be in a game using a pot-limit betting structure. Following player A's initial bet of 100 chips, player B decides to raise by the amount in the pot, the maximum bet permitted. To make the raise requires 400 in total from player B, 100 to call player A's bet, putting 300 chips in the pot, plus 300 to match the pot total. Player C now makes a pot-limit raise as well, betting 400 to cover player B's bet and 1,000 more to match the new total in the pot. The action is then on player D who must bet 1,400 chips merely to call.

THE SHOWDOWN

In poker, there are two ways to win the pot. If a player should make a bet that is not called by any opponent, that player claims the pot and is under no obligation to show the winning hand. Alternatively, if two or more players are still contesting the hand at the end of the final betting round, then those players should reveal their cards simultaneously in what is termed the showdown. The player judged to possess the highest-ranking hand of those on display then wins the pot. If one or more hands are tied, then the chips in the pot are divided equally between the winners.

Above: Amid the excitement of a game it can be all too easy to misread one's hand. This is merely an A-high straight and not, as it might appear, a royal flush.

Above: This A-high flush in hearts is superior to the straight pictured above and shows the value of the showdown. It allows everyone to determine the winner in the event that a player misreads a hand, perhaps by claiming a royal flush when only an A-high straight exists.

Above: At the showdown, it is customary for those players still contesting the pot to reveal their cards face up on the table. The player holding the royal flush in clubs here can be confident of victory.

ACTING IN TURN
♦ ♣ ♥ ♠

It is essential that players remember to act only when it is their turn to do so. Betting out of turn may seem a minor infringement, but it unnecessarily presents opponents with information regarding the potential strength of a hand. Those players whose decision has been pre-empted will obviously modify their betting intentions based on such a mistake, and folding out of turn presents similar advantages to opponents. A player acting first often has little information upon which to base a strategy, but if a couple of opponents fold out of turn, that player's situation immediately improves.

Declarations

At a showdown between two players, it is quite common for the player calling an opponent's final bet to ask that opponent to reveal his cards first rather than for both hands to be revealed simultaneously. Should the caller recognize that the opponent's hand is superior he may legitimately muck his cards and thus conceal information concerning his own hand. In regular poker, this procedure occurs quite frequently, as experienced players have little difficulty in identifying whether they hold a winning hand.

It is quite possible, however, particularly in poker played with wild cards, for a player to misread the value of a hand and declare that it is higher or lower in value than is actually the case. To avoid this situation it is worth applying the 'cards speak' poker rule such that, when the hands are exposed at the showdown,

Left: Steve McQueen and Robert DoQui discuss play in *The Cincinnati Kid*. Commentating on proceedings at the table and debating the hand in progress, though often tolerated during an informal game, is generally regarded as taboo. Antagonistic or disparaging comments regarding an opponent's play are also discouraged in most card rooms.

Below: Frank Sinatra, as Frankie Machine in United Artists' *The Man with the Golden Arm*, shown in the marathon 36-hour poker session, one of the highlights of director Otto Preminger's production.

the winning hand is adjudicated solely using the cards on display. Players who make mistakes in verbally declaring the value of their hands are thus prevented from winning or losing as a result of their error.

Split-pot, high-low games

This popular form of poker involves the players with the highest hand and the lowest hand both claiming a share of the pot. Ideally, players aim to win all the chips, or 'scoop the pot', by holding both the high and low hands simultaneously. When betting is completed but before hands are revealed at the showdown, players must declare whether they are competing for the high hand, low hand or both. This declaration, best made simultaneously, usually involves a procedure as follows. Players take a couple of their chips and place their hands under the table to conceal any activity. At a given signal from the dealer, all competing players then reveal the number of chips in their hand to indicate their declared intention. No chips in the hand symbolizes a low call, one chip indicates a high call and two chips means the player intends to call both high and low. Once again, to avoid confusion over identifying the best hands, both high and low, it is advisable to adopt the cards speak ruling.

ACCEPTABLE TABLE TALK
♦ ♣ ♥ ♠

Debating events during the play of a hand is generally frowned upon, irrespective of whether a player is still participating or awaiting the next deal. Careless comments by players regarding which cards they folded may provide clues to the strength of the hands still in contention for the pot. Making abusive or critical comments regarding an opponent's play while contesting a hand is known as 'coffeehousing'. While it is not necessarily impolite, it is not always considered a breach of etiquette. In America, it is widely accepted as an integral part of poker culture, whereas in Europe, the opposite tends to be true, certainly at a formal level. On the international tournament circuit, currently attracting widespread television coverage, the debate over what constitutes acceptable table talk continues. Some of the more notable professionals who regularly appear on television, among them Phil Hellmuth, Mike 'The Mouth' Matusow and Tony G, are extremely vocal during play. As arch competitors, they are inclined to use every tactic to try and obtain an edge over their opponents which, though it may at times seem unethical, can provide entertaining television for the viewer.

CASH OR RING GAMES

Cash games, or 'ring games' as they are sometimes called, are the mainstay of poker, both in casinos and online. Characteristically, they involve players competing against each other, typically for several hours, in games with constant betting structures. In tournament poker, the betting levels increase as play progresses, to force players into confrontations that might see them eliminated. By contrast, the level of the compulsory bets – the antes and blinds – in cash games remains the same throughout, as do the upper and lower betting limits applicable. This difference is influential in the long-term and short-term strategies players need to implement in order to play profitable cash game poker, but there are many other factors equally worthy of consideration.

Adopting the right approach

Most regular home games played for cash have their own protocols governing the poker variations played, the minimum and maximum amount of the buy-in, and the level of the betting. Casinos and online poker sites will also have regulations covering these aspects of the game, while offering a much wider range of cash games to match the personality and the financial means of every player. And since these may be operated around the clock, any one table will see players regularly cashing out to be replaced by others buying in.

Given such choice, a player's first decision concerns which poker variation to play, it being advisable to limit this to the game or games the player understands best. The next factor to consider is the scale of the betting, as determined by the antes or blinds, since this will dictate the size of a player's buy-in. Most experts recommend buying in for the maximum permitted, since this provides a player with the resources to exploit early winning opportunities while offering a safeguard against a run of poor cards.

The next objective is to find a suitable table at which to play. Personal preference will dictate whether a player selects a full-handed game of up to ten players, or opts instead for a short-handed game with as few as two or three opponents. In a full-handed game, having the patience to wait for a strong hand before betting is immensely important, given the

Above: 'Splashing the pot' by dumping your chips in among the others already staked can lead to confusion. Ordinarily, players should each make a bet by placing the required number of chips in a neat stack just in front of them.

Right: Joseph Hachem competing in the WSOP world championship poker tournament which he went on to win. Here he is shown piling up his chips during the event at Binion's Gambling Hall and Hotel in July 2005.

number of players and potentially better hands in opposition. A short-handed game, on the other hand, is likely to feature looser betting, with players more prepared to gamble on marginal hands.

General advice

Aside from the practical aspects of playing cash game poker, there are also some general points that should be considered by those eager for poker action. Most professionals insist that, to play the game at the highest level, players need to be aware of their own strengths and weaknesses, whether physical, mental or emotional. The reasoning is that without understanding oneself and one's motivation for playing, it is difficult to set clear and realistic poker objectives.

The professionals also advocate some very basic principles for improving play, key among them being not to drink alcohol, to avoid playing when tired or feeling stressed, and never to play with frightened money – that is, money that is reserved for other purposes. Additionally, while rebuying chips may be permissible in a cash game once a player's stack is exhausted, borrowing money from other players in order to do so is rarely, if ever, a good idea.

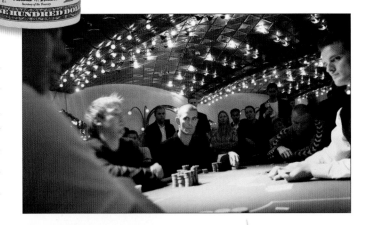

THE BANKROLL
♦ ♣ ♥ ♠

A player's bankroll is the money set aside specifically for playing poker, which, for the serious player, may represent a substantial capital sum to be invested in the game. Whether siphoned from a regular income or shrewdly accrued from poker itself, the state of this bankroll serves as a barometer for a player's fortunes at the table. Disciplined cash game players adopt a long-term view, regarding the outcome of any single session as incidental to the overriding objective of securing a profit.

Above: The increased popularity of televised tournament poker has led to an increase in the number of regular tournaments held by casinos and card rooms around the world. As players new to the game seek to mimic what they see on television, so the casinos have responded by offering tournaments with low entry fees to attract more players keen to experience tournament play for themselves.

Left: Carlos Mortensen celebrates becoming the 2001 WSOP world champion following his victory in the US$10,000 no-limit Texas Hold 'em tournament at Binion's Horseshoe Hotel and Casino, Las Vegas. As is traditional, the winner's prize is presented on the table, in cash, as photographers capture the scene for posterity. The 29-year-old professional gambler beat Dewey Tomko into second place in order to claim the US$1.5 million prize for winning.

TOURNAMENT PLAY

Tournament play has many attributes that make it appealing, not least of which is that anyone with sufficient money to buy in to a major competition can find themselves competing on level terms against the stars of the contemporary game. Equally, there are a prolific number of online tournaments that, for a very modest outlay, offer the chance to win seats at some of the major events including the US$10,000 WSOP world championship game itself. Lower down the scale, tournament poker provides the opportunity for players to participate in a competitive and possibly profitable game for a fixed fee, making it easier to gauge potential losses. Indeed, there are even freeroll tournaments that require no entry fee at all, although the prizes for winning sometimes consist of tickets to more lucrative tournaments rather than cash.

Tournament structures

A variety of different tournament structures exist, although they are all based on the same knockout principle, by which one player accumulates all the chips as opponents lose theirs and are eliminated. During play, the antes or blinds are increased at regular intervals, thus dictating increases in the minimum bet. This mechanism propels even cautious players into betting action, since the alternative is to witness their chip stacks being eroded by the ever-increasing compulsory bets. The most popular games are well represented and the cost of entering a tournament need be no more than small change. Ordinarily, an additional house charge of up to ten per cent of the entry fee may be levied by the club or casino that plays host. Anyone wishing to contest a US$10 event contributes that sum to the prize pool,

Above: Age Spets (right) competing in the Poker Stars World Cup in 2005, a televised tournament featuring heads-up poker. This format involves two players only, facing each other across the table in poker combat, the object being to acquire all the opponent's chips to win the game.

Left: Dealers take a break during the 2005 WSOP. Often taken for granted by the players, the huge 24-hour casinos of Las Vegas employ an army of dealers, croupiers and waiting staff to meet the needs of their clients. Historically, Vegas dealers have rarely earned extravagant wages and it is customary for players to offer a small tip, known as a 'toke', to the dealer when they win a hand.

Left: Competitors at the British Open await the floor manager's command to 'shuffle up and deal' which will signify the beginning of the tournament. As can be seen, a well-subscribed tournament can develop into a slightly claustrophobic affair with opponents and other tables all in close proximity.

the cash that will be divided between the tournament's highest-placed finishers, and pays a further US$1 to the house to cover incidental costs. To win a share of the prize pool itself, a player will usually have to finish within the top ten per cent of all entrants, which, in a field of a thousand or more starters, represents a major examination of anybody's poker skills.

Freeze-outs, rebuys and add-ons

In freeze-out tournaments, all players begin with an equal number of chips but they are not allowed to buy any more at all during play. Players who lose all their chips are eliminated from the game. Rebuy tournaments, as the term suggests, are those in which players are permitted to buy additional chips after the game has started, subject to restrictions that vary from one tournament to another. Typically, rebuys are limited to the first hour or two of a tournament and are often only permissible if a player has fallen below a certain number of chips. For example a player who began with 1,500 chips may only be able to purchase more if down to 500 chips or less during the specified rebuy period. When this ends, it is common for players to have an additional chance to buy more chips, irrespective of their current chip status. This is termed the add-on. Following this, the rebuy tournament proceeds to a conclusion in freeze-out fashion.

CARD HANDLING

A general point of etiquette to remember when playing poker, especially in a formal and competitive environment, is that all those active in a hand should have their cards on the table immediately in front of them. This helps clarify exactly who is still participating in a hand, any folded cards having already been added to the muck.

In stud poker, the structure of the game naturally contrives this situation as it involves cards being dealt face up as well as face down. But many other poker variations involve players being dealt cards face down only. The value of these concealed cards, otherwise known as hole, or 'pocket cards', is unknown to opponents. Players often physically hold their cards to assess their opening hand, but it is recommended that they be replaced on the table as the betting begins.

BASIC POKER SKILLS

Absorbing the practical conventions of poker that govern the rules and patterns of play is obviously the first step along the road to becoming an above-average player. But beyond the mechanical processes of the deal and the betting structures lie the more esoteric elements of poker that make the game so challenging. These are the focus of attention in this chapter, which highlights the various skills that must be employed at the table in order to be competitive. Of course, many social players may consider that participating in an occasional poker game is of more importance than actually winning. Such opponents are regarded as 'fish', 'pigeons' or 'sheep' by the mercenary player who adopts a predatory approach, deploying the skills detailed here. Chief among these skills is an understanding of the theory of probability as it applies to poker, knowledge of which immediately gives the studious player an edge.

Right: Acknowledging that poker is a game of skill in which chance plays a part represents the first step on the way to becoming a better poker player. Anyone wishing to improve their game should always take a little time to consider the implications of any betting decision before committing their chips to the pot. Consistently successful players, while aware of the element of chance, make rational decisions based upon the information available at the table, and that is an acquired skill.

POKER ODDS: THE THEORY

The theory of probability was devised by 17th-century French philosophers and mathematicians Pierre de Fermat and Blaise Pascal after they had responded to a nobleman's query regarding a gambling game played with dice. They realized that it was possible to calculate the likelihood of an event happening by chance when a finite number of potential outcomes existed. To understand this, consider rolling a pair of dice with the aim of hitting a double 6. Each die presents six possible outcomes, so to calculate the total number of outcomes from rolling both involves multiplying the first six possibilities by the second set of six possibilities. This produces 36 potential outcomes in total, of which just one will realize a double 6, making the odds against this happening 35 to 1. Assuming a fair game, probability theory therefore suggests that in 36 rolls of the dice, a double 6 can be expected to materialize once; in 36,000 rolls, a pair of sixes can be expected to appear 1,000 times. This leads to an important point concerning probability in that the greater the sample of repeated events with multiple possible outcomes, the likelier it is that the results will more accurately reflect the probability of their occurrence. It is possible that in 36,000 rolls of the dice, a pair of sixes may result on anything from none to all 36,000 occasions, but the probability is that it will occur 1/36th of the time.

Above: A basic grasp of probability theory is an asset in poker and a simple example of the concept in action can be found when rolling a pair of dice. Each die presents six possible outcomes so the total number of combinations occurring when rolling a pair of dice can be calculated as 6 x 6. The chances of rolling a double 6 are therefore 1 in 36, representing odds of 35 to 1 against this event occurring.

Profitable knowledge

Understanding the significance of odds and probabilities in poker is absolutely crucial for anyone wishing to prosper at the game. Possessing such knowledge and applying it judiciously at the poker table inevitably gives a player an advantage over weaker opponents whose decisions are governed by instinct or a profound belief in luck alone. Being able to compare the probability of seeing beneficial cards with the odds of reward offered by the pot – the pot odds – enables a player to judge situations more clinically, something that is particularly useful when the stakes are high. It leads players into the realm of rational and reasoned decision-making which, in the long term, is likely to prove profitable, as they are readily able to distinguish the relative values of poker hands and bet accordingly.

Learning the basics

Although a keen knowledge of mathematics is an asset, the key elements of probability theory applicable to poker are simple enough to understand. First, the probability of an event occurring plus the probability of it not occurring must add up to 1. For example a 1 in 10 chance of securing a winning card represents a probability of 0.10 or 10 per cent, while the chances of it not occurring are 0.90 or 90 per cent. Whenever a 1 in 10 chance does present itself, it is sometimes worth recalling that a loss can be expected nine times as often as a win.

To calculate the probability of multiple events occurring in succession, often a requirement in poker, multiply the probability of the first by the probability of the second, then by the probability of the third and so on. The chance of receiving pocket aces – a pair of aces as hole cards – in Texas Hold 'em, therefore, can be expressed as the product of 4/52 x 3/51. Here it is crucial to bear in mind that the second probability is dependent on the player's first card being an ace. The product of 4/52 x 3/51 represents 0.45 per cent and equates to 1 chance in 222 of a pair of aces being dealt. Three aces appearing on the flop – the first three community cards that are dealt face up in the centre of the table all at one time – represents a probability of 4/52 x 3/51 x 2/50, which is 0.018 per cent. That

GIVE IT A WHIRL

Above: Odds are 4/52 = 0.076

Above: Odds are 4/52 x 3/51 = 0.0045

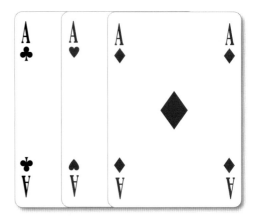

Above: Odds are 4/52 x 3/51 x 2/50 = 0.00018

equates to one flop in every 5,555. Computing the probability of either of two events occurring requires that the probability of each be *added* together before subtracting the probability of both taking place. So, if any ace, 7 or heart will offer a winning hand with two cards to come, the subtraction counteracts the possibility of counting the ace and 7 of hearts twice if these cards are among those unseen. Though it may seem daunting for the novice, the ability to make these calculations improves quickly with practice and experience.

Calculating probabilities

By way of illustration, imagine a game of seven-card stud in which, after six cards have been dealt, a player requires one more heart to secure an ace-high flush. If a player has seen 17 cards already – the player's own six cards and 11 others dealt face up to the player's opponents – of which six are hearts, then seven hearts remain among the 35 cards unseen by the player. This outcome has a 1 in 5 (20 per cent) chance of occurring, making the odds against a heart being dealt 4 to 1.

CALCULATING PROBABILITIES

PLAYER A

Right: In this seven-card stud example, a sixth card has been dealt to the three players contesting the hand. Player F shows the best hand and is first to act, betting 100 to make the pot total now 875. To win, Player A needs a heart with the final card to make an ace-high flush. With seven hearts remaining among the 35 unseen cards, he has a 1 in 5 chance of this occurring. A bet of 100 chips to win at least 875, meaning pot odds of nearly 9 to 1, makes calling for 100 a decent option as the odds of reward are greater than the odds against making the flush. Should player B call too, then player A has even better value in gambling on the 5 to 1 chance.

POKER ODDS: THE PRACTICE

Estimating probabilities requires speedy and often rough calculations, though these are usually enough to guide a player's betting decisions during a game. Experience will show that recurring themes arise during a session, leaving any player with three key questions to bear in mind when assessing the chances of winning. First, how many cards are needed to obtain or retain a winning hand? Second, how many unseen and potentially available cards remain to secure such a hand? Third, how many chances are there to be dealt the required cards?

Applying the knowledge

Whichever form of poker is played, players will frequently need one or more cards for a winning hand, but the odds against this occurring vary from game to game. In draw poker, a player holding two pairs, aces and sixes, may already hold a winning chance, but drawing a third ace or 6 to make a full house would make victory highly likely. To do so requires drawing one of four cards – the remaining aces and sixes – from among the 47 unseen cards, the probability of which is 4/47, showing odds fractionally better than 11 to 1 against. Yet holding the same hand in five-card stud with one more card to come presents a different betting proposition, as the player will have seen numerous cards face up on the table during play. If 15 opponents' face-up cards have been seen, of which none are aces or sixes,

Above: Professional poker player Carl Olson considers his next move as the hand unfolds. At this level of the game, players are highly skilled in evaluating the number of cards required to win and whether it is cost-effective to pursue them.

APPLYING THE KNOWLEDGE

PLAYER C

Right: Player C may already have the best hand, with two pairs, in this draw poker game, though there are 4 chances in 47 of drawing an ace or 6 to improve to a full house, reflecting odds of just under 11 to 1.

then the player has just 33 unseen cards from which to find a winner. The chances are 4/33, or fractionally more than 1 in 8, that an ace or 6 will be dealt to complete the full house, showing odds of just over 7 to 1. While the scenarios are similar, the odds against hitting a full house are much lower in the five-card stud example, but the player is likely to have negotiated more betting rounds to reach this position.

Judging situations

Using the concepts of probabilities and pot odds is crucial for serious poker players. Having a rough idea of the odds against securing a winning hand is better than betting blindly. Crucially, players are advised to focus on the chances not just of improving a hand, but of holding the eventual winner. Opponents also receive other cards as the game progresses, and in games such as Texas Hold 'em, a card that strengthens one hand may also improve another quite dramatically. This is a key aspect of community card games, like Hold 'em, in which all players combine exposed cards on the table with their own cards to form the best possible hand. Being aware that a hand can improve but still be beaten by another player is also worth considering.

Implied pot odds

Speculative gambles do occasionally pay off in poker, with players confounding the odds by betting when perhaps folding was a likelier option. Even world-class players sometimes bet speculatively, although usually after assessing the implied pot odds on offer during a hand. This means that a player considers the potential pot odds that might arise as a result of subsequent bets during the hand in play. For instance, betting 100 chips into a 500-chip pot may seem inadvisable when the odds against winning are 7 to 1. However, only two more callers would be required to expand the pot to 800 chips and thus improve the pot odds sufficiently to justify the decision. If successful, the player stands to win 700 chips for the bet of 100, accurately reflecting the odds against being dealt a card that can guarantee a winning hand. Given seven additional similar situations, the probability is that the player will be successful once, which will be sufficient to break even. By contrast, if the potential winnings on those seven occasions remain at 500 chips only, then even the single expected success would result in a net loss of 200 chips. This underlines how betting when the odds are favourable is the key to success.

APPLYING THE KNOWLEDGE

PLAYER C

Left: In this five-card stud example, player C also has the two pairs, aces and sixes, but the odds against securing a full house have improved to just over 7 to 1. This is the case because, since no aces or sixes are visible among the other players' hands, player C is now seeking any one of four cards from just 33 remaining unseen to improve to a full house.

CARD READING

Playing successful poker involves interpreting many strands of information that may be available. A grasp of probability theory is important but it can only be confidently implemented when a player is capable of reading the cards on display. This means being able to identify the strength of one's own hand and its chances of being improved, as well as considering the cards that may be held by opponents. Aside from draw poker, most variations involve several cards being revealed during a hand and this information, in addition to the betting patterns in evidence, can help a player to deduce the cards an opponent currently holds or is trying to obtain.

Assessing a hand

When assessing the qualities of any poker hand, players must first have an awareness of the average winning hand required in the poker variation played, this in turn being affected by the number of players competing at the table. For instance, in a full-handed Texas Hold 'em game, meaning one that involves nine or ten players, two pairs or three of a kind represent

decent hands with fair chances of winning, since players hoping to make straights or flushes are often forced out of the betting before their hand materializes. Yet in Omaha, which is structured very similarly to Texas Hold 'em, the prevalence of straights, flushes and full houses is much greater, since players receive four hole cards face down on the table, with which to begin play, not two. Although the players are

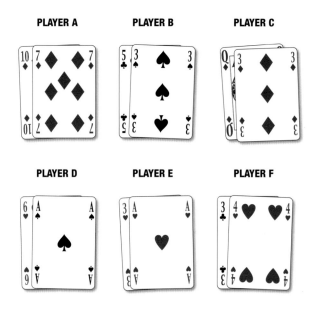

ASSESSING A HAND

Right: Reading the cards is an essential skill, as shown in this example where player A's two pairs, ordinarily a good hand in Texas Hold 'em, are leading but remain vulnerable to a flush. A substantial bet from player D, due to act first, suggesting the flush has already been secured, might be sufficient to encourage player A to fold the leading hand.

required to combine exactly two hole cards with three of the board cards dealt face up to make a hand, the greater number of possible combinations available to each player presents more opportunities to secure a high-ranking poker holding. As a general rule, winning hands naturally tend to be of greater value the more players there are involved in a game.

Reading opponents

Combining information from the cards in play with knowledge of a specific opponent's mannerisms helps a player to gauge the meaning behind events at the table. To this end, it is worth underlining the value in observing as much as possible even after folding a hand. Inferences obtained from the betting of those still contesting the pot can be tested, at no further cost, when the hand is resolved at the showdown. Indeed, most experts recommend that anyone wishing to participate in a game, at a casino or online, should watch the action for a while rather than immediately begin playing. This helps condition a player to the rhythm of a game and provides time to identify whether the potential opponents are strong or weak poker players. Equally, those who play aggressively or

who are inclined to bluff too often may be distinguished from the 'calling stations', these being loose players who do not raise much, and repeatedly call other players' bets, irrespective of their chances of winning. The comments and general behaviour of the players may also provide clues to their current mood. For instance, anybody who seems distracted during play but suddenly starts concentrating on the game may be indicating possession of a good hand.

ASSESSING A HAND

Left: This Omaha example illustrates that, with more cards in circulation around the table, the chances of at least one player obtaining a flush with a flop such as this are greatly increased. Player C can count the As and Qs for a possible ace-high flush, but must now worry about a pair appearing on the board as this could furnish an opponent, player D for instance, with a full house or even four of a kind.

ATTENTION TO DETAIL

By now it will be evident that keeping abreast of events at the poker table is a prerequisite for success, although regular social games typically include at least one player who always needs prompting when the time to make a betting decision arrives. Other factors that warrant attention, particularly in club and casino games, include the rake (the casino's commission fee), the general house rules and, of course, the betting structures applying to the games themselves. Regrettably, as befits a pastime historically referred to as 'the cheating game', it is worth remembering that not everybody plays fairly. Various sharp practices might be perpetrated by other players, ranging from short-changing the pot to playing with a marked deck of cards. Vigilance is therefore recommended, even if only to police the minor infringements taking place during a game.

The importance of memory

Many of the lessons to be learned from poker are best absorbed from experience. Being able to benefit from such experience, however, will depend on a good memory, another essential asset possessed by most of the top players. Contrary to popular myth, it is possible to train and develop one's memory, a process that often involves coding information by breaking it down into recognizable patterns. Telephone numbers,

for example, are usually remembered as small groups of numbers rather than as a long string of digits. Similarly, acronyms are commonly employed as shorthand terms for words and phrases. At the poker table, there are many patterns observable during play that, if remembered and understood, may be brought to bear either later in the game or at a subsequent session.

The three prime components to focus on are the cards themselves, the betting habits of opponents, and, most importantly, one's own playing style. Although it is useful to identify the various revealing mannerisms, or 'tells', of opponents, controlling one's own betting moves or gestures is also beneficial. In this respect, adopting a flexible attitude and varying the style of play during a session makes it more difficult for habitual behaviour to be recognized.

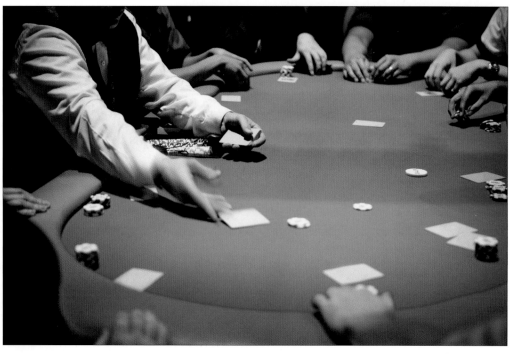

Above right: Allan Dyrstad in action at the Poker Stars World Cup in 2005, a tournament featuring heads-up poker – a two-player confrontation. Both players will pay an ante or blind in heads-up games, investing chips in every pot. This is enough to generate the betting action as players cannot afford to be too patient in waiting for good cards. They have to take risks with mediocre hands and this makes such one-to-one poker combat a highly specialized form of the game.

Right: The key to successful poker is to be able to decipher your opponents' actions from the moment the cards are dealt. At every level, when players fold, call or raise, there is a reason behind their decision. By observing, astute players recognize behaviour patterns that can offer clues, giving them a tactical edge over their opponents.

Left: The 2003 WSOP world champion Chris Moneymaker became the first player to win the main event having qualified via the Internet. Despite not having played in a live tournament of this magnitude before, Moneymaker successfully made the transition from the online game.

Below: Success at poker depends to a degree on a player's ability to deceive opponents regarding the strength or weakness of a hand. Possessing a 'poker face' is considered an asset. However, many players take the precaution of shielding their eyes from opponents when having to contemplate a decision.

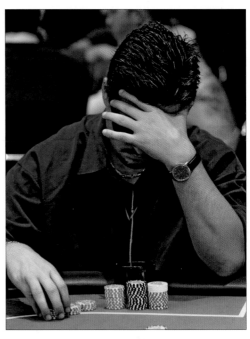

Assessing a player's moves

Information obtained from the cards during a game only represents part of the story when playing a hand. Other clues emanate from the actions and mannerisms of other players at the table, and recognizing the significance of these moves is a very helpful skill. In regular poker schools, players will be comfortably familiar with each other's characteristics, but when encountering new opponents, online or in a casino perhaps, it can take time to decipher their actions.

There are some playing styles that can usually be identified after a short while at the table, certainly at amateur games. Beginners are often very difficult to bluff since they are not skilled enough to recognize what an opponent's raise is supposed to imply. Even if having only a remote chance of winning, such players often stay in the pot simply because they enjoy the betting action. Similarly, players known as calling stations will insist on calling bet after bet, either because they overestimate their chances of winning or because they are intrinsically sceptical by nature.

Adjusting one's play to take account of such players, perhaps by adopting a stricter policy on which hands to support, is a sound strategy. Equally important to recognize are the cautious players, the 'rocks', who regularly fold before the betting becomes serious, choosing to preserve their chips for the moment when they can bet aggressively with a very strong hand. It pays to be wary of calling a large bet made by such a player unless possessing a very strong hand oneself.

COUNTING CARDS

It is in stud poker that this skill is most readily applied, since the game features many cards dealt face up to the players. These cards are subsequently turned face down as and when players fold throughout the game. Retaining a clear idea of how many cards have been seen, and their value, is essential for any player wishing to calculate the probability of being dealt the card or cards needed to win.

CONCENTRATION

Being able to draw accurate inferences from play during any session requires high levels of concentration. Assimilating information by memorizing cards in play, assessing fluctuating probabilities and observing the actions of opponents is of great benefit in guiding a player's own decisions. But this can only happen if a player is focused on the game. Aside from the strategic benefits of concentrating on play, it is also conducive to any game for all players to be aware of the basic proceedings, such as who dealt, whose turn it is to bet and how many players remain active in the later betting rounds.

Pacing the game

Poker is most enjoyable when played at a decent pace, there being nothing more frustrating for the average player than to fold a hand and then have to wait several minutes for slow, distracted players to resolve the outcome. Casinos will seek to deal 40 or more hands per hour, particularly if the rake is a fraction of every pot, which underlines how most hands take just a couple of minutes to complete. The inherent speed of online poker means that rates of over 60 hands per hour are not uncommon in that form of the game.

Although a quick conclusion to each hand is appreciated by most players, it is also true that the majority will anticipate any poker session lasting several hours. For those earning a living from the game, such time spent playing is simply regarded as work. But for the casual player and professional alike, engaging in a marathon poker session brings with it certain pressures. Pacing oneself to handle the mental and physical challenge is as important as any strategy. Taking advantage of mistakes induced by tiredness or stress is all part of the game, so, to avoid falling victim to this possibility, players should be prepared to take breaks or even cash out of a game if their concentration levels lapse for any reason.

Avoiding distractions

In emphasizing the skills employed in poker, the guiding principle is to outline how best to minimize losses and maximize winnings while assessing the risks that are a natural element of the game. To that end, intense concentration is sometimes required, which implies that unnecessary distractions be avoided. In home games, television, background music and protracted conversations among friends are common

Above: Playing poker well requires a high degree of disciplined application to the game. Concentrating is essential which means that any distraction could have a negative impact on play. Anyone seriously involved in a game will surely be unwilling to respond to regular mobile phone calls if intent on being competitive.

Left: Clonie Gowen exudes apprehension at the WSOP in 2004. Like most players, even the winner of the 2003 WPT Ladies Night tournament can be unpleasantly surprised at having either misread an opponent's hand or suffered what is known as a 'bad beat'. The latter occurs when an opponent defies the odds to make the winning hand.

Above left: Despite its general popularity, poker has always had to compete for space in casinos with other gambling games such as blackjack, roulette, craps and slot machines. All these, unlike poker, involve fixed-odds payouts for various winning outcomes, meaning that the house can guarantee itself a profit margin.

Above: Mike 'The Mouth' Matusow engages in banter at the poker table while competing in the 2005 WSOP. As his nickname suggests, Matusow chats incessantly during play, a trait that so divides opinion that he is considered both the most entertaining and the most annoying player in the game.

Left: The celebrated illusionists Siegfried and Roy, pictured with one of the trademark white tigers that were an integral part of their show. In 1990 Siegfried Fischbacher (left) and Roy Uwe Ludwig Horn were offered over US$50 million a year to perform at the Mirage Hotel and Casino.

features of a poker session, along with breaks for food and drink. Such elements enhance sociability, of course, but divert attention from the cards and slow up the game. The distractions on offer in the major casinos, by contrast, include slot machines, roulette tables and the sports betting bar, all of which could easily claim a poker player's bankroll during moments of weakness. For the best results in poker, focusing on the task in hand is vital, since not doing so invites failure.

Similar considerations apply at home when playing online poker. The familiarity of the home environment, coupled with the fact that there is no risk of being physically distracted by opponents at the table, can induce a sense of complacency. Surfing the Internet or writing emails while playing at an online poker site is possible for those with a genuine ability to handle multiple tasks, though this is likely to have a negative impact on a player's results.

External pressures

As with any aspect of life, playing poker to the best of one's ability is generally easier and much more enjoyable when not burdened by other serious concerns. Illness, tiredness and emotional stress are all likely to have a negative impact on play, whatever the source of the problem. Such pressures can be expected to inhibit concentration, the effect of which is likely to result in costly mistakes being made. Problems at work or within the home may dull the competitiveness required at the table in order to prosper and, just as importantly, could reduce the pleasure obtained from simply playing the game. Of course, approaching a poker session in a relaxed and positive frame of mind is a sound policy, but there will always be those players who can successfully immerse themselves in a game precisely because this helps them forget their other concerns.

BODY LANGUAGE

Much has already been made of the information to be gained from shrewd observations at the poker table, particularly with regard to the cards in play and the betting patterns of opponents. But assessing other players also involves understanding their mental and emotional state, since this is likely to have an overriding impact on their performance. This becomes easier the more frequently the same players gather together to play, as is the case in regular amateur games. Typical things to note include the postures adopted by opponents and their general demeanour at different stages of the game, as these are likely to reflect their true feelings. Players dispiritedly slumped in their chairs after a series of losing hands might be understandably frustrated. Although unremarkable in itself, this could also advertise the intrusive presence of doubts in their own ability or even a loss of interest in the game, something that could easily be exploited by an aggressive opponent.

There are also a few specific signs of tension or nervousness that might inadvertently betray the strength of an opponent's hand. For example players who bet out of turn because of their eagerness to be involved are probably holding decent cards.

Also, those whose hands literally shake as they make a substantial bet may be revealing excitement at the proximity of victory. Making sense of such clues is another skill that can improve any player's chances of success. Pulling them all together when the adrenaline is flowing represents a serious challenge, but this is definitely one of the reasons poker retains its appeal.

Poker tells

Players must deceive each other in order to improve their winning chances, but this practice of deliberate misrepresentation often infringes the moral codes learned since childhood. The internal pressure generated can manifest itself in particular mannerisms that, if witnessed and understood, could give away the strength of a player's hand. These are known as 'tells'. Former world champion Doyle Brunson maintains that the pulse in a man's neck is a good source of information. Often visible when the heart is pounding, this usually betrays a bluff since the heart is more likely to race at the prospect of a deception being uncovered. The reasoning is that a player betting with a strong hand is less likely to fear a call and will be more relaxed at the prospect of this happening.

Above: Paul Wasicka fails to stifle a yawn at the final table of a WSOP tournament in 2006. The world championship extends over several days during which even the most experienced professional will suffer fatigue.

Right: Jac Arama celebrates a win at the Grosvenor Victoria Casino in London. Many players wear sunglasses or tinted spectacles to obscure their eyes from opponents since our pupils dilate when excited, whether that emotion is fear or pleasure.

The denomination of chips used when betting may also offer clues to a player's hand. Low denominations casually added to the pot could suggest weakness from a reluctant caller prepared to speculate only with small change. Alternatively, confident bets with high-denomination chips usually emanate from players who fully expect to reclaim them at the showdown. Admittedly, some of the more obvious tells are easily faked. Feigning indifference when possessing a powerful hand, for example, or staring intently at an opponent when bluffing in order to intimidate the player into folding, require a minimal deployment of acting skills. In addition to reading other players' poker tells, of course, is the need to restrict giving away clues to one's own hand, which is dependent on maintaining consistency in one's actions throughout the game, whether winning or losing.

Online poker tells

Without the ability to see opponents when playing online, the scope for identifying poker tells is obviously restricted, but there are still a few pointers worth considering. Comments typed into the chat box may reveal something of a player's age, mood or skill level, though it is unwise to take them all at face value. More significantly, the speed at which players make their betting decisions can provide clues,

Above: Carl Olson pictured in classically pensive mode with his elbows on the table and his head resting on his hands. Olson's pose is typical of a player keen to avoid betraying the quality of his hand with an inadvertent comment or movement.

especially given that some online players will be competing on several tables at once. Those who repeatedly delay their actions are likely to be distracted by events elsewhere. By contrast, players who ordinarily act promptly but delay in calling a particular bet may be trying to infer that they face a difficult decision when, in fact, they hold a winning hand. Once again, the key is for players to stay focused on events and act consistently themselves, to prevent opponents from reading any significance into their own actions.

Above: Allen Cunningham of Nevada blows on his hands during the latter stages of the 2006 WSOP world championship tournament. He finished fourth behind the winner, Jamie Gold.

Left: Eddie Scharf rubs his head as he contemplates the action at the table. Though this may typically represent a player being puzzled by the betting so far, such deliberations can easily be faked. In this instance, Scharf could well have by far the best hand and yet be trying to convey an air of indecision.

THE ART OF BLUFFING

Ordinarily, a bluff involves a player with poor cards betting to represent possession of a strong hand, with the aim of causing opponents to fold. Successfully achieving this is undoubtedly one of the most thrilling and rewarding features of a game in which deceiving one's opponents is integral to success. However, there is an art to bluffing that is framed by the nature of the poker variation played, the stakes that are involved and the quality of the players at the table. For instance, in low-stakes, fixed-limit games, it is difficult to execute many bluffs because the cost of calling any bet is rarely enough to force everyone to fold, particularly when the pot is large, relative to the size of the stakes. On the other hand, no-limit poker features more bluffing opportunities, since players can bet sums substantial enough to create real concern in the minds of players holding good but not unbeatable cards. The key to the success of any bluff lies in identifying the right moment to bet against opponents who will understand the message that the bluffer is attempting to convey.

Seeds of doubt

There are two important benefits to be gained from bluffing in poker. In the short term, a successful bluff can convert a weak hand into a winner, enabling a player to acquire a pot unexpectedly by representing sufficient, though actually non-existent, strength. Obviously, this will not happen every time a player bluffs, yet losing a pot when having a bluff called also offers positive long-term benefits, even as the weakness of a player's hand is revealed. Once a capacity for deception is exposed, doubts surface in the mind of

THE IMPORTANCE OF TIMING

PLAYER A   **PLAYER D**

Above: In this Texas Hold 'em game, Player A's bet after the flop in support of the pair of aces is read by player D who calls with an inferior hand – the pair of fives – knowing that the bet could be interpreted as a bid for a flush draw in clubs. The presence of another club on the turn followed by a strong bet from player D could be enough to persuade player A to fold.

Above: The turn card is the Qc meaning that player A now holds two pairs, aces and queens. However, player A's bet with what is currently the strongest hand is immediately raised by player D to suggest that the flush has been obtained. This has the mark of a credible bluff and may cause player A to fold rather than to try drawing for the full house that might now be assumed necessary to win. The odds against achieving this are 11 to 1, greater than the current pot odds on offer.

Right: Another Texas Hold 'em example shows the concept behind the semi-bluff. Player D, who needs a 4 for a straight, bets 100 chips after the flop hoping to take the pot immediately. Player E's call indicates possession of a strong hand, a pair of kings in this instance, but though player D's initial bluff at the pot did not succeed, the possibility still exists that a 4 will come on the turn or the river to provide the winning hand.

each opponent over the meaning behind any subsequent bet from the known bluffer. The second reason for bluffing, therefore, is to enhance the likelihood of opponents contributing chips to a pot they have little or no chance of winning, simply because they wrongly suspect another bluff is being executed.

The importance of timing

The majority of poker variations involve several cards in play being exposed for all to see, the exception being draw poker and its derivations. This fact creates many viable bluffing scenarios, as players can generate inferences regarding the hand they hold, which are clearly recognizable to opponents. But to do this successfully requires a good sense of timing. For example, as the diagram at the top of the opposite page illustrates, a player holding Ad, Qd in Texas Hold 'em when the flop reveals Ac, Jc, 7h, may bet on the strength of the pair of aces, only to be called by a single opponent. One logical assumption could be that the caller is drawing to a flush in clubs, which, when the turn card is revealed as Qc, presents the player now holding two pairs with a serious problem. If the player bets and is immediately raised by the opponent, the clear inference is that the flush has been secured, leaving the player in need of another ace or queen on the river, the final community card dealt face up to the board, for a full house. The opponent does not need to possess the flush in this situation to stand a chance of taking the pot, since representing it with a bluff, a possibility established by calling on the flop, could easily be enough to win.

SEMI-BLUFFS

E   F

CALL
100   275
POT TOTAL

3♥ 3♥   K♦ K♦   5♣ 5♣

D   D   A

BET
100

C   B

PLAYER D

6♠ 7♠ 7♠

PLAYER E

K♥ A♦ A♦

♦ ♣ ♥ ♠ SEMI-BLUFFS ♦ ♣ ♥ ♠

Players who bet in the knowledge that their hand cannot win are said to be making 'naked bluffs', which can only succeed when everyone else folds. Distinct from such occasions are those when a player bets in support of a weak hand that has an outside chance of improvement with cards still to come. David Sklansky, poker expert and author of several books on the game, coined the term 'semi-bluff' to describe such situations. Using another Texas Hold 'em example, (above) a player holding 6s, 7s, when the flop is 3h, Kd, 5c, might bluff to take the pot there and then without holding even a pair. Should an opponent call, immediately suggesting a superior hand, there remain two opportunities to hit a 4, offering a 17 per cent chance that the semi-bluffer will be rewarded with a winning straight.

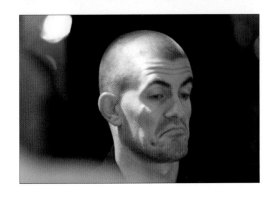

Right: Gus Hansen, known as the 'Great Dane', seen competing in the no-limit Hold 'em tournament at the Danish Poker Championships in 2005. Though only fourth on this occasion, Hansen has earned a reputation as a formidable tournament player since his breakthrough victory in the WPT's Five Diamond Poker Classic in May 2002.

EXERCISING JUDGEMENT

The ability to exercise sound judgement obviously comes with experience, but putting into practice some of the skills briefly described in this chapter will improve anyone's poker game. How much it improves depends upon a player's level of competitiveness and the quality of their observations at the table. Those who have a strong desire to win possess all the incentive they need to take note of patterns emerging during play in order to distinguish the good players from the poor ones. Indeed, one of the key factors to successful poker is being able to identify the right level at which to play in terms of the abilities of opponents and the sums being contested. Being the shrewdest player at a regular game may be enough to earn a modest extra income, something that might satisfy the ambitions of many amateur players. On the other hand, no player should be ashamed to preserve their bankroll by cashing out of a game in which it is evident that the opponents are superior or in which the stakes are simply too high. Accurate judgement exercised in this situation can protect a player against unnecessary losses.

The importance of position

Although the importance of a player's position during a betting round varies slightly from one poker variation to another, it is accepted as typically more advantageous to act later, when more information is available. Yet this commonly acknowledged fact can be utilized by players in early positions to work against their opponents. Since it is expected that players will check or bet cautiously the earlier they are to act, a maximum bet from an early position will often be respected as representative of a very strong hand. Bluffing and semi-bluffing opportunities therefore exist in these situations, although, as with any tactical move, it is wise not to employ it indiscriminately.

By the same token, betting in a late position offers greater chances to steal pots from opponents who have shown a marked reluctance to become involved in the action earlier in the round. Since their reticence usually suggests weakness, a player in late position may find that even a modest bet is enough to persuade everyone else to fold.

THE IMPORTANCE OF POSITION

PLAYER F

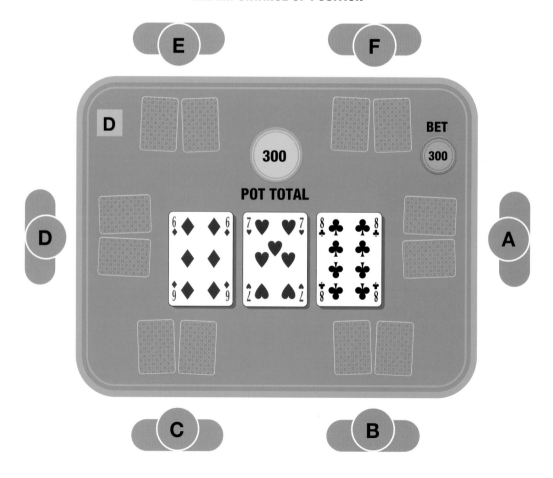

Right: In this no-limit Texas Hold 'em game, each player has paid the minimum of 50 chips to see the flop. As first to act after the flop, player F bluffs with a pot-sized bet of 300. Since a large bet in this situation is generally acknowledged as risky, the aim here is to suggest that a strong hand such as a straight or three of a kind is already held, enough perhaps to intimidate opponents into folding.

Assessing chances

Judging one's chances of winning any pot always needs consideration of three key elements to the game, namely the cards in play, the betting patterns of opponents and the odds of probability at work. As each hand lasts only a couple of minutes, however, accurately analysing the fluctuating scenarios presented during a game sometimes calls for educated guesses on the part of each player. Some general patterns of play are repeated sufficiently, however, to make this process a little easier. For example, a player drawing three cards in draw poker can be expected to be retaining a pair, whereas a one-card draw is likely to indicate that a straight or flush is being targeted. In Texas Hold 'em, a pre-flop raise (the matching of or increase on a previous bet before the three community cards are dealt) is rarely considered unless the player holds an ace, king or high-value pair. Similarly, when playing stud poker, it is prudent to accept that any player who continues betting in the face of an opponent's showing pair is likely to hold superior hole cards. Understanding the implications of such betting patterns enables a player to make swift but generally sound assessments of the play before hastily committing chips to the pot.

Pot management

Successful pot management incorporates both attacking and defensive measures, which a player can use to accentuate winning hands and diminish the impact of losing hands. In simple terms, pot management means contributing less in support of hands that will probably lose, and betting in a style that will build a big pot when holding a hand that is virtually certain to prove the best. For instance, needing to draw a card or two to fill in a straight or a flush is a common situation, but the odds against this occurring usually prohibit calling any significantly large bet by an opponent.

The idea, obviously, is to preserve a chance of an unlikely win as cheaply as possible, either by checking or only calling minimum bets. By contrast, when the cards fall favourably enough for a win to appear likely, it pays to disguise the fact by checking, or betting the minimum, to encourage opponents to remain in the pot and thus boost the probable winnings. Raising the pot is a viable strategy in this situation as well, provided an opponent or two can be relied upon to call the bet. Since some opponents will fold, this offers the dual benefit of increasing the pot and reducing the opposition at the same time.

THE IMPORTANCE OF POSITION

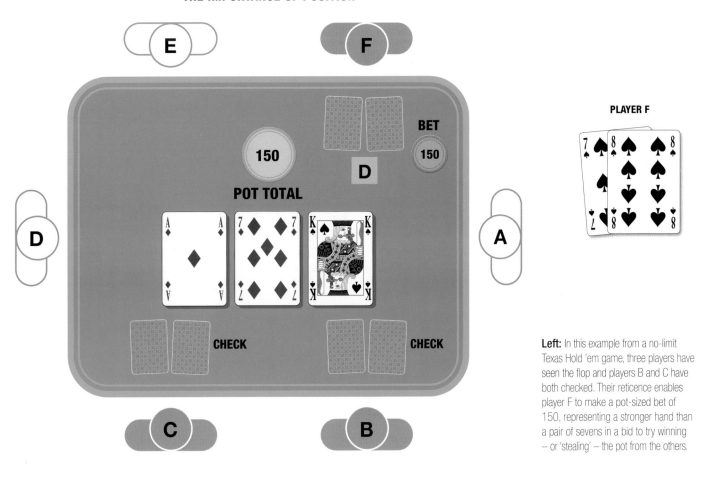

PLAYER F

Left: In this example from a no-limit Texas Hold 'em game, three players have seen the flop and players B and C have both checked. Their reticence enables player F to make a pot-sized bet of 150, representing a stronger hand than a pair of sevens in a bid to try winning – or 'stealing' – the pot from the others.

POKER VIRTUES

Assimilating all the advice on sensible poker play before tackling a game is a rarity, as the majority of players only tend to discover the relevance of such advice through experience. Learning from one's mistakes, however, is certainly a virtue that is as applicable to poker as to any other endeavour. Irrespective of a player's level of ability, exercising patience and some personal discipline also brings its rewards at the poker table. Players who enjoy early success during a session can easily start betting a little more loosely and fritter away hard-earned chips in a misguided effort to capitalize on their skilful play or simple good fortune. This contravenes one of poker's maxims, which states that players should not try to beat opponents, but should, instead, allow their opponents to force the issue by trying to beat them. The more they lose, the more desperate they are likely to become, with the likely result being that they will make increasingly poor decisions as play continues.

Patience

The need for patience becomes unavoidable when each poker session is considered as part of a lifelong poker game. Although it is always preferable to be ahead when any session concludes, this is highly unlikely to occur on every occasion. Nevertheless, this simple fact does not prevent some players from betting loosely and taking more chances than necessary in order to stay involved in the action. Quite often this stems from the mistaken belief that contesting the majority of hands offers a greater chance of success, which is rarely the case.

At the serious end of the scale, the reality is that most successful poker players contest few pots and save their chips for those betting confrontations in which they have the edge. This helps ensure that the pots they do win are much bigger than average, which means they need to win fewer of them to stay ahead. Such strategy is employed by what the professionals refer to as tight-aggressive players, predatory types who bide their time and wait for the right moment to pounce on unwary or impulsive opponents.

Discipline

Having the discipline to remain patient, perhaps by folding a strong hand in the face of a convincingly large bet, can be a major test. Equally, when the textbook moves consistently fail to achieve the desired

Right: A view of the 1950s pinball game 'Queen of Hearts'. Rocking the pinball machine in order to keep the ball in play often causes it to 'tilt' which results in the control mechanisms shutting down. The player responsible is thus penalized by the ending of the game. This term has been adopted by poker players to describe those moments when they similarly lose their discipline and start betting recklessly, behaviour which is usually a prelude to severe defeat.

Right: Retaining the discipline required to play effectively is a major test of a player's ability. A succession of unlucky defeats can easily cause a player to lose control – to tilt – and make even more costly misjudgements under pressure. In this Texas Hold 'em example, the player holding 8, 9 offsuit has a chance of securing a straight with a 7 or a Q on the turn or river, but to pursue this hand in the face of a bet from an opponent is probably to be avoided. Any Q will simply furnish someone holding an A with a higher straight (A, K, Q, J, 10), while it is also possible an opponent holds A, Q already.

PLAYER'S HOLE CARDS

FLOP

result, it is easy to lose faith and make questionable betting decisions in a bid to recoup short-term losses. This is often the prelude to a player 'tilting', a term borrowed from pinball, where machines that have tilted do not function. It refers to the deterioration in a player's game to the point where ever more frequent losses trigger irrational and usually costly betting decisions. Under such pressure, it is far more likely that players will misjudge the situations confronting them. For example a player holding 8s, 9c in Texas Hold 'em when the flop is 10h, Js, Kd, could easily fall prey to pursuing the 7 or Q that would realize a successful straight draw. Yet a Q on the turn or the river would also complete a higher straight for any opponent holding an A, a detail that is easy to miss if not fully concentrating on the game.

Having the strength of character to walk away from a losing session, rather than throw good money after bad, is another essential poker discipline. During any session itself, the key to maintaining a sound strategy is to have strict standards regarding which starting hands to play, to trust in the odds of probability and to treat each hand on its merits as play develops. In adopting such a disciplined approach, players can expect to reduce losses to a minimum and remain competitive, although a sense of humour is also an asset to cope with any series of bad 'beats'. These are occasions when opponents consistently defy the odds in drawing the cards that they need to win.

A LONG-TERM GAME
♦ ♣ ♥ ♠

Learning the basic poker skills offers the chance to obtain a lifetime of pleasure from the game, whether as an amateur or as a budding professional. Most players will spend more of their disposable income on the game than they are ever likely to recoup, but adopting a patient, disciplined and objective approach will at least help to keep down the cost of their gambling pleasure.

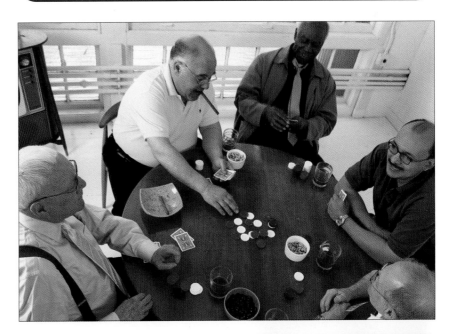

Above: As with so many card games, the skills absorbed from playing poker can be maintained over a lifetime through regular participation in a game. To obtain the most from a session a player needs to possess some semblance of competitiveness, a quality that need not diminish with age.

Right: A player at the 2004 WSOP waits patiently for the right time to make a move. Highest-level tournament poker is sometimes characterized as hours of inaction punctuated by moments of extreme excitement. Lengthy periods of time may be spent waiting for a suitable chance to become involved in a pot, The consequence of making a misjudgement could be elimination from the event.

PRACTICE MAKES PERFECT

To become skilled in any pursuit obviously requires practice as well as experience. Fortunately for the legions of players new to poker, there exist many opportunities to both study the game and put into practice what they have learnt, either live or online. The benefit of online poker sites is that they offer play money tables, which, as the name implies, enable players to warm up for a session before risking any real cash. Beginners use these tables in order to gain experience, and they help condition new users to the configurations of the poker site. The betting strategies exhibited on these tables may be erratic, given that no cash is at stake, but the scenarios enacted help attune a player to the general patterns of the game. However, whether live or online, it is always worthwhile warming up with a few hands dealt out before play, simply to remind oneself of the different possibilities that can emerge.

Available resources

Taking advantage of the vast amount of written and recorded material concerning poker is obviously of benefit to anyone's play, irrespective of their level of experience. Both the World and European Poker Tours were established to help meet the interest in televised poker and these have supplemented the many other tournaments that have appeared on television. The predominant game featured in these is no-limit Texas Hold 'em, so students of that variation are well served, but those wanting guidance on how to play the other popular poker games need only scour the bookshelves or the Internet for information. The majority of professionals who have written about the game, generally offer tips on how to play draw, stud, Omaha and their various high-low derivations, as well as Texas Hold 'em. World champions such as Doyle Brunson, Phil Hellmuth and Tom McEvoy have all offered their

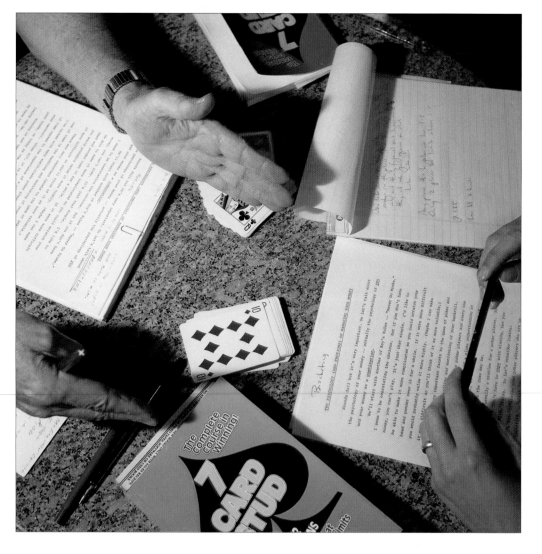

Right: As with any pursuit, becoming more skilled at poker requires studying the game as well as obtaining playing experience at the table. The concept of the 'poker school' emanates from players regularly convening to enjoy a game and informally analysing each other's play. While this constitutes enough of an education for some players, more serious students of the game will absorb the lessons to be learned from many of the books and websites dedicated to poker.

Above: Keeping even a basic record of poker income and expenditure is always advisable for those who play regularly and wish to improve their game. A simple record of wins and losses, complete with notes on which variations were played and the level of stakes involved, can help players to identify their strengths and weaknesses.

own insights into how to play winning poker, although professional gambler David Sklansky and gaming expert John Scarne are two other respected writers whose work covers most aspects of the game.

Analysing the game

All players have different motivations behind their wish to play poker, but those who take the game seriously enough to consider improving their techniques can only do so by analysing their previous performances. Remembering each hand contested during a session is improbable, though there are often key hands, usually involving big pots, which can be recalled later when considering why a particular ploy either succeeded or failed. If, despite winning several

sizeable pots during a session, a player still finishes with a loss, an objective review would probably reveal that too many chips are being squandered playing hands that have a poor chance of success. Acknowledging that possibility is a positive step towards eradicating loose and costly betting strategies. A general analysis of the game is central to the concept of the 'poker school', usually involving a regular group of players who not only compete against each other, but discuss the game and help further their poker education as a result.

Keeping records

Poker is first and foremost a gambling game with chips and, by extension, cash, being the obvious means by which players can assess their ability. Relatively few people make a substantial living from playing poker, but that does not negate the value of lesser-skilled players monitoring their own performance by keeping accurate records of their play and their finances. Doing so helps players to analyse their game and enables them to build up a picture of their strengths or weaknesses. Making a note of the variations played during a session and recalling which of these proved most successful is obviously useful when deciding which variations to play in future. Similarly, comparing one's performance in tournament poker with that in cash games might highlight which of these best suits an individual's own temperament or playing style. Most of all, keeping a record of play promotes an objective approach and ensures that the game remains at the forefront of any player's mind.

THE POWER OF OBSERVATION

♦ ♣ ♥ ♠

At the poker table there is always plenty of information on offer, which, if observed and interpreted correctly, can give any player an edge during the game. Apart from the visible cards in play, the betting patterns of opponents and how they play certain hands should be mentally noted. Most importantly, players are encouraged to stay focused on the game at all times, even when not participating in a hand. By watching events unfold to the showdown, when competing hands are revealed, it is possible to gain an insight into how others play, what type of hands they are willing to support, and whether they favour a tight or a loose betting style.

Above: Prior to attending any poker game, players may find it worthwhile dealing out a few hands to themselves as a way of warming up beforehand. If the session is likely to include several variations then someone who is used to playing Texas Hold 'em, for example, may wish to refresh their memory regarding the subtle differences between that game and Omaha. Winning hands in Omaha are usually of higher value than those in Hold 'em so a quick revision of the potential impact this might have on play could safeguard a player against making costly mistakes when the action starts.

POPULAR POKER VARIATIONS

In its earliest recognized form, poker was played with a deck of just 20 cards and was limited to four players, who each received five cards before betting on the strength of their respective hands. Since the introduction of the 52-card deck, the game has undergone a substantial period of evolution, with the simplistic nature of the 'bluffing game' giving way to hundreds of variations on a theme. The purpose of this chapter is to introduce the five most popular poker variations – draw poker, five-card stud, seven-card stud, Texas Hold 'em and Omaha – and explain the basic rules and patterns of play for each, beginning with the oldest recognized form of the game, draw poker.

Right: A typical hand following the deal in draw poker, the oldest form of the game. Players receive five cards each and can expect to see at least a pair, such as the sixes illustrated, in two out of every five deals.

DRAW POKER

Of all poker games, this is likely to be the version familiar to anyone who has ever spent time playing cards with friends or family, and it fits the profile of what is often referred to as 'kitchen-table' or 'penny-ante' poker. It is the traditional game which has been passed down through the generations over the past 150 years. As such, it has historically been the starting point from which keener players go on to discover the many other forms of poker that have emerged since the 19th century.

Origins of the game

Draw poker became widely recognized as a game in its own right some time after the American Civil War (1861 to 1865) and remains popular to this day, though arguably more as a parlour game played for nominal stakes than as a serious betting medium. Before the draw element was introduced, poker was regularly played as a no-limit betting game with the size of bets and raises unrestricted. This made it far more a test of nerve than a matter of judgement, there being few clues to the composition of an opponent's hand throughout play and numerous opportunities to bluff. The gradual adoption of the draw – allowing players the option to discard cards they do not want in exchange for new cards during a game – and the acceptance of limits on the betting changed poker sufficiently between 1850 and 1900 to secure its immediate future as a game of skill. These developments made draw poker much more appealing to cautious players who wanted to gamble without being reckless. Further discipline was imposed on the game with a restriction that is believed to have originated in Toledo, Ohio. Under this rule, a player

Above: The great game of poker. This illustration, dating from 1884, shows four players participating in a game while a fifth looks on. By this time, draw poker was well established as a popular pastime, a status that was greatly accelerated during the American Civil War which ended in 1865.

POKER HAND PROBABILITIES

Draw poker begins with each player being dealt five cards and, while in the majority of cases players will need to utilize the draw in order to improve their hands, the chances of being dealt a recognized poker hand in those initial five cards are detailed below.

HAND	CHANCE
Royal Flush	1 chance in every 649,740 deals
Straight Flush	1 in 72,193
Four of a Kind	1 in 4,165
Full House	1 in 694
Flush	1 in 509
Straight	1 in 255
Three of a Kind	1 in 47
Two Pairs	1 in 21
One Pair	1 in 2.5
No Pair	1 in 2

Right: Royal Flush – there is one chance in every 649,740 deals that a player will receive this hand in the first five cards dealt.

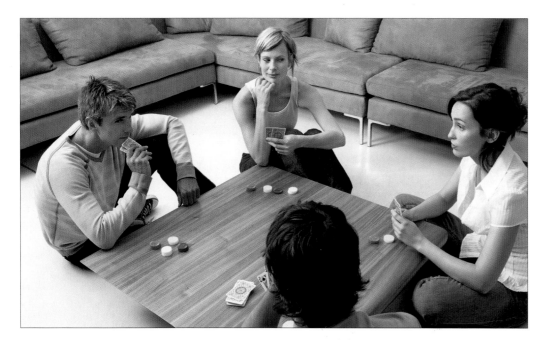

could only open the betting after the deal if in possession of a hand comprising a pair of jacks or better. Players who wildly gambled on their first five cards, irrespective of what they held, were denied the opportunity to intimidate opponents with an unpredictable and loose betting strategy. The game using this rule became known as 'jackpots' and it was soon adopted as the favoured form of draw poker. It tested a player's mathematical and observational skills to a greater degree and is the form of the game under consideration here.

Number of players

Ordinarily, draw poker is a game best suited to no more than six players, since this represents the maximum viable number that can be satisfactorily accommodated with a single 52-card deck. To avoid the possibility of having to recycle discarded cards at the draw stage, players are typically limited to exchanging no more than three cards in an effort to improve their respective hands. Given the lack of any substantive rules for the game, there are poker schools and online poker rooms that will permit a player to exchange all five

cards at the draw if desired, especially if there are five or fewer participants. This is a questionable tactic and most players with a hand poor enough to warrant being completely replaced are probably best advised to forfeit their ante by folding and awaiting the next deal.

CHIP DENOMINATIONS

The denominations of the coloured chips used in poker vary from one establishment to another but the values indicated here are typical of those used in many casinos and online poker sites.

VALUE	COLOUR
1	White
2	Yellow
5	Red
10	Blue
20	Grey
25	Green
50	Orange
100	Black
250	Pink
500	Purple
1,000	Burgundy
2,000	Light Blue
5,000	Brown

SEQUENCE OF PLAY

Once the compulsory bets have been made, usually with everyone adding an ante to the pot, the dealer deals five cards each, face down, to all players. A round of betting follows, provided at least one player holds a pair of jacks or better. After the betting round, those players who are still competing for the pot may discard the unwanted cards from their hands, subject to any limits in place, and replace them with others from the deck. After the draw, a second round of betting ensues, leading to the conclusion of the hand. A player who makes a bet that is unmatched by any opponent, whether in the first or second betting round, can win the pot without having to expose the winning hand. If two or more players match bets to the end of the game, they reveal their cards in a showdown and the best hand claims the spoils.

Antes

Draw poker requires all players to ante a nominal sum to create the pot, usually set at between 10 and 20 per cent of the minimum bet for the game. In a 25/50 fixed-limit game for instance, in which bets are set at 25 chips during the first round and 50 in the second, a typical ante would be 5 chips.

An alternative approach for instigating the pot is to have the dealer contribute a sufficient sum to cover the antes for all players since, as the deal moves around the table, the net contribution from each player will remain the same, provided each shares an equal number of deals during the session. These conventions apply in live games, but the online version of draw poker uses the blind betting system, whereby the two players to the dealer's immediate left contribute compulsory bets before the deal, known as the small blind and big blind respectively.

THE ANTES

Above: In this example of a 25/50 fixed-limit draw poker game, each player is required to ante 5 chips to generate the initial pot. After the deal, players may bet and raise in denominations of 25 chips only. During the second round, the bets and raises are set at 50 chips.

The deal

After the cards have been shuffled and cut, the nominated dealer discards or 'burns' the top card before dealing one card at a time to each player in turn, working clockwise around the table, until they have five each. The remainder of the pack is then placed face down in readiness for the draw that follows the first round of betting.

THE DRAW
♦ ♣ ♥ ♠

Should two or more players have matched bets to the conclusion of the first betting round, they next have the option to draw further cards from the deck to improve their hands. Working clockwise, each player may discard up to three cards face down and request replacements from the dealer, who should discard the top card of the deck before commencing the draw to prevent any player gaining an advantage from recognizing the first card dealt. Once the first player has had any discards replaced by the dealer, the next player still involved in the game exercises the option of the draw. This process continues until all remaining players have been accommodated, at which point, the second and final betting round occurs.

In all poker games, it is the dealer's responsibility to direct proceedings during play, ensuring that players act in turn, bet the correct amounts and are aware of the rules. And since accidents do happen, if any card is inadvertently exposed during the deal, it is customary to declare the hand dead. Once the misdeal occurs, the cards should be gathered together by the dealer before being shuffled, cut and dealt once again with no additional antes required.

Opening the betting

The opportunity to bet passes clockwise around the table, starting with the player to the left of the dealer. Any player unable to meet the requirement of at least a pair of jacks to open the betting must check, but a player whose hand does meet the opening requirements has the choice either to check or to make the first bet. In the original draw poker game of jackpots, the first player to declare possession of a hand comprising a pair of jacks or better was compelled to make the opening bet, but this rule soon lost its appeal and is rarely applied now. Once an opening bet has been made, the remaining players must decide whether to fold, call or raise. If nobody opens the betting, the hand is declared dead, with the pot remaining in place and players obliged to pay a further ante in readiness for the deal. Evidently, with no compulsion to open the betting, even when holding a suitably high pair, a game between extremely cautious players could be stiflingly short of action.

THE DEAL

Above: After the antes have been paid, the dealer discards or "burns" the top card in the deck before distributing cards, face down and one at a time, to each player in turn, until they have five each.

OPENING THE BETTING

PLAYER A

PLAYER B

PLAYER C

Above and left: After the deal, the player to the dealer's left – player B – is the first to act but must check since the opening requirement of holding a pair of jacks or better is not met. The option to bet then passes to player C, who, with a pair of kings, now opens with a bet of 25 chips. Players D, E and F all fold, but the dealer, player A, calls the bet. The action is now on player B, who decides to fold.

FINAL BETTING ROUND

The player who opened the betting is also the first to act in the second round and has the option to fold, check or bet. Should all players decide to check, then each player reveals their hand to determine the winner. Once a player bets then the other active players must decide whether to fold, call or raise. Any player who makes a bet that is not called wins the pot and is under no obligation to show the winning hand. But if one or more opponents call the bet, then all active players should lay their cards face up on the table to determine the winner.

The showdown

There are several conventions that are typically applied at the showdown at the end of the second betting round. If nobody bets and all players check, then the participants should reveal their cards in turn, beginning with the player who opened the betting in the first round, known naturally as the opener. Working clockwise around the table, all active hands are therefore exposed, one at a time, with the winning hand being readily identified. When there has been some action during the second round and a bet or raise is called, then the bettor or raiser is first to reveal their

THE DRAW

PLAYER A   **PLAYER C**

Above: As player A is dealing, player C is the first to draw further cards. Retaining the pair of kings and the A kicker, player C discards the remainder and draws two additional cards. Player A does the same, retaining the pair of nines and the K.

FINAL BETTING ROUND

PLAYER A   **PLAYER C**

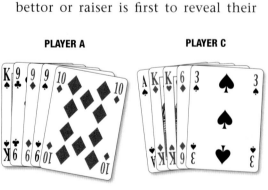

Right: While showing no improvement on the pair of kings, player C bets the minimum of 50 chips and is called by player A whose hand has improved to three of a kind ('trips'). Player A could have raised as any three of a kind is a strong holding in draw poker, but calling represents a safe option. Player C opened the betting originally and must have been holding a higher pair than player A's nines which could similarly have improved to three of a kind.

cards. In this situation, many callers are reluctant to show their cards if they know they are beaten, thus depriving opponents of any clues to their betting strategy or the quality of hand they are prepared to support. Although accepted as a legitimate ploy, most guides to poker suggest that all active hands should be exposed at the showdown at the request of any player still contesting the pot. To avoid disputes, players could agree to reveal their cards simultaneously. Finally, cards speak at the showdown because, although players normally announce what they are holding, this rule restricts the possibility of players winning – or losing – by wrongly declaring the value of a hand.

Similar variations

While jackpots is commonly regarded as the dominant draw poker game, there are numerous other versions played throughout the world. For example in California many players tend to favour incorporating the joker, which is often referred to as 'the bug', to make a 53-card deck using the joker as a wild card. This card may be counted as an ace or as the fifth card needed to complete a straight, a flush or a straight flush, so it has limited value. A player may obtain a hand of five aces, ranked above a royal flush in this game, but may not use the joker to make five of a kind in any other rank below aces.

Outside California, draw poker with the joker wild sees the joker unlimited regarding which card it may represent. Similarly, playing deuces – twos – wild sees the four twos in the deck counting as wild cards of any value, with five of a kind becoming the highest-ranked hand attainable. Involving wild cards in a game can often improve the chances of players obtaining a strong hand, which, in turn, generates more betting action.

Left: A player should expect to be dealt a hand such as this J-high straight only once in every 255 deals. Though not the best possible hand, it is strong enough for a player to 'stand pat' by declining to draw any further cards and therefore constitutes a 'pat hand'.

A Pat Hand
♦ ♣ ♥ ♠

A player who declines to exchange any cards at the time of the draw is said to possess a 'pat hand', with the decision not to draw further cards known as 'standing pat'. Evidently, players who opt to do this cannot help but suggest that they possess a strong hand, a move that is inclined to suppress the opposition's willingness to bet. Very strong hands, therefore, may often secure relatively modest pots. However, standing pat also represents a viable bluffing opportunity that may be sufficient to win a few pots with poor cards. Better still, being caught bluffing in such a situation on occasion increases the possibility that, when the pat hand actually is powerful, it will be paid off with more callers and a bigger pot.

THE SHOWDOWN

Above: Since player A has called player C's bet, the hand is concluded with both players revealing their cards at the showdown. Player A wins the pot of 180 chips with three nines, beating player C's pair of kings. It is worth noting that both players retained their pairs but drew just two cards, not three, when given the chance. To have kept just two cards would have clearly signified to opponents that a pair, and no more, was currently held.

FIVE-CARD STUD

Although draw poker's success as a gambling medium saw it become a hugely popular game during the 19th century, it was not long before poker players devised a variation to extend poker's appeal. Five-card stud emerged to compensate for the perceived deficiencies seen in draw or 'closed' poker by those who felt that the original game offered far too little information upon which to make any betting decisions. Stud or 'open' poker, where players receive the majority of their cards face up, remedied this problem. The game also involved four, not two, betting rounds, which presented the potential for gradually building sizeable pots with players better able to gauge the relative merits of their opponents' hands during play.

Origins of the game

The first mention of five-card stud appears in the 1864 American version of Hoyle's famous guide to card games, lending credence to the notion that, alongside draw poker, it developed during the American Civil War. Having spread from the states of Ohio, Illinois and Indiana, it grew in popularity among those players who found draw poker to be a stifling game with little scope for implementing subtle betting ploys. The increased number of betting rounds and the exposure of cards during play created a game that encouraged players to stay involved, thus leading to pots that were worth contesting. In draw poker, building a pot large enough to generate interest often involved high antes, a discouraging factor for players unwilling to risk money before seeing their cards.

Despite the opportunities presented by the game to implement viable bluffs and betting strategies, five-card stud declined in popularity following a ruling in 1910 by the Attorney General of California. He declared it a game of chance and thus illegal, while draw poker was adjudged a game of skill and was exempted, in California at least, from the widespread prohibition of other forms of gambling. Though five-card stud continued to be played, it became viewed as a mechanical game lacking dynamism by those

Left: Three poker players in Ohio, *circa* 1870. Draw poker had developed into a game distinct from its European origins by the mid-19th century but, by the time this photograph was taken, five-card stud poker was also increasing in popularity.

Below: These antique ivory poker chips may not be to everybody's taste although the popularity of the game has led to a boom in the sales of poker chip sets which, along with a deck of cards, constitute the basic equipment required for a game. Nowadays most good quality chips are made of clay or, more usually, a heavy durable plastic.

Right: Karl Malden (centre) deals as Steve McQueen and Edward G. Robinson engage in their heads-up, five-card stud confrontation in *The Cincinnati Kid*. Though two players can easily play the game, there is usually more cut and thrust when five-card stud is played by eight to ten players.

Right: Karl Malden (centre) deals as Steve McQueen and Edward G. Robinson engage in their heads-up, five-card stud confrontation in *The Cincinnati Kid*. Though two players can easily play the game, there is usually more cut and thrust when five-card stud is played by eight to ten players.

players who had absorbed the basic, conservative strategies required to reduce potential losses. It was not until the 1950s that stud poker once again overtook draw poker as the most popular variation, but it was the seven-card version, not five-card stud, that had become pre-eminent by then.

Number of players

As there is no draw to consider and many players can be expected to fold before the latter betting rounds, up to ten players can comfortably play five-card stud utilizing a single deck of cards. The game is characterized by low average winning hands and this, allied to some disciplined betting strategy, can make it rather dull if there are five or fewer players. For this reason, experienced five-card stud players prefer games between eight to ten competitors since, with more cards in play, better hands may develop and this is likelier to prompt the betting confrontations that are the essence of poker.

THE CINCINNATI KID

The celebrated showdown in *The Cincinnati Kid* features a high-stakes game of five-card stud, the structure of which lends itself to the building of dramatic tension in a fashion not matched by draw poker. Eric Stoner, played by Steve McQueen, has an A in the hole and a pair of tens showing when he bets US$1,000 and is immediately raised a further US$1,000 by his opponent, who shows Qd, 8d. Lancey Howard, as portrayed by Edward G. Robinson, also possesses the Jd, offering an outside chance of a straight or a flush, but is trailing so badly that most poker commentators believe he ought to have folded. Stoner calls and ultimately the pot increases to US$25,000 by the time of the showdown with Stoner, the eager new kid on the block, showing a full house. Remarkably, the poker master's luck is in and Howard secures a queen-high straight flush (Q, J, 10, 9, 8 of diamonds) to win the pot, retain his status as 'The Man', and break the spirit of the young pretender.

Left: *A Winning Hand*, a poker representation dating from the late 19th century by which time five-card stud had begun to rival draw poker as the most popular form of the game. It is less commonly played today, as shown by its absence from the numerous tournaments staged at the WSOP, although a specific variant of the game called *Sökö* is very popular in Finland. The term derives from 'Minä Sökötän' which, in Finnish, means 'I check'.

SEQUENCE OF PLAY

As in all poker games, five-card stud begins with the dealer shuffling the cards and having the deck cut before, typically, each player antes a nominal amount to instigate the pot. Players receive one card each face down (their first hole card) and a second card each face up before the first round of betting commences. Those paying to remain in the game are dealt a third card, also face up, at which point a second betting round takes place. Should the pot still be contested, a fourth card is dealt face up to each participant before the next betting round when the minimum bet is often doubled. If a fifth card is required to decide the destiny of the pot, then this too is dealt face up to each player, following which the fourth and final betting round occurs. The pot is won by any player making a bet unmatched by an opponent at any stage during the game or, in the event of a showdown, by the player with the best poker hand. Importantly, players who fold during play should turn all their cards face down to indicate they have dropped out of the hand.

The antes and the deal

Prior to the deal, it is customary for all players to ante a small sum to initiate the pot and confirm their willingness to participate in the hand. In a 25/50 fixed-limit game of five-card stud a nominal ante of 5 or 10 chips will usually be sufficient to generate a pot, particularly if there are as many as ten players in competition. For beginners, a low-stakes, fixed-limit game along these lines is recommended until the nuances of stud poker are understood. However, since good players soon master the rules of sound five-card stud strategy, playing the game for small stakes and with fixed betting limits can render it somewhat

THE ANTES

Above: In this example, bets for the first two rounds are set at 25 chips before rising to 50 chips for the final two rounds. Before then, however, all players must pay the ante, set here at a nominal 5 chips, in order to participate in the game. At this point, the dealer, player B, may then deal the cards.

THE DEAL

Above: Once the antes have been paid, the dealer burns – discards – the top card and then deals one card face down to each player in turn, followed by one card face up, known as the 'door card'. Player E, showing a Q, is compelled to bet first, by virtue of possessing the highest card on display.

formulaic. It is recognized, therefore, that five-card stud benefits more than many other variations from being played as a no-limit or high-limit game. Such betting structures offer players the chance to make large bets, relative to the size of the pot, encouraging creative play from those at the table. Aggressive betting strategies and bluffs are more likely to work when opponents realize that calling a bet may mean going all-in with their remaining chips.

Once the antes have been paid, the dealer burns the top card and then deals one card each, face down, to every player, working clockwise around the table. Each player receives a second card dealt face up. Since the remaining cards to be dealt during the hand will also be face up, it is crucial that players keep their hole cards obscured from opponents.

Opening the betting

Following the deal, the player holding the highest first face-up card, known as the 'door card', has to make a compulsory opening bet. This may be set at the minimum betting level for the game or may also, like the ante, be a nominal bet for a sum less than the minimum. Using the 25/50 fixed-limit example once again, this means that the opening bet may be set at 25 chips or, to offset the obligation to the opening bettor, reduced to, say, 10 chips. Thereafter, beginning with the player to the opener's left, the other players must decide whether to fold, call or raise. Should the compulsory opening bet – the 'bring-in' – be set at 10 chips, it is possible for players to call for that sum or raise to the stipulated minimum of 25 chips, an act known as 'completing the bet', as the action circulates around the table. Should two or more players hold a door card of the same rank, then the opening bet is made by the first of those to the dealer's left.

Above: The purpose of the ante in poker is to create a pot for which players can compete and to stimulate their interest by ensuring they already have a small investment in the hand. It is also a mechanism for ensuring that cautious players who are reluctant to risk their chips will see their stacks steadily eroded unless they actively try to win a pot now and again.

OPENING THE BETTING

Above: As the player with the highest-value door card, player E bets 25 chips with the Q showing. The remaining players, beginning with player F, must now decide whether to fold, call for 25 or raise by entering 50 chips into the pot. Player F folds, player A calls, then players B and C fold. Finally, player D calls for 25 chips to conclude the betting for this round.

THIRD STREET

At the completion of the first round of betting, those players still contesting the pot receive their third card dealt face up. On 'third street', as it is known, there is sufficient information for players to begin assessing their chances of winning. Assuming a six-player game in which all are still participating, each player will have seen 13 of the 52 cards, representing a quarter of the deck. These are the 12 cards so far dealt face up to each player, plus their own individual hole cards. Possessing a high pair at this stage of the game is generally advantageous, particularly if the hole card is paired with an up card. If the pair is comprised of both up cards, making it an open or showing pair, then the strength of the hand is plain to see. The opening bet in this round is made by the player with the best visible two-card hand and, again, if there are players with hands of the same value then the honour falls to the player nearest the dealer's left. Unlike in the first round, from third street onwards no player is compelled to bet and all players may check, if they wish, prior to receipt of a fourth card. In most forms of limit stud poker, the minimum bet applying to the first two betting rounds is doubled for the latter two rounds. However, if an open pair materializes on third street, the player in possession is permitted to double the bet at this stage of the game, thus protecting the hand by making it more expensive for speculative callers to try outdrawing it.

Fourth and fifth street

Once the betting on third street is complete, a fourth card is dealt, face up, to those still in the game, after which it is the player showing the highest-value hand who has the option to bet first. The final round of betting occurs after

THIRD STREET

Above: The three players remaining in the hand now receive a third card, face up, prior to the next betting round. With an Ah showing, player D is the first to act in this round, but any bet is optional, not compulsory, so player D may defer a betting decision by checking. In the event, player D bets 25 chips and is called by both opponents.

FOURTH STREET

Above: On fourth street, the betting levels now double with player D showing a pair of aces, leading player E's pair of queens and therefore facing the first betting decision. Player D bets 50 chips, confident that the pair of aces is leading, but both players E and A call, holding a pair of queens and aces respectively.

the fifth card has been dealt, by which time anyone still contesting the hand is in possession of five cards, one face down and four face up. Betting once again starts with the player in possession of the best visible hand. Obviously, inferences from the betting allied to the visible cards on the table during play mean that players will have a clear idea of what their opponents hold, or are suggesting they hold, during the concluding round.

The golden rules

One of the reasons that five-card stud has succumbed to the popularity of other poker variations is that the application of some simple strategic rules reduces the likelihood of large pots being contested to a showdown. On many occasions, hands fail to progress beyond third street since the pot odds rarely justify players with drawing hands seeking the cards they need to improve, particularly in the face of an open pair.

This represents the first rule of sensible play in that it is very rarely worthwhile to call a significant bet made by a player whose board cards alone outrank one's own hand. Playing a three-card flush or straight with two cards to come, for instance, is rarely advisable and is regarded as folly if an opponent bets with an open pair. The odds against completing the flush or straight are usually far too prohibitive to warrant calling, particularly when the betting levels are set to rise in the next two rounds. Similarly, it is dangerous to continue supporting an open pair after third street when an opponent with a higher-value board card calls a bet. A player showing a pair of tens and with a Q as a hole card, for example, is entitled to be wary if, having bet on third street, an opponent with an A and a K calls or raises. The inference is clearly that the

FIFTH STREET

Above: The players now receive their final card, giving them four cards face up and one – the hole card – face down, so each player is able to gauge the potential strength of their opponents' hands. Player D still shows the best hand and bets while player E, knowing that the queens are beaten, folds. Player A, also holding a pair of aces, calls and wins the pot at the showdown because the 9c is a higher kicker than the 8s held by player D.

opponent's hole card is either an A or a K and that the pair of tens represents little threat. While a disciplined application of these guidelines may help a player to conserve chips, since they are quickly absorbed with experience, they can render a session of five-card stud rather mechanical and somewhat short of serious confrontations.

Above: Showing the Ac as a door card, this player finds that the hole card is another A for the top pair and the best possible starting hand. The odds against this occurring are fractionally over 220 to 1 against though, in five-card stud, the hand presents a strong opportunity to take the pot.

SEVEN-CARD STUD

Once poker players had come to terms with the concept of five-card stud, it was not long before a seven-card version of the game materialized. More cards and more betting rounds generated greater interest in this stud variation, which left its five-card precursor behind in terms of popularity. From the beginning of the 20th century until the end of the World War II, during which the game was widely played by US servicemen, seven-card stud gradually acquired a reputation for being a testing but rewarding form of poker. After the war, the players of Las Vegas were similarly in thrall to the game and, up until the 1980s, it was twice as likely to be played in Nevada's casinos as all other variations combined. Only in the last 30 years has Texas Hold 'em managed to challenge seven-card stud as the pre-eminent poker game.

Development of the game

The game of seven-card stud, also known as 'seven-toed Pete' or 'down the river', is regarded by many as the quintessential poker variation. With each player ultimately receiving seven cards with which to form a hand, three face down and four face up, the game combines aspects of both open and closed poker. There are enough visible cards in circulation throughout play to formulate clear ideas concerning the composition of an opponent's hand, favouring those who are reluctant to bet blindly. However, with each player having three cards unexposed at the showdown, there is also enough scope for subterfuge and for some strong hands to develop away from the prying eyes of opponents. In addition, there are five betting rounds to negotiate, so that even a low-stakes game between

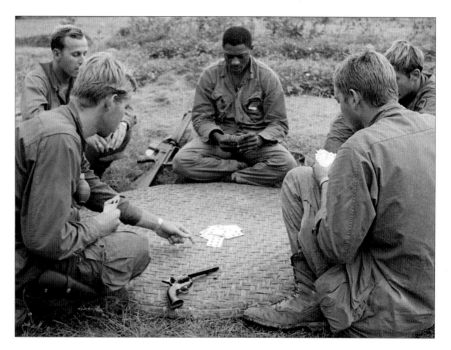

Above: US servicemen take time out to play poker, a pastime that naturally infiltrated military culture from the time of the American Civil War. By the time of World War II, seven-card stud was the preferred game for most servicemen and this played a part in it becoming the most popular poker variation in the immediate post-war era.

THE NUMBER OF PLAYERS

Above: Up to eight players can play seven-card stud and it is common for casinos and card rooms to cater for this number at a sitting. In a typical game, several players will have folded before the latter betting rounds, so the deck is rarely in danger of being exhausted during a single deal. This illustration represents the position after the initial deal when players receive three cards, two face down and one face up. Each has anted 10 chips to the pot and the compulsory bet (known as the 'bring-in bet') falls to player E, who possesses the lowest door card.

conservative players can generate plenty of betting action and large pots. The key to successful seven-card stud is, as ever, to monitor the ever-changing probabilities of receiving the card or cards needed to improve a hand by keeping a close eye on the up cards in play and those already folded during the game. Although difficult to master, seven-card stud maintains its appeal because it is a challenging game that rewards the dedicated application of all poker skills to an extent not replicated by draw poker or five-card stud.

Number of players

Seven-card stud is a game for between two and eight players, with casinos and clubs limiting participation to the higher number, which is the most that can be accommodated using a single deck. Although players may receive up to seven cards, the prospect of the deck becoming exhausted during the play of a hand is remote, since some players can be expected to fold long before the seventh and final card – the river card – is dealt. In low-stakes home games, it is possible that more players will retain their interest in the pot for longer. Therefore, if there is likely to be pressure on the deck during a game of seven-card stud, it is advisable to restrict the number of players to seven at most.

POPULAR BETTING STRUCTURES

♦ ♣ ♥ ♠

In common with the majority of other poker variations, seven-card stud can be played using any one of several different betting structures. Fixed-limit or spread-limit games are the most prevalent, with raises being limited to three, or perhaps four, per betting round, but pot-limit stud is popular among aggressive players and at tournament level. Choosing the right structure is important to the dynamics of the game, although this depends on the preferences and financial means of the players involved. The lower the betting limits, the more likely it is that several players will see a hand through to the showdown. This sort of structure is common in regular home games where competitiveness is secondary to the inherent entertainment value to be gained from playing. Serious players will, of course, seek games with much higher stakes, but casinos, real and online, usually offer a range of betting limits to suit all tastes and temperaments.

Left: A player takes a look at his hole cards following the deal in a casino game. Note the care taken to restrict any possibility that an opponent might see them and so gain free information. Players can often be sat quite closely together at the table so shielding the cards in this fashion is recommended.

THE FINAL ROUND

Above: This illustrates a typical scene prior to the final betting round of a 25/50 fixed-limit game, with four players having a full complement of seven cards. As will be apparent, estimating what each player holds at this stage from the cards on display and their betting behaviour throughout is a major test of skill and observation. Player A, for example, could hold any value hand between a pair of eights and a Q-high straight flush in hearts. The potential of the hands belonging to players D and G is more easily recognized.

SEQUENCE OF PLAY

Assuming a fixed-limit game, all players typically ante a nominal sum, after which the dealer distributes the cards one at a time to each player in turn until they have three cards, two face down and one face up. After the first betting round, those remaining in the game receive a fourth card, face up, prior to the second round of betting. Further betting rounds ensue after the fifth and sixth cards are dealt, also face up, following which a seventh card is dealt face down to each remaining player. Anyone participating in the game to the showdown now has seven cards from which to make a five-card poker hand, four face up and three face down. The winner, as always, is the player who either makes a bet that is uncalled or who displays the best hand at the showdown once the fifth and final betting round has concluded.

The antes and the deal

The size of the antes depends on the betting limits applied and the house rules in operation, but a figure approaching 20 per cent of the minimum betting level is quite normal. In a 50/100 fixed-limit game, the ante to be paid by each player will therefore be 10 chips. If seven-card stud is the only game to be played during a session, it is recommended that the dealer pays the antes for each player. This can help speed up the game

and nobody is disadvantaged as the deal circulates around the table one hand at a time. After the antes are in the pot, the dealer burns the top card and deals one card at a time to each player until they have three cards, the first two face down and the third, referred to as the door card, face up. At this point, the first round of betting is ready to commence.

Early betting rounds

In seven-card stud, the player with the lowest-ranked first exposed card or 'up' card on the board (otherwise termed the door card) is obliged to make a bet known as the 'bring-in'. When two or more players possess the low card, the suits come into play on the only occasion in poker when they are ranked, with clubs counting lowest followed by diamonds, hearts and spades in ascending order of value. A 2c is lower than a 2d, which, in turn, is lower than a 2h. The size of bring-in may vary from one card room to another, but it is typically set at twice the size of the ante. If the ante is 10 chips, the bring-in is likely to be 20 chips, still below the level of the minimum bet. The betting continues clockwise around the table, with the player to the left of the bring-in next to act. This player may fold, call the bring-in or raise the betting to the minimum level for the first two rounds, which, continuing with the 50/100 fixed-limit example, would be 50 chips. If this occurs, it is known as

Right: In this fixed-limit seven-card stud game, bets for the first two rounds are set at 50 chips before rising to 100 chips for the final three rounds. But first, all players must pay the ante of 10 chips before the cards are dealt. This immediately gives them a stake in what is initially a small pot but, with five betting rounds to go, this can be expected to grow substantially prior to a potential showdown.

THE ANTES

'completing the bet' and sets the level for the rest of the round, with bets and raises now in denominations of 50 chips. From fourth street onwards, the first player to bet is the one who shows the best visible hand, and the option to check is available to all players if no bets are made. Also, as in five-card stud, if a player holds an open pair on fourth street, then betting during this round may be doubled to the higher limit – 100 chips in this case – by any player still contesting the hand. Holding the best visible cards does not always imply the best possible hand, but the number of cards to have been displayed at this stage should help players to assess their own chances of winning. Since players who fold will turn their up cards face down to confirm their decision, remembering the cards that have already been dealt is a skill that can help shape this assessment as the hand progresses.

PLAYABLE OPENING HANDS
♦ ♣ ♥ ♠

To win a pot in a full-handed, eight-player game of seven-card stud normally requires a hand of at least two pairs, with straights, flushes and full houses occurring frequently enough at the showdown to make them worth pursuing. It makes sense for players to conduct a quick assessment of their first three cards to determine the chances of making a potential winning hand. Having three of a kind is obviously beneficial, since this may be sufficient to win the pot without any further improvement. It also offers a player the chance to drive opponents holding potential flush and straight draws out of the game with some confident, aggressive betting. High-value pocket pairs (two cards of the same rank) are also worth playing, while other hands that warrant consideration in the early stages of the game are three-card flushes and open-ended three card straights such as 8, 9, 10, for instance. It is possible for any starting hand to improve sufficiently to win, but the examples detailed here offer by far the best chances of success.

Left: The first three cards dealt in seven-card stud offer a range of opening hands that offer plausible chances of developing into winners. Any three of a kind, such as the three tens seen here, represents an immensely strong starting hand and could easily prove good enough to win even if it fails to improve.

THE DEAL

Left: This shows the position after the deal, with each player having received two cards face down and one – the door card – face up. The player with the lowest door card is now obliged to make a nominal bet known as the bring-in, which, in this case is set at 20 chips – double the ante. Player F, showing a 3h, is therefore compelled to open the betting, or bring it in, for 20 chips. Following player F's compulsory bet of 20 chips, the action moves clockwise around the table, beginning with player A. Players may fold, call the bring-in of 20 chips, or raise the bet to the stipulated minimum of 50 chips, this being known as completing the bet.

FIFTH STREET

The crucial point in seven-card stud for those still involved in the pot comes on fifth street, the moment when a fifth card is dealt to each player, face up, in readiness for the third round of betting. With just two cards to come, everyone should have a sound idea regarding the composition of their opponents' hands and whether or not it is worth continuing to bet against them. This decision is crucial because the betting typically increases on fifth street with the minimum bet for the final three rounds being twice that applicable during the first two. In general, any player who has already secured a high straight or better on fifth street will probably bet modestly to keep opponents interested. The time for a larger bet to build the pot comes on sixth street, when a player's sixth card is dealt and when those still needing cards to win are more likely to call.

Increased betting limits

From a strategic point of view, this is usually the last moment in a fixed-limit game when a large bet or raise might induce opponents to fold, although this is difficult to achieve in a restrained, low-stakes affair. Although the minimum bet usually doubles on fifth street, anyone with a realistic chance of making a good hand is unlikely to fold in the face of a bet unless there are one or two raises to indicate that much better hands already exist. In pot-limit stud,

Right and above: Following the bring-in, player A calls for 20 chips before player B, holding a pair of tens, completes the bet by putting 50 chips into the pot. Players may call or raise in denominations of 50 chips only. With the Ac showing, player C calls, as does player D, while player E chooses to fold. Should players F and A both call by adding a further 30 chips to make up the deficit, then the first round of betting will be concluded.

PLAYING A LEADING HAND
♦ ♣ ♥ ♠

Since most seven-card stud hands are not fully realized until at least the sixth card has been dealt, having a made hand on fifth street is obviously advantageous. A high-ranking straight or better will win around half the hands played in a seven-handed game featuring plenty of callers at the showdown. When holding such a hand it is therefore regarded as sensible to wait until the fourth betting round before making a raise, since those remaining in the pot are more likely to call for the final card, in hope as much as in expectation. The key for any player in a winning position, of course, is to make it costly for opponents to catch the cards they need, and timing such a move is also important in maximizing winning chances. Any player who holds a vulnerable leading hand such as two pairs or a low-ranking straight must consider betting on fifth street to eliminate some of the opposition and reduce the risk of being outdrawn by those with the apparent potential to do so. Should such a move not prove successful in eliminating the majority of opponents, it is usually advisable to sit tight and play the remaining rounds as cheaply as possible.

THE FIRST BETTING ROUND

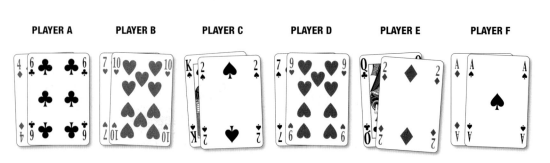

players are more inclined to try reducing the field with a big bet on fifth street, relative to the size of the pot. Bluffs and semi-bluffs are much more likely to succeed, especially when a player has three cards to a high-ranking straight or flush showing. A large bet on fifth street from someone in this position may cause opponents to fold potential winning hands because they are unwilling to risk calling even larger subsequent bets when they could already be beaten. Understandably, when the stakes are higher, players tend to be much more selective in which hands they support beyond fifth street.

Pot management

As in all poker games, managing the pot when holding a strong hand in seven-card stud needs a clear assessment of the opposition's visible cards and betting patterns. The style of game is important, since players are more likely to bet to the showdown with speculative hands in a low-stakes, fixed-limit game than they are in pot-limit stud, a game characterized by heavy betting in the closing rounds. Generally, the more players that continue beyond fifth street, the stronger the winning hand is likely to be. A player holding three of a kind or two pairs of high value will usually bet the maximum allowed to encourage those with straight and flush draws to fold.

If possessing a lock hand (a hand that cannot lose), or something close to it, then the strategy normally applied is to bet the minimum required to keep other players in the pot. This helps build the pot gradually by preventing players from receiving cards for free, as well as offering opponents a chance to improve their hand and yet still be trailing. If they do improve, they are more likely to call subsequent bets and raises which further increases the chance of winning a substantially inflated pot.

FOURTH STREET

PLAYER E

Above: Players F and A call the first-round bet, adding a further 30 chips each before the fourth card is dealt. Player C, showing the highest-value up cards, opens the second betting round by checking with a weak hand. Player D bets 50 in support of the pair of sevens only to be raised by player F, who doubles the bet to 100 chips. Player A, who needs two cards for a flush or straight, calls for 100, along with player B, who holds a vulnerable pair of tens. Player C folds, D calls, and the round is complete.

FIFTH STREET

PLAYER C

Above: As the fifth card is dealt, player B bets first due to showing a pair of jacks, but checks as it is difficult to show a strong enough hand to drive others out of the pot, with the other two jacks already visible in other hands. Player D, holding two small pairs, also checks, while player F, currently leading with two pairs of aces and threes, applies further pressure by betting 100. Player A, without a pair, folds, at which point both players B and D decide to call for 100.

CLOSING ROUNDS

At the completion of the third betting round on fifth street, each remaining player receives a sixth card, face up, and the option to bet passes to the player showing the top-ranked four-card hand. It is not unusual for half the players in a full-handed, fixed-limit game to remain involved at this stage, with every aim of betting to the end. Once the betting is complete, the dealer distributes a seventh and final card, face down, to those still participating. The final betting round then proceeds, with the option to bet, once again, falling to the player with the best visible hand.

Sixth street

The betting action on sixth street depends on the nature of the game and the players involved. In an aggressive pot-limit game, it is rare for more than two players to be in opposition by the sixth card, while a fixed-limit variation is more likely to see three or four players still in contention. At this point, each player has four of their final seven

Right: Player F receives a 5s, face down, which does not improve upon the full house of threes over aces. Of more concern is that both players B and D called when the three threes became evident, which means, from player F's perspective, that player B could have a bigger full house if holding pocket tens, as could player D with the relevant down cards. Player F opens the betting and is raised by player B, who cannot beat player F's board cards, so can only win by attempting a bluff. Player D folds while player F contemplates whether to call the dealer.

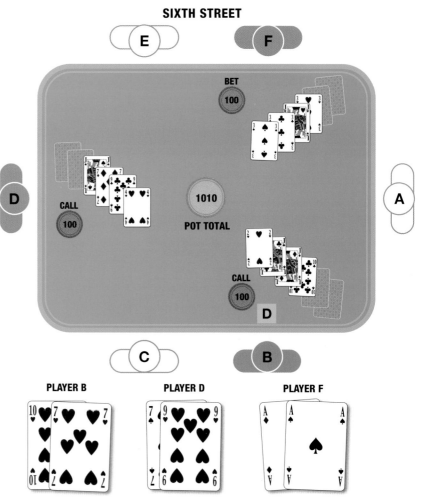

Above: The pot now contains 1,010 chips which, with the minimum bet being 100, offers attractive pot odds of 10 to 1. Player F is first to act by virtue of showing three threes and bets 100 chips. Players B and D know that player F cannot have another J for a full house, but must fear that the remaining 3, not yet seen during play, may be among their opponent's hole cards. If correctly deducing that player F instead has a pocket pair for a made full house, both will realize that they may still draw a card to acquire a better hand. One of the two unseen tens in the deck will help player B, while player D requires either a 7 or a 9 for a full house that may yet win.

cards face up on the table. In conjunction with the betting patterns they have already exhibited in the previous three rounds, this information offers clues as to the hands each player holds or is hoping to obtain. Having three or four cards of one suit suggests a flush, while someone betting with a four-card straight in view is indicating that the hand is completed by one of their pocket cards. The value of having the strength of one's hand disguised amid those pocket cards, especially with a further down card to come, is thus underlined.

Seventh street

The seventh and final card is dealt face down to each player once the fourth betting round is complete, providing those still in the hand with three cards face down and four face up. In terms of strategy, a couple of simple guidelines apply during the final betting round, since certain situations can be expected to recur. Players holding an obvious winning hand should bet, particularly if it uses two or all three down cards. Opponents who have played to the showdown will often call with hands that have improved but are inferior.

By contrast, when the strength of a potential winning hand is clearly visible from the up cards, then a bet is rarely advised. An opponent who cannot beat the hand at the showdown will fold, so there is nothing further to be gained from the pot. Someone who can readily beat it will probably raise in the face of a bet, perhaps triggering a reluctant and costly call only to confirm possession of the second-best hand. The problem here is that it is easy for a player to feel justified in calling given the amount committed to the pot. Also, even though the call may be made in expectation of defeat, it can seem a small price to pay just to be certain that an opponent who re-raises a bet on the river is not bluffing.

Similar variations

The huge popularity of seven-card stud has given rise to variations that are as challenging as the original. English stud poker follows the structure of seven-card stud as far as fifth street. For the final two rounds, however, players may draw a replacement card from the deck with an up card replaced face up, and a down card replaced face down. More popular variations include the low only game, known as razz, and the high-low, split-pot seven-card stud games, of which there are several. In all cases, straights and flushes are discounted in compiling a low hand with A, 2, 3, 4, 5 – a wheel – the lowest hand attainable. In the split-pot variation, this hand would have a sound chance of winning both high and low to scoop the pot.

PLAYING A DRAWING HAND
♦ ♣ ♥ ♠

A drawing hand in poker is one where a player needs a specific card to complete a legitimate poker hand – four-card straights and flushes are typical examples. A player in this position, with two cards to come, in seven-card stud, will hope to pay the minimum for the chance to catch the card. With two rounds of betting to negotiate, this will be a severe test of skill. In limit poker, players will check or merely call an opponent's bet, rather than raise in this scenario. It is essential to avoid 'drawing dead', which occurs when a player tries drawing a hand that, if obtained, still cannot win.

THE SHOWDOWN

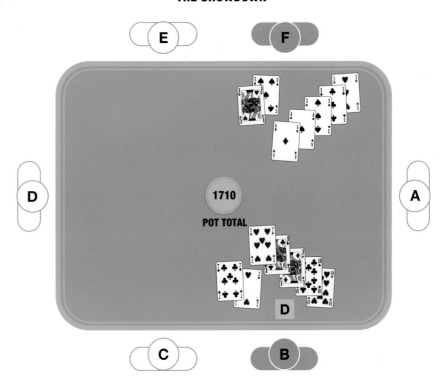

Above: Player B's attempted bluff failed as player F called the raise of an extra 100 chips after player D, with only two pairs, folded. As the betting is now concluded, players B and F expose their seven cards and reveal their poker hands, with player F's full house of threes over aces outranking player B's two pairs, jacks and tens, to claim the pot worth 1,710 chips.

TEXAS HOLD 'EM

Texas Hold 'em, often referred to simply as Hold 'em, is currently the most widely played of all poker variations, having surpassed seven-card stud as the game of choice. This situation has arisen as a direct consequence of the game's exposure on television, which has managed to exploit the entertainment value presented by top-class tournament players in action. Almost invariably, televised poker features no-limit Texas Hold 'em, which lends itself extremely well to the medium and is recognized by professionals as the most demanding of poker games. At a lower level, Texas Hold 'em is played for fixed limits and low stakes, which, naturally, helps maintain the amateur player's interest in a game regarded as simple to learn, but difficult to master.

Origins of the game

Following the development of stud poker, Texas Hold 'em was one of a number of games that utilized community cards, dealt face up on the table, that could be used by all players to make their respective poker hands. One of the first such community card games was termed 'wild widow' and this gave rise to usage of the word 'widow' to describe the common cards on the table that are available to all. Since players ultimately have seven cards from which to choose their best five, it is accepted that Texas Hold 'em is also a variant of seven-card stud. The game emanated from the southern states of the USA, possibly originating in Robstown, Texas, at the turn of the 20th century, before reaching Dallas around 1925. Hugely popular with southern professionals, it naturally spread to Las Vegas, where, in its fixed-limit guise, it was shaded by seven-card stud in terms of popularity. Then, in 1971, Benny Binion decided that the WSOP World Championship should be a knockout tournament and, with the approval of the experienced players who entered, no-limit Texas Hold 'em was chosen for the main event. From that point onwards, the expansion in tournament play, allied to the volatile characteristics of the game, ensured that Texas Hold 'em maintained its place in the public eye.

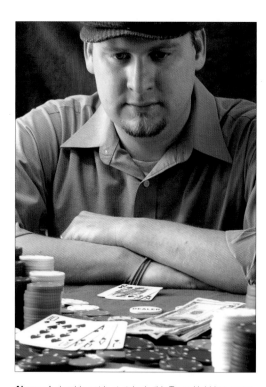

Above: A sizeable pot is at stake in this Texas Hold 'em game as the showdown reveals the dealer has made the best possible hand – the nuts – on the river as the ten gives him a royal flush. The outcome is highly improbable, but anyone who plays the game long enough may well encounter a hand that plays out in this fashion at some stage during their poker career.

Below: Recognizing the best hand available is crucial in forming a viable Hold 'em strategy. Here, with all five board cards revealed, a 5-high straight would constitute 'the nuts', meaning that a player holding 4, 5 as pocket cards could bet knowing that the hand was unbeatable.

IDENTIFYING THE NUTS

Number of players

Since players are dealt just two cards each, it is feasible to accommodate as many as 20 people in a game. In truth, such a number renders it almost impossible to manage. Clubs and casinos generally limit participants to a maximum of ten, which, even in a tight and cautious game, will create plenty of betting action. Any number between two and ten players can enjoy a competitive game. As with all poker variations, the average value of the winning hand decreases, the fewer players are involved. Consequently, in a full-handed Hold 'em game, this being one featuring the accepted maximum of nine or ten players, a patient and conservative approach is usually recommended. This is particularly the case in cash games when players should expect to fold well over half their hands before the flop. When the game is 'short-handed' with five or fewer players in competition, it is more likely that the betting action will be loose, as players gamble a little more freely in support of marginal hands and bluffs.

Above right: Players receive just two cards in Texas Hold 'em, not much upon which to base the first serious betting decision. A pocket pair represents one of the strongest of the 169 possible two-card combinations that could be dealt, pocket aces most of all. Conversely, holding a hand of 7, 2 'offsuit' (of differing suits), is usually a prelude to folding at the first opportunity.

Right: The value of the nuts changes with each hand, with an A-high flush in hearts being the best possible hand in this example. Anyone holding an A-high straight, by virtue of holding any A and 10, would be concerned at the possibility of an opponent holding a flush. With no pair on board, a full house is impossible.

THE NUTS

A player who holds an unbeatable hand during a poker game is said to hold 'the nuts' or a 'lock hand'. This is advantageous since it allows the player to focus his or her attention on building the pot without fear of losing the hand. In the many open poker variations in which several cards are exposed during play, determining the nuts and the likelihood of someone holding the best possible hand available is therefore a crucial factor when considering whether to bet. According to folklore, the term emanates from the Wild West era, when players were supposedly inclined to bet their wagons and horses on the outcome of a hand. To underline the integrity of such a bet and the strength of belief behind it, the nuts from the wagon wheels would be placed in the pot, a tactic considered inconceivable without possession of an unbeatable hand.

IDENTIFYING THE NUTS

SEQUENCE OF PLAY

To begin the game, each player is dealt two cards face down, these being referred to as 'hole' or 'pocket' cards. A round of betting ensues before the dealer reveals three cards, face up, on the table. This is called the 'flop'. Following the flop, a second betting round occurs and then a fourth card – the 'turn' – is dealt, after which there is further betting. The fifth and final card, known as the 'river', is revealed by the dealer prior to the last round of betting. The objective is to make the best five-card poker hand possible from their two hole cards and the five community cards on the table. Players may discount their hole cards entirely when finalizing their hand, in which case they are said to be 'playing the board', their hand comprising now all five community cards.

The deal and the blinds

Prior to the deal, the two players to the dealer's left must make compulsory bets, known as 'posting the blinds'. The first player bets the 'small blind', usually set at half the minimum stake of the opening betting round, while the second player makes a full bet known as the 'big blind'.

As the deal moves clockwise around the table, each player faces the prospect of making these forced bets. The deal itself sees players receive two cards each, face down, prior to making their first betting decision. After the blinds, the next player to act may fold, call the big blind or raise. Players cannot check in this round, since the betting has already been opened, courtesy of the blinds. If the betting has not been raised by the time the action returns to the players in the blinds, they may raise if they wish. Although the blinds have late betting positions in the pre-flop betting round, this early advantage is lost after the flop when they will be the first players to act.

STARTING THE GAME

Above: To start the game, the players to the immediate left of the dealer must post the blinds. Here, the small blind is set at 50 chips, while the big blind is 100 chips, the set level for a bet in the first two rounds of this game, which is a 100/200 fixed-limit example. The dealer is indicated by the dealer button that moves one place to the left after each hand.

Left: A button used to indicate which player is obliged to pay the small blind, a compulsory bet that is paid by the first player to the dealer's left. As the first to act in all betting rounds following the flop, the player in the small blind should be cautious when choosing whether to call any substantial pre-flop bets made by opponents. To do so usually requires possession of a strong starting hand.

IMPORTANT OF POSITION
♦ ♣ ♥ ♠

In Texas Hold 'em, a player's position relative to the dealer is a crucial factor in any betting decision, since the earlier a player is required to bet during a round, the less information there is to help shape that decision. The dealer, as last to act, has a distinct advantage, because the checks, bets or raises made by opponents can all be taken into account when the time comes to act. Typically, players in early positions are best advised to support only premium hands, while those in the later betting positions may take more chances with poorer quality hands, particularly if the betting is light.

Starting hands

Judging which starting hands to support is crucial in Texas Hold 'em, as each player initially receives just two cards. Any two can win, but being dealt high-ranking cards or a pair is advantageous. High pocket pairs such as aces, kings or queens are strong enough to take the pot at the showdown without help from the board. They are not invincible starting hands, so players holding them often raise the betting before the flop to drive out weaker hands that retain a chance of improving sufficiently to win.

STARTING HANDS

♦ ♣ ♥ ♠

There are 169 possible starting hand combinations in Hold 'em: the most valued are the high pairs of aces, kings and queens. Also strong are the unpaired holdings of A, K; A, Q and A, J, especially if of the same suit. Players with such hands will often raise the betting before the flop to encourage players with weaker hands to fold, thus strengthening their grip on the pot.

Pre-flop betting

Strategies for betting before the flop vary. In a fixed-limit game for small stakes, many players will pay to see the flop, irrespective of their hole cards, hoping to improve their hands. At the other extreme, high-stakes Texas Hold 'em characteristically sees most hands folded before the flop, especially in the face of the first substantial bet. A player raising the maximum infers possession of a premium hand. Calling such bets in a high-stakes game is risky, unless the caller also holds a viable hand with good chances of improvement.

Right: Once the cards have been dealt, player D folds before player E raises with a strong hand, doubling the bet to 200 chips. Player F folds another weak hand and the dealer calls the 200 with K, Q offsuit. After player B sacrifices the small blind of 50 chips by folding, player C in the big blind calls the raise, by adding 100 chips to the pot to conclude the betting round.

THE DEAL

Above: Players receive two cards each from the dealer and must base their initial betting decisions on these alone. Estimating the value of a starting hand based on the likelihood of it proving successful is therefore essential. Here, player E's pair of tens and player C's A, Q suited represent strong hands worthy of support. Player A's K, Q offsuit is not as valuable as it might appear, while the remaining hands are uniformly poor.

PLAYER A	PLAYER B	PLAYER C	PLAYER D	PLAYER E	PLAYER F

PRE-FLOP BETTING

THE FLOP

After the flop, each player is able to see five of the seven cards from which they might ultimately make their respective hands, these being their two hole cards plus the three community cards on the table. This is the key point in the game, as players can visualize the best hand they might achieve if participating in the showdown and, most importantly, assess whether this is likely to prove a winner. Continuing in the game beyond the flop, though, not only depends on the value of the cards, but on the action at the table as the betting round proceeds.

Betting on the flop

The player to the dealer's left is first to act and may fold, check or bet. Should all players check, the turn card is dealt, becoming what is known as a 'free' card since nobody has paid to see it. Any post-flop betting strategy must take account of several factors, including a player's position, the betting structure in operation and the number of opponents still in contention. The scale of bets made before the flop also needs to be considered. A raise is usually indicative of a strong two-card holding, particularly if emanating from a player in an early position. For example if a flop comprises As, Ad, Kc and a pre-flop raiser bets again, a natural assumption would be that the player holds an A, a K or possibly both as hole cards. Even an opponent holding a pair of kings for a full house of kings over aces, a very powerful hand, might baulk at calling, for fear of trailing a bigger full house of aces over kings, or possibly even four aces.

Right: Since player C has a good chance of hitting an A-high straight or flush, a bet of 100 tests the strength of the opposition. Player E is leading and calls when another raise may have been in order to emphasize a strong hand. Player A is content simply to call.

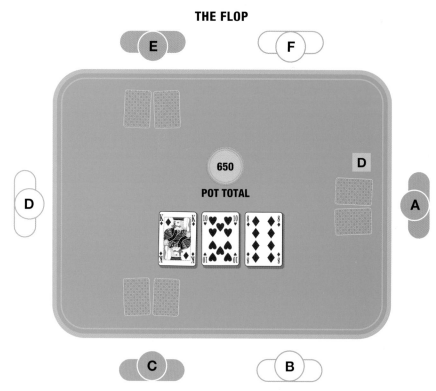

Above: Following the flop, player A as last to act may feel confident with the top pair of kings. The flop offers good chances for progress to player C's hand with a slightly better than even-money possibility that a straight or a flush will materialize on the next two cards. Player E is in a strong position, currently leading with three tens.

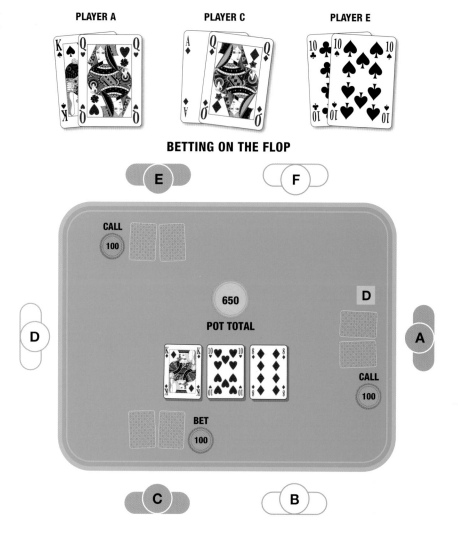

Leading hands

It is rare in Texas Hold 'em for the flop to provide a player with an unbeatable hand, but the flop will normally clarify whether a player possesses a hand that is currently leading. A player holding Kd, Kh when the flop comes Kc, Qs, 6h, would be in a commanding position with three of a kind and a probable winning hand, but danger might still exist if an opponent holds Js, 10s. Needing an A or a 9 for a straight, and with an outside chance of making a flush, such a hand is tempting enough to warrant support. Under these conditions, therefore, it makes sense for the holder of a leading hand to bet, forcing those with 'drawing hands' – those needing a specific card to complete a legitimate poker hand – to pay dearly for their next card. By contrast, when holding a leading hand on the flop that looks unlikely to be beaten, it generally pays to bet lightly, to encourage opponents to stay in the game. Such a strategy conceals the strength of the hand and helps to inflate the pot, thus increasing potential winnings.

Drawing hands

Hands in which a player needs one more card on either the turn or the river in order to improve to a winning position are called drawing hands. Typically, this involves players seeking straights or flushes as these are consistent winners in Texas Hold 'em. Adopting the correct strategy in this situation depends on the probability of hitting a relevant card and the cost of staying in the game, making an awareness of pot odds essential. When the odds against drawing a required card exceed the pot odds available, it is prudent to fold, but if the reverse is true, then it is advisable to stay in the game. Overall, drawing hands are generally pursued only if the cost of doing so is relatively small.

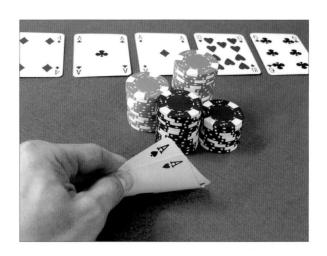

Right: A player with pocket aces peeks at his hole cards once again after the flop to confirm possession of four aces. The hand is definitely guaranteed to win meaning that the player can focus on trying to keep as many opponents involved as possible in order to swell the pot and make a profitable outcome.

THE SIGNIFICANCE OF POT ODDS
♦ ♣ ♥ ♠

Being able to calculate the number of cards that might help a drawing hand or hurt a leading hand is an essential poker skill. It helps a player to distinguish whether the odds of reward for making a bet are justified or not. For example a player who is trailing after the flop may recognize that hitting any one of five cards on the turn or the river will guarantee a winning hand. The odds against this occurring are 4 to 1, so, in this situation, a bet would normally be considered only when the total in the pot offers odds of 4 to 1 or better.

LEADING HANDS AND DRAWING HANDS

Above: In strategic terms, when possessing a leading hand such as the three tens held by player E here, it is generally advisable to bet, forcing those with drawing hands to pay for the privilege of seeing more cards. Conversely, when in player C's position, the usual strategy is to stay in the game as cheaply as possible until or unless a favourable card appears on the turn or the river.

THE TURN AND THE RIVER

In a typical Texas Hold 'em game, the minimum bet doubles after the turn card has been revealed. Those players who continue betting beyond the flop can therefore be assumed to have a reasonable chance of securing the best hand, since the cost of playing has risen. With just one more card to come, identifying the best hand available from the cards in play and estimating the possible hands held by other players is a straightforward task. However, it is also true that a player needs to be realistic in assessing the chances of obtaining a winning hand. This is particularly the case in pot-limit and no-limit Hold 'em, when the scale of the betting tends to increase dramatically in the last two rounds, making it potentially expensive if frequently calling with the second-best hand. Should two or more players match bets after the turn card is exposed, then the dealer reveals the river card, this being the fifth community card on the table and the catalyst for the last round of betting.

POT MANAGEMENT

♦ ♣ ♥ ♠

Of all the skills common to good poker players, being adept at pot management is one of the most crucial. This means betting in a way that maximizes winning opportunities when holding good cards, but moderating potential losses when holding poor cards. For instance, when possessing a pocket pair in Hold 'em which is matched by a card on the flop to make three of a kind, a large bet might persuade opponents to fold. Since such a hand will usually win, try to build the pot with a minimum bet or a small raise, to keep other players involved.

THE TURN

Above: The turn card (Kh) has now been revealed, and, with 950 chips already in the pot, the bets and raises in this fixed-limit game are now set at 200 chips each. Player E currently leads with a full house of tens over kings, while player A has improved to three kings but is still trailing.

BETTING ON THE TURN

Above: Having failed to make a straight or a flush, player C checks at this stage. Player E bets 200 chips, indicating that the two kings on the board seem to bear no threat, and player A calls because trip kings is ordinarily a very strong hand in Texas Hold 'em. At this, player C folds, since neither a straight nor a flush will beat the full house that players A and E may possess.

Final betting round

At this point in the game, all remaining players can adjudicate their poker hands from the seven cards available to them. Once more, the first active player to the dealer's left has the option to fold, check or bet after the river card has been dealt. If all players check, the winner is determined by a showdown, which also occurs if a player makes a bet that is called by at least one opponent. In terms of strategy, decisions during the final betting round are few. A player holding a powerful hand, if not the nuts, should be aiming to extract as much as possible from opponents who, having sustained their interest to the river card, will often have hands sufficiently strong to tempt them into calling a bet. If the river card does not help a player's hand and an opponent makes a maximum bet, it is often sensible to fold, irrespective of how many chips the player has contributed to the pot already. Above all, the single most important factor to remember in widow games like Hold 'em is that any community card that improves one player's hand may strengthen that of an opponent to an even greater degree.

Playing the board

Occasionally, players who bet through to the river will find that the best poker hand they can make comprises the five community cards alone, their hole cards proving redundant in terms of improving their hand. When this is the case players are said to be 'playing the board'. This is generally a weak position to be in, but, since a player's hole cards are unknown to opponents, it is still possible to bluff at this point in the game, should the opportunity arise. Indeed, for players faced with such a situation, bluffing is normally the only means of claiming the pot, although this should only be contemplated when a player detects weakness in an opponent's hand.

THE RIVER

Above: Unluckily for player E, one of only four cards remaining in the deck that could help player A to improve to a winning position has materialized on the river, the Qc now providing player A with a superior full house of kings over queens. This shows how Hold 'em hands can quickly change in value and explains why players with leading hands after the flop often bet aggressively to prevent situations such as this from arising.

THE SHOWDOWN

Above: Player E bets 200 chips in the belief that player A may have three kings but not a full house. However, player A does have a superior hand and justifiably calls to claim the pot of 1,750 chips at the showdown. However, by calling rather than raising, player A has missed an opportunity to exploit an unbeatable hand since a raise may have prompted player E to call and so lose even more chips.

OMAHA

This poker variation is one of the more recent examples to have captured the imagination of players, with references to the game almost non-existent prior to 1980, after which it started appearing in the card rooms of Las Vegas. Now it is one of the more popular forms of online poker, regarded as ideal for social players who enjoy a game with loose betting action and high-value winning hands. Although similar to Texas Hold 'em in terms of its betting structure and pattern of play, Omaha differs from its close poker relation in two key respects. First, players are dealt four cards to begin the game instead of two, and they are required to use two, and only two, of their hole cards, with three from the board to make their hands. These differences have a profound effect on the nature of the game. Players experienced in Texas Hold 'em, in which the average winning hand is much lower, sometimes take time to adjust their strategic thinking.

Origins of the game

Occasionally referred to as Omaha Hold 'em, the game, unsurprisingly, emanates from Nebraska. According to Bob Ciaffone, author of *Omaha Holdem Poker*, it was normal for players in Omaha to insist that a legitimate Texas Hold 'em hand must include both hole cards and three community cards. This concept was retained in the new variation, where players receive four hole cards, from which any two must form part of their final poker hand. The game first appeared at the WSOP in 1983, when professional gambler and poker theorist David Sklansky won the US$1,000 fixed-limit Omaha contest, taking the first prize of US$25,500. Since

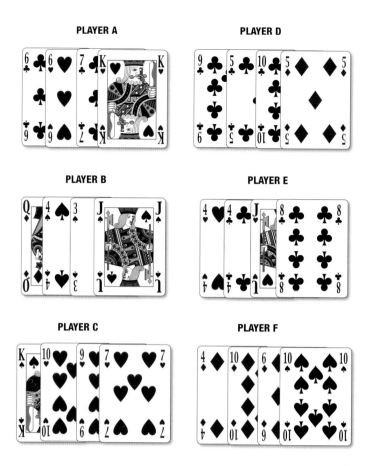

TWO FROM THE HAND, THREE FROM THE BOARD

Above: To form a viable hand in Omaha, players must use two of their pocket cards and three from the board. In this instance, player A makes the winning hand of a full house, sixes over eights, by combining the pocket sixes with the 6 and pair of eights on the board. The apparent full house of sixes over kings is not permissible because this would use three pocket cards and just two board cards. Player B has only a pair of eights since the J-high flush in spades would also require three pocket cards, while player C is similarly unable to make a legitimate straight or flush from what is available. To complete the picture, the best hands for players D, E and F are two pairs (eights and fives), three of a kind (trip eights), and two pairs (tens and eights), respectively.

then, Omaha has become an established part of the poker scene, with a high-low, split-pot variation also having evolved.

Number of players

Between two and ten people can play the game, with card rooms and casinos inclined to cater for the maximum. Some simple arithmetic will confirm that a full-handed, ten-player game will see virtually the whole deck in play during each hand. Since the game is characterized by plenty of calling but little raising before the flop, especially within a fixed-limit betting structure, the number of cards in circulation almost guarantees high-value winning hands. Straights or better win in the majority of cases and players can assume that if the board suggests that a bigger hand than theirs is possible, then an opponent will probably already have it. Poker theorists maintain that success at Omaha is simply a case of finding a lock hand, or the nuts. Only when holding the best possible hand, or facing favourable pot odds in trying to draw to it, should a player consider betting.

Legitimate hands

The crucial difference between Omaha and Texas Hold 'em is that players must combine two of their hole cards with three from the board to form their poker hand. Experienced Hold 'em players who are unfamiliar with Omaha sometimes forget this ruling. One of the key implications is that being dealt three or four of a kind is counterproductive, since only two of those cards will be used in the final reckoning. Similarly, holding any four cards of the same suit offers little advantage in securing a flush, since two of the hole cards are redundant and the chances of seeing three more of that suit among the community cards are greatly reduced.

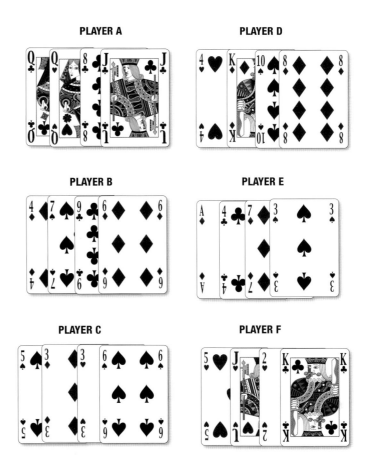

TWO FROM THE HAND, THREE FROM THE BOARD

Above: In this example, player C has the weakest hand, with just two pairs, threes and twos, while the K-high straight held by player A is only fifth best. Players B, D and E are all able to use the three diamonds on the board, with two in their hand, to make flushes, but player E holds the A, 7 of diamonds for the best of these. However, to underline the typically high value of winning hands in Omaha, player F's full house of twos over kings is the best of the six hands dealt.

SEQUENCE OF PLAY

In Omaha, the action begins with the small blind and big blind being posted by the players to the dealer's immediate left, as with Texas Hold 'em. The dealer then deals the cards one at a time to each player, clockwise around the table until everyone has four cards face down prior to the first betting round. The dealer then reveals the flop: three cards face up on the table, which all players can use towards finalizing their hand. A second betting round then takes place, after which the turn card is dealt. Betting limits usually double at this stage of the game, and, following a third betting round, the river card is revealed. This acts as a prelude to the final round of betting. The winner is the player who either makes an unmatched bet during the game or holds the best poker hand at the showdown, comprising exactly two hole cards and three from the board.

The blinds and the deal

Rather than having every player ante before the deal, Omaha mimics Texas Hold 'em in that the compulsory bets are confined to the two players to the left of the dealer. The first bets the small blind, normally half the minimum stake unit for the first betting round, while the next player must pay the big blind, which is equivalent to a full bet. In a 50/100 fixed-limit game, therefore, the small blind would be 25 chips and the big blind 50. The dealer burns the top card before dealing four cards face down to each player. These hole or pocket cards should be kept hidden from opponents during play.

Playable opening hands

As always, the first crucial element of the game comes when players are dealt their opening four cards. Only two of

THE BLINDS AND THE DEAL

Above: As player C is the dealer, players D and E have to bet the small blind and the big blind, since they are the two players to the dealer's immediate left. This example features a 50/100 fixed-limit Omaha game, so the blinds are set at 25 and 50 chips, respectively. After the blinds have been posted, the cards are dealt one at a time to each player clockwise around the table, beginning with player D, until all players have four cards face down. These are their hole or pocket cards and should remain unseen by opponents.

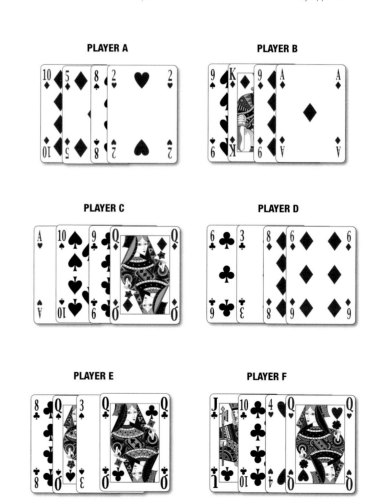

these may be used in forming the eventual hand, but these four cards offer six different combinations of two cards each. The key to successful Omaha play is to recognize when any one of these six two-card combinations may blend with the board cards to provide a winning hand. For example, while high pocket pairs are much less valuable than in Hold 'em, having Ad, As, Kd, Ks is beneficial for several reasons. Should any A or K appear on the flop, the chances of hitting a full house are greatly increased, particularly considering that there is a 50 per cent chance a pair of a lower value will materialize among the five board cards. If the board contains three diamonds or three spades, then the best possible flush would be held, and if any Q, J, 10 should appear, then the player will secure the high straight. The key, therefore, is to support only those opening hands in which four, five or all six two-card combinations offer genuine chances of blending with the board to create a winning hand.

The flop

Once the pre-flop betting round is complete, the dealer burns the top card and reveals the next three cards from the deck, face up in the centre of the table. Since seven cards are available to each player at this point, they should have a clear idea of the best possible hand they can attain and, most importantly, whether this is likely to prove good enough to win. The first player to bet after the flop is the one to the dealer's left, whose options are to check, to bet or to fold. The action then continues clockwise around the table in the usual fashion, as each active player in turn decides whether to remain in the hand or drop out. Should all players check, the dealer reveals the turn card prior to the next betting round.

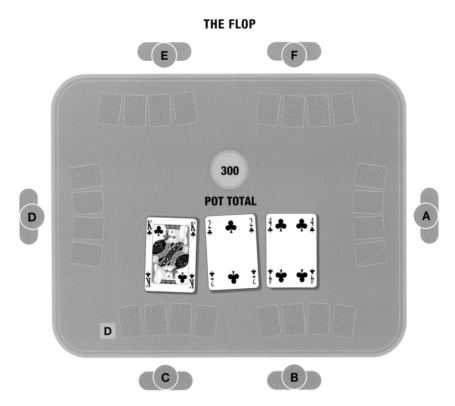

THE FLOP

Above: All six players called the bet of 50 chips before seeing the flop, generating a pot of 300 chips. The flop itself shows the K, 2 and 4 of clubs, making K-high flushes for players D, E and F. All three have two clubs amid their pocket cards, with player E currently best at this stage by virtue of the Qc. Players A and C have little or no chance of beating a flush, rendering their own prospects of winning remote. Player B, meanwhile, has an outside chance of securing a full house.

Left: A button to help signify that the second player to the dealer's left is compelled to bet the big blind. In Omaha, as in Texas Hold 'em, the big blind is normally the same as the minimum bet for the first two rounds of betting. In a 50/100 game therefore, the big blind will be a compulsory bet of 50 chips.

PRE-FLOP BETTING
♦ ♣ ♥ ♠

In a full-handed game, it is unusual for players to bet aggressively in order to reduce the field before the flop. Few initial holdings are powerful enough to justify a pre-flop raise, which is, in any case, unlikely to eliminate a sufficient number of opponents to greatly help matters. Even the most unpromising of hole cards may ultimately combine with the board cards to produce a strong hand, this being one of the game's most appealing characteristics. Consequently, pre-flop betting is often restrained, with several players calling to see what develops. The net result of this is an increase in the size of the pot and therefore improved pot odds for those still involved as the game unfolds.

THE TURN AND THE RIVER

Following the second round of betting, the dealer reveals the turn card, having previously discarded, or burned, the top card from the deck once again. Typically, the betting limits double at this stage, so any player who has yet to hit the nuts or who has little prospect of doing so should realistically consider folding. The game itself becomes simpler to analyse, however, since players are readily able to identify the likely winning hand and whether they have a chance of obtaining it. In fixed-limit Omaha, betting on the turn to ward off those with drawing hands is rarely successful, although in pot-limit games, this is the moment when those already holding strong but not unbeatable hands will try to exert pressure with pot-sized bets. Once the third-round betting has concluded, the dealer reveals the river card and the final betting round occurs prior to the showdown. The player with the best poker hand comprising two hole cards and three from the board wins the pot. Alternatively, the pot can be won earlier in the game if a player should make a bet that is not called by opponents.

Right: After the turn card, all players decide to check and so the river card, the 5d, is revealed by the dealer, with the pot total remaining at 500 chips. Player D rightly suspects that the low flush comprising Kc, 6c, 4c, 3c, 2c is beaten by either a higher flush or a full house, and checks. Player E holds the best hand, but knows it is not the best possible – the nuts – and also checks. Player F bets 100 chips, the minimum bet having increased for the last two rounds, following which, players B and D fold.

THE TURN

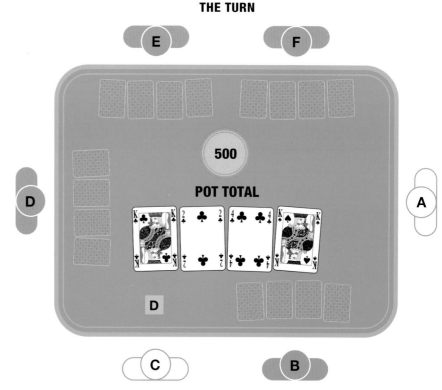

Above: After player D bets 50 chips in support of the flush, players E, F and B call to boost the pot to 500 chips. Players A and C fold. The turn card is then revealed as the Ks, giving player B three of a kind and a chance of a full house should an A or 9 appear on the river. Player E's flush is leading as the betting for this round begins.

THE RIVER

PLAYER B

PLAYER D

PLAYER E

PLAYER F

Identifying the nuts

As mentioned earlier, experienced poker players regard Omaha as a game that is consistently won by the player holding the nuts. With this in mind, recognizing the best possible hand available at each stage of the game is an essential skill that can help guard against the costly error of calling with the second-best hand. For example, when a pair appears on the flop, it is highly likely that one or more full houses will already have been secured. Pursuing a flush in this situation is therefore pointless and even drawing for further cards to obtain the best possible full house – known as the nut full house – offers only a 50 per cent chance of success. With no pair on the flop but two or three cards of the same suit evident, then players may assume that a flush is the likeliest winning hand, immediately devaluing any potential for hitting a straight.

Omaha high-low, eight or better

Evidence of the flexibility of poker and the enthusiasm among players for devising new forms of the game comes in the shape of Omaha high-low, eight or better, a split-pot variation that is arguably more popular than high-only Omaha. The pattern of play is the same, as governed by whichever betting structure is in place, but the pot is divided between the holders of the best high hand and the best low hand. To qualify for the best low hand, however, players must have all five cards of the relevant hand ranked 8 or lower. Also, in compiling a low hand, players can disregard straights and flushes, making the nut low hand (the best possible low hand available) a straight of A, 2, 3, 4, 5, known in the game as a 'wheel' or a 'bicycle'. A 5-high straight flush, therefore, could conceivably provide a player with the best low hand and the best high hand simultaneously. This

represents the ideal situation, since a player who wins both high and low scoops the pot by taking all the chips bet during the hand. Should no low hand qualify for a share of the pot during a game, the winning high hand takes the entire pot. One of the factors that makes this game so appealing is that, with some players chasing high hands and others aiming low, pots can become so large that even winning a half share represents a good result. However, players need to avoid 'quartering' the pot by tying a hand, either high or low, as the half share of the total pot on offer will be divided in half again.

STRAIGHTS, FLUSHES AND FULL HOUSES
♦ ♣ ♥ ♠

The reason why Omaha is considered a game of straights, flushes and full houses becomes clear when examining statistical facts about the likely composition of the board cards, sometimes referred to as the widow. Half of the time, at least one pair will appear and, when this occurs, a full house or better will be held by someone on two out of every three occasions in a full-handed game. Similarly, the board will contain three or more cards to a flush, 40 per cent of the time, with the result that a flush will be present on around nine out of ten occasions. Seeing three cards on the board that help fill a straight occurs 80 per cent of the time, which, with so many combinations possible among the players' pocket cards, makes a straight almost as likely.

THE SHOWDOWN

Above: Following player F's bet, player E reluctantly calls for 100 chips, despite knowing that the hand could be beaten by a higher flush, a full house or even four kings. At the showdown, the players reveal their cards and player E's Qc proves decisive in securing the pot of 700 chips, with a higher value K-high flush in clubs than that of player F.

POKER STRATEGY

The various different poker games that have developed over the past two centuries have given rise to many theories regarding poker strategy. To an extent, many of these are extrapolated from the mathematics behind the game, since, with a single deck in use there is always a finite number of possibilities at work, however large. Yet poker is played by and against people, which gives rise to a host of other factors that have to be taken into account when assessing the chances of winning a hand, securing a profitable session, or emerging triumphant from a tournament. The style of the game being played, the betting structure in operation and the stake levels applicable will all influence a player's decisions, as will the characteristics of the opponents themselves. This chapter focuses on the five standard forms of poker, high-only, and outlines some of the key factors that newcomers and experienced recreational players alike must consider if they are intent on improving their poker-playing skills.

Right: A player commits his remaining chips to the pot by betting 'all-in'. This move is a familiar sight to those who have seen poker on television, which almost invariably features no-limit Texas Hold 'em, a game in which players may risk all their chips on a single hand whenever it is their turn to bet.

DRAW POKER

Draw poker begins with all players contributing an ante to the pot. Working clockwise, the dealer deals one card at a time face down until each player has five cards. The option to open the betting falls upon the player to the dealer's left, but only if holding a hand that has a pair of jacks or better. If not, the option moves around the table until someone with a qualifying hand commits chips to the pot. After the first betting round, players may discard up to three unwanted cards and replace them with others from the deck. After the draw, a second round of betting ensues, the first player to act being the player who opened the first betting round. If two or more players match bets in this round, the game ends with the showdown when they reveal their cards to identify who has the winning poker hand. The pot may also be claimed if, during either the first or second round of betting, a player makes a bet and the opponents all fold.

PLAYER A **PLAYER B**

PLAYER C **PLAYER D**

PLAYER E **PLAYER F**

Above: A typical range of hands after the deal in a six-player game where player A is dealer. Players B and C cannot open the betting since their hands do not qualify, but player D can with the pair of kings. A two-card draw for a flush is unlikely to be successful, so player D should keep the kings and discard the other three cards which are not high enough as kickers. Player E has no pair and should fold. Player F could raise any opening bet and take the pot now with two pairs, aces up. A call is safe, as the odds are against anyone improving enough to beat the hand. Any betting should prompt players A and B to fold but player C could call to draw one card to a straight – either an A or a 9 will suffice.

As the original poker variation, draw poker was initially played as a no-limit betting game, which made it suitable as a gambling medium for the wealthy and those who possessed an uncanny ability to bluff. The imposition of limits on the betting broadened the game's appeal, while the adoption of rules governing who opened the betting for each hand further transformed draw poker. With the advent of jackpots, the variation in which a player who opens the betting must possess a pair of jacks or better, draw poker became a much more mechanical game that rewarded sound strategic play. Although still popular in California's card rooms, where for nearly a century it has been the only poker game permitted by law, elsewhere, draw poker has diminished in significance compared to seven-card stud and Texas Hold 'em. Nevertheless, the game provides a solid foundation upon which beginners can gradually expand their poker knowledge, it being the first form of poker most people learn to play. Online poker sites that feature draw poker host games without the requirement for opening the betting with a pair of jacks or better. As such, this deprives players of one of the elements essential to formulating a strategy, namely the certain knowledge that one opponent holds at least a pair of jacks. For this reason, attention here will be focused on jackpots, the draw poker variation that invokes the opening requirement and in which the draw is limited to three cards.

Starting hands

In order to have a clear concept of a good starting hand, it is necessary to contemplate what is ultimately likely to win in a full-handed game of six or even seven players. Anyone dealt two pairs or better in their first five cards immediately possesses a hand that has about an even-money chance of winning without improvement. Two small pairs might prevail, but combining a pair of aces with a lesser pair is preferable. This is because the hand has only an 11 to 1 chance of improving to a full house, assuming a one-card draw, so anyone not holding a pair of aces is vulnerable to opponents who draw two cards to a pair with an A kicker – the highest unpaired side card in that player's hand. They have a 4 to 1 chance of achieving two pairs – with aces up – or better, leaving an opening hand of two low-to-medium pairs as the likeliest to be leading before the draw but trailing afterwards. Holding a pair of aces presents a player with a 3 to 1 chance of improving the hand after a three-card draw and wins frequently enough in its own right to warrant support, particularly in a light betting heat. Pairs lower than jacks are considered risky propositions when calling the opening bet, since such a hand is evidently already trailing. Anyone holding a higher pair has the same chance of improving as the player with the lower or underpair. So a three-card draw to a pair of nines, for example, has a 3 to 1 chance of improvement, generally speaking, and a 7 to 1 chance of becoming three of a kind, known as 'trips'. Yet such improvement may still leave the hand second-best at the showdown, a prospect that is even more likely, given that the opener will occasionally have much better than a pair of jacks.

Seeking information

Players who have developed an understanding for the game soon recognize the inferences to be drawn from the bets made by opponents. Although up to a fifth of all deals may feature no hand good enough to open, when a player does possess such a hand, there is a strong likelihood that another is in circulation. Should the first player to the dealer's left choose to open the betting, taking the earliest position or acting 'under the gun' as it is known, then it is fair to assume that a pair of aces or kings is the minimum hand being advertised. Players opening with anything less in an early position find it hard to justify calling a subsequent raise, since they are almost bound to need improvement on the draw. In mid and late positions, players are inclined to open with jacks or queens, but will also be wary of anyone who then raises. Such aggression would signify the raiser probably holds at least a pair of aces, and more probably two pairs or three of a kind. In a fixed-limit game, raising with less than a pair of tens is hardly worthwhile, since it is difficult to bet a sufficient amount to prevent the opener from calling with what is, by definition, a better hand. Only a tight player known for only raising with rock-solid hands might perpetrate a successful bluff under such circumstances, underlining the importance of understanding one's opponents and their playing styles.

Above: When dealt two pairs, such as the jacks and eights shown here, a player has an even-money chance of winning even if the hand does not improve. Discarding the 6d in an effort to draw an additional J or 8 for a full house is a logical move, though the odds against the full house being completed are 11 to 1 against.

Above: Being dealt a pair of aces offers a player the chance to open the betting in any position, even when first to act. If an opponent should raise an opening bet made under the gun, however, they are likely to be holding two pairs or better. Therefore, if choosing to call, the player holding this hand will probably discard the 8h, 5d and hope to find a K or preferably another A to have any chance of winning the pot. There is also the chance that both cards drawn could be an additional pair to go with the pair of aces.

Above: Whether to play a pair of queens will depend on a player's position at the table. If the option to open has been checked around to a player in late position with this hand, a bet is advisable, if only to collect the antes. If an opponent raises, the player holding the pair of queens must expect to be losing, since the opponent is likely to have at least a higher pair and possibly much more. Calling with a fairly good hand, while knowing that any improvement may not be enough to win, is one of the consistent features of the game.

Betting clues

Prior to the draw, the only clues available regarding any player's hand come from the betting. Those with an early advantage will normally bet to emphasize it, the one exception being when a player holding a 'pat hand' – an outwardly strong hand since he or she opted not to exchange any cards at the draw – calls the opener, rather than raising, to encourage others to do likewise and boost the pot. But with only two betting rounds, it is usually best to press home an advantage by forcing opponents either to fold or to inflate the pot in their own efforts to find a winning hand. In a fixed-limit game, therefore, although a player with an average hand – a low pair, perhaps – may call the opener and trust to fortune, anyone who subsequently raises is unlikely to be bluffing. To raise with less than a high pair, which could be vastly inferior to the opener's hand, invites disaster when players need only call one more bet before the draw. Pursuing this strategy will virtually guarantee heavy losses in the long run, since the pot odds will rarely match the odds against securing a winning hand. In other words, when successful, the chips won will not compensate for those lost in the inevitably frequent defeats. Players who favour pot-limit draw poker have a little more scope for a speculative call and the occasional bluff, but in order to beat the odds they will normally have to read their opponents exceptionally well.

Playing the draw

Deciding how many cards to draw after the first round of betting is often straight-forward, particularly if the betting itself has offered a few clues as to the potential strength of opponents' hands. Understandably, it is sensible to draw the number of cards needed to

FIG A

Above: When contemplating how many cards to draw, players need to balance the likelihood of improving sufficiently to win against the cost of obtaining more cards. Holding two medium pairs prior to the draw puts a player in a probable winning position, but it is 11 to 1 against drawing to the full house that would make victory almost certain.

FIG B

Above: Players who hold four-card flushes have a 5 to 1 chance of completing the hand, but the one-card draw should only be contemplated when there are several callers in an unraised pot.

FIG C

Above: Any players hoping to draw two cards to complete a straight are trying to beat odds of 22 to 1, making it a speculative play, at best.

maximize the chances of securing the best hand possible, although there is an exception to this rule when a player holds three cards of the same value, also known as 'trips' – a potential winning hand even without improvement. Two-card draws to straights or flushes are rarely worth considering, whether playing a fixed-limit or pot-limit game, while one-card draws for the same hands are best played cheaply against several opponents. The possibility of some vigorous betting in the second round makes the implied pot odds more attractive in this situation, especially as the hand is likely to be a winner if it hits. Against just one opponent, drawing one card to a straight or flush is much less appealing, since the odds of reward rarely justify the risk. To improve upon two pairs requires drawing one card for a full house, but the odds against this occurring are an unattractive 11 to 1. This is why players holding two pairs usually raise the betting in the first round to drive out weak hands and reduce the chance of being outdrawn.

As mentioned earlier, a player holding trips is best advised to draw one card, as opposed to two, even though this reduces the chances of making a full house. Such a move disguises the value of the hand and makes it more likely that an opponent will call a second-round bet with a losing hand, having assumed, wrongly, that the player possesses two pairs or is bluffing with a busted straight or flush. If an opponent decides not to draw further cards or 'stands pat' as it is termed, then anyone holding trips will definitely draw two cards in the expectation that a full house may be necessary to win. Players who are dealt pat hands of a straight or better can usually assume they are in a winning position, leaving them free to concentrate on building the pot.

FIG D

Above: Finding 'trips' – three of a kind – after the deal is something of a rarity, and such a hand is a regular winner. Rather than discard the two odd cards in a bid to improve the hand, it is often worth a player retaining one to help disguise the hand's real strength. Opponents may read a one-card draw as indicative of an attempted straight or flush, or that the player holds two pairs at best.

FIG E

Above: While holding trips is beneficial, being dealt a pat hand such as a 10-high straight should safely see a player claim the pot; extracting the most chips possible from opponents then becomes a matter of pot management.

Observing opponents

Apart from the information to be gleaned from bets made in the first round, the draw is the only other point in the game when players may gain an insight into the hands held by opponents. Remembering how many cards were drawn and by whom can provide clues to the value of hands in competition for the pot. Discounting an outright bluff, anyone choosing to stand pat with their original five-card hand is obviously confident that they possess a probable winner. Otherwise, players typically draw as many cards as necessary to give themselves the best chance of improving their hands. Those making three-card draws are almost certainly retaining a pair, the value of which can be reasonably estimated if the opener opts to do this. Two-card draws suggest trips or a pair with a high kicker – the highest unpaired side card in that player's hand – since drawing two for either a straight or a flush will bring success on fewer than 1 in 20 occasions, making this an unattractive proposition to most players. Finally, players who draw a single card are perhaps the most difficult to read, since they could be holding anything from a currently worthless four-card straight to a virtually unbeatable four of a kind. Generally, it is best to assume that a player who opens or raises the betting and then draws one card probably has at least two pairs and maybe even trips. In an unraised pot, players drawing one card are more likely to be trying to buy a potentially lucrative flush or straight as cheaply as possible.

Right: Following the opening bet, players A and D fold, but the remainder all call for 25 chips. The fact that no opponent raised could indicate several things. First, they may each hold a pair that was too low with which to open, leaving them a 4 to 1 chance of improving past a pair of aces. Alternatively, they may have four-card straights or flushes that they are hoping to fill as cheaply as possible. The worst-case scenario is that at least one opponent has a powerful hand and is simply trying to build the pot.

THE DEAL

PLAYER F

Above: This example hand of a 25/50 fixed-limit game highlights some of the likely thought processes facing a player throughout a typical game. After the deal, the option to open the betting is checked – or passed – around the table until player F, holding a pair of aces, bets 25 chips. On the assumption that nobody is slow-playing a stronger hand, this high pair may even prove good enough to win without any further improvement.

THE BETTING

Above: Having opened the betting and indicated possession of at least a high pair, player F keeps the J kicker to help disguise the true value of the hand. Opponents are then forced to consider that player F may well hold three of a kind. Had the Jc been discarded as well, it would be much clearer to all that player F holds a high pair and no more at this stage.

Odds against

Players who prosper at the game are generally well versed in the probabilities applying at the deal and before the draw. The odds of being dealt a pair of aces or better, for example, are 8 to 1, which emphasizes the need for patience while waiting for a playable hand, as even a pair of jacks and above will only materialize once in every five deals. Against five opponents, a pair of aces has a better-than-even chance of being ahead, which makes it worth playing in most cases. At the other extreme, receiving at least a straight directly from the deal will occur once in every 132 occasions, underlining the rarity of a genuine pat hand. To put this into perspective, a six-player game could see the deal circulate 22 times around the table before anyone is dealt a straight or better. Of the other key opening hands that offer good prospects of winning, two pairs or better will happen once in 13 deals, while a hand of at least three of a kind will appear once in every 35 deals.

Any player who draws cards to a hand with potential rather than to a hand that is already made is said to be 'on the come'. The term can apply to players with two pairs, for example, who may draw one card to try catching a full house but, in a game where two pairs is often good enough to win, such a holding could be described as a made hand already. It is more usually associated with four-card flushes and straight draws that need one more card to complete the hand. In the best of such situations, namely holding an open-ended straight flush draw, the odds against hitting any one of the 15 cards that will complete – or fill – either a straight or a flush are 2 to 1. At the other extreme, needing one card for an inside straight draw is 11 to 1 against being successful, odds which preclude anything but a cautious betting approach.

THE DRAW

160

POT TOTAL

PLAYER F

Above: Player B now draws two cards while players C and E draw just one card each. The latter two, by virtue of their betting position and their reluctance to raise earlier, could both be drawing to straights or flushes, but player B's draw is more difficult to read. If slow-playing trips, it is unlikely that player B would discard two cards, since discarding one would better disguise the hand. As a two-card draw to a flush or a straight is unlikely, it is therefore more likely that player B has a medium to high pair with a high kicker. If so, player F is still in good shape and discards two.

Pursuing value

Only by comparing the relevant pot odds with the chances of improving a hand sufficiently to win can players ensure that they bet in support of good-value propositions. In fixed-limit games, the implied pot odds before the draw rarely exceed 3 to 1, less than the chance a player holding a low pair has of beating an opponent holding a pair of aces. Opportunities to bet when the pot odds are in favour of drawing a probable winning hand are therefore rare in a game where players with weak hands sensibly fold, leaving two or possibly three players to contest the pot. Players holding a four-card straight or flush are definite underdogs against just a couple of opponents and will be unlikely to win a pot sizeable enough to justify the risk of playing. The situation changes when the opener has several callers, since more bets can be anticipated in the second round, thus increasing the pot odds. A one-card draw to a flush or an open-ended straight has a 5 to 1 chance of completing the hand, which makes this a much more attractive proposition in a multi-handed pot.

Following the draw

Betting strategies following the draw are dependent on several factors as players try to assimilate the various strands of information obtained so far. A player opening in early position is advised to bet again in the second round only with an improved hand, otherwise a check is recommended. Anyone who is already beaten will not call a bet, while those who have improved to a possible winning position will call or even raise, perhaps prompting a call from the opener that simply compounds the loss. In fixed-limit poker, the cost of calling is rarely enough to make bluffing in the second round a serious option. Those bluffs that are successful tend to be set

THE DRAW (SECOND-ROUND BETTING)

160
POT TOTAL

BET
50

PLAYER F

Above: As the opener, player F has the option to act first in the second round but, having seen no improvement following the draw, the only sensible option is to check. When player B bets 50, player F immediately has doubts that the pair of aces is still strong enough to win, since, if reading player B's hand correctly, it is only 3 to 1 against it having improved from one medium pair to two pairs or better. This would make the bet justifiable in terms of the available pot odds, while a bluff in this situation is unlikely.

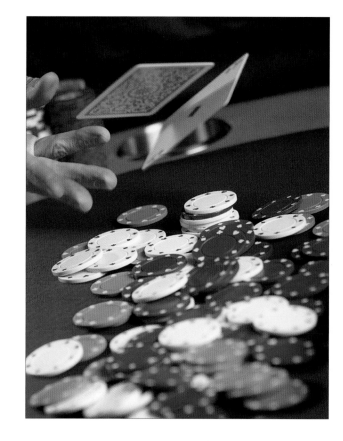

Right: A player theatrically tosses his cards away to indicate that he is folding, even though there is a massive pot at stake. Folded hands should always be added face down to the 'muck', this being the pile of discarded cards that accrue during the play of each hand that is the responsibility of the dealer.

up with a strong pre-draw bet or raise, a move that could be enhanced by subsequently not drawing any cards, or 'standing pat' as it is otherwise known. Another general rule is not to bet with anything less than a premium hand, an A-high flush or better, for example, when one or more opponents have drawn one card without previously having raised the pot. Anyone who completes a straight or better will raise any second-round bet, while those who missed their hand will inevitably fold.

Straights and flushes

Holding a straight or a flush, especially A-high, puts a player in a strong position, as such hands can be expected to win, or hold up, on most occasions. How the hand is played after the draw will depend on the circumstances beforehand.

If a made flush is dealt to a player who then opens the betting, then another bet in the second round is almost obligatory. Players who have improved to three of a kind, for instance, may call just to be certain that the opener is not bluffing. Checking merely allows players who fear they have not improved enough to check too, and this reduces the potential winnings.

If an opponent opened, then there are other possibilities for a player with a pat straight or flush. A call will probably keep other players involved, but a raise is not out of the question if the game is loose with plenty of action. When a player successfully draws to a straight or flush, calling the opening second-round bet is generally a sound policy. Those players whose hands remain inferior despite having improved, may well be tempted to call, or perhaps even raise, in the face of perceived weakness. A raise at this point, however, will probably eliminate players who would otherwise call and, once again, reduce the potential winnings.

Above: A player raises the betting by adding more chips to the pot. The raise is an aggressive move, of course, and usually indicates possession of a strong hand although this perception allows players to employ it as a bluffing technique too. When choosing to raise, players should announce their intention clearly before committing their chips to the pot. Adding sufficient chips to call the previous bet and then announcing a raise is known as a string bet and is not permitted.

THE SHOWDOWN

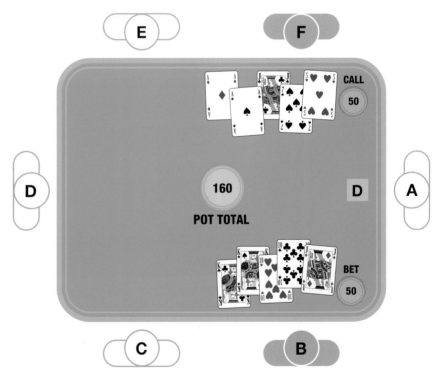

Above: The fact that players C and E quickly folded suggests that they completely missed their draws, leaving player F to decide whether the pot odds, now 4 to 1, justify calling player B's bet. In the event, player F does call, suspecting that player B may hold a lower pair than aces, which did not improve. At the showdown, player B is the winner, but player F's earlier check is vindicated. A bet would surely have been re-raised by player B, meaning that player F would probably have contributed 50 more chips just to confirm defeat.

FIVE-CARD STUD

The pattern of play for five-card stud permits from two to ten players to engage in a game which begins with each player contributing the ante to the pot before being dealt two cards, the first face down and the second face up. The player with the highest-ranking face-up card, otherwise known as the 'door card', opens the first round of betting with a compulsory bet known as the bring-in, following which opponents may fold, call or raise. When the first round of betting is completed, those still involved in the game are dealt a third card, also face up, and a second betting round follows. Again, the player showing the best hand opens the betting with this honour quite often falling to a different player in each round as successive cards are dealt. The game continues with a fourth face-up card being dealt, followed by another betting round and then, if necessary, competing players receive a fifth card face up as a prelude to the final betting round. As ever, the winner is decided either at the showdown when those still involved reveal their hands or by a player making a bet at any stage of the game that is not called by opponents.

Five-card stud represented a major departure from draw poker, the first recognizable form of the game. Although the introduction of betting limits and restrictions on which player opened the betting expanded draw poker's popularity, the paucity of information available upon which to base any betting decisions led to the development of open poker, of which five-card stud is the oldest surviving example. Open poker games are those in which several of the cards in each player's hand are exposed for all to see. In five-card stud, each player ultimately receives one card face down and four face up, if participating to the fourth and final betting round. The structure of the game therefore enables players to modify their strategic thinking after each successive round, as more cards are exposed and the inferences behind opponents'

Below: This is a typical scene after the final card has been dealt. Three players have survived the first three betting rounds and the action is on player F who boasts the best visible hand, a pair of aces. This could be enough to win but, since player A has obviously called on fourth street when both opponents were already showing open pairs, it is possible that player A has a concealed 9 and has successfully completed a J-high straight. This would be enough to beat the others who can only hold three of a kind at most.

As they appear to the opposition

As they appear to the player

TYPICAL FINAL-ROUND SCENE

710
POT TOTAL

Above: To be dealt a pair in the first two cards usually provides a player with an immediate advantage, although high-ranking pairs are obviously of more value since they are more likely to win the hand without any improvement required. The odds against being dealt any pair are 16 to 1, but seeing queens or better in the first two cards will happen around once in every 74 deals, while receiving a pair of aces is a 220 to 1 chance.

betting patterns become more apparent. In addition, since there is no draw to put pressure on the deck, five-card stud can accommodate up to ten players, which is the number of participants considered ideal by experienced players and poker professionals. Such a game is likely to create betting confrontations that are essential to an enjoyable session. Adopting a pot-limit or no-limit betting structure will also help to counteract the mechanical facets of five-card stud that are prevalent in a conservative fixed-limit game. Bluffing becomes a more attractive possibility when bigger bets are permitted and the pots can escalate sufficiently to tempt players into staying with hands that might usually be folded in a fixed-limit contest.

Starting hands

In common with all poker variations, judging which opening hands to play and which to fold is the first important element of five-card stud. After the deal, this decision is based upon the receipt of just two cards, of which one is visible to opponents. This might initially seem to present a player with too little information upon which to decide whether to fold or play, but an understanding of the odds affecting the game emphasizes

why this decision is important. Any player who stays to the showdown has an even-money chance of obtaining a pair. In a six-player game, therefore, if all players see five cards the likelihood is that three of them will possess at least a pair, with one of these likely to be queens or better. Possessing a pair of aces or kings gives any competitor an advantage, and the earlier that pair materializes during play, the better. The ideal situation is to be dealt a pair in the first two cards, since a player in this position can exercise more control over the betting. When holding two unmatched cards, the general advice is to be cautious and fold immediately, unless both cards are ranked 10 and above. The only exception to this rule is when a player has a hole card, one that is held face down on the table, that is higher than any door cards (the first exposed or 'up' card) on display. A player can expect to see a pair of aces once in every six deals, so an A in the hole with a 7 showing, for example, presents a player with a fair possibility of making the high pair. If this occurs and there are no other aces or open pairs among opponents' up cards, then the hand has a good chance of winning at the showdown, supposing the player is unable to force opponents to fold beforehand by betting aggressively.

Above: A pair of queens, often referred to as 'ladies', is a strong opening hand in five-card stud. After the deal, a player holding a pair of queens should expect to be leading since only a pair of aces or kings could be beating the hand at this stage. If there are no door cards higher than a Q on show, then the player will be aware of holding an immediate advantage over the opposition when contemplating the opening bet.

THE VALUE OF PAIRS
♦ ♣ ♥ ♠

The value of being dealt a pair in five-card stud can hardly be overstated. Although possessing a pocket A or K to match the door card is desirable, even lower-ranked pairs can be valuable to some extent. In a tight game where players are exercising caution, a raise from a player showing a 7c, for example, may cause the opener and any callers holding higher-value door cards to fold, for fear that a pair has already been secured.

After the deal, a six-player game presents any player with odds of just over 3 to 1 against pairing the high card in this situation, odds that worsen considerably if one of those cards is dealt to an opponent. That unfortunate situation may be enough to induce conservative players to fold. Whether one is dealt a pair or not, in a high-stakes or no-limit game of five-card stud, bluffing with a big first-round bet to suggest a pair is a plausible tactic. However, it is rarely considered by players holding unpaired cards, either of which is ranked below a 10.

Door cards

Before the first round of betting takes place, the first exposed or 'up' card dealt to each player – the door card – offers the only clue as to the potential of each hand. The player with the highest-value door card opens the betting, but this obligation may fall to a player holding a 7 or an 8 on occasion, in which case several callers can be expected. If the door cards are low, it increases the chance that players will have high-value hole cards – those dealt face down and thus unseen by opponents – which could encourage them to stay in for a round or two. A raise from a player showing a low door card normally indicates a pair is held, and a similar assumption may be wise if the player merely called the opener.

Social players are not always aware of the probabilities at work, so the skill of the opposition needs to be considered when seeking a link between the exposed cards and any bets. Poker is a gambling game, and many players are prepared to pay over the odds for the thrilling, if unlikely, possibility of making a powerful hand.

Likely winning hands

As suggested, the average winning hand in five-card stud is much lower than in other poker variations, with a high pair usually being enough to claim the spoils. Finding such a hand within the first three cards is an advantage, particularly if the pair includes the hole card, as it offers the chance to raise the betting and drive opponents out of the pot. In doing so, many hands with the potential to win will often be folded before they are complete. For example players who hold three-card flushes or straights will hardly ever encounter the pot odds to make it worthwhile to continue with the hand, especially when an opponent has an open pair. Such hands are rarely seen, while even three of a kind has only 1 chance in 35 of being dealt in a

OPEN PAIRS

Left: Three examples of hands after the dealing of the third card face up – third street – all showing an open pair. Typically, the minimum bet for the first two rounds in five-card stud is half that of the last two rounds. Any player holding an open pair on third street, however, is entitled to protect it by doubling the minimum bet, making it more expensive for opponents to try beating the hand. If choosing not to exercise this option, any opponent not showing a pair may also bet at the higher level, if desired.

Below: Workers playing a game of poker in 1940 at the Fort Blanding site, Florida, used by the US army as an infantry replacement training centre during the Second World War. At least eight players are involved making it likely that five-card stud will be one of the poker variations considered for the evening's entertainment. With more cards in circulation the chances of players formulating good hands is increased, thus helping to make the betting action much more competitive.

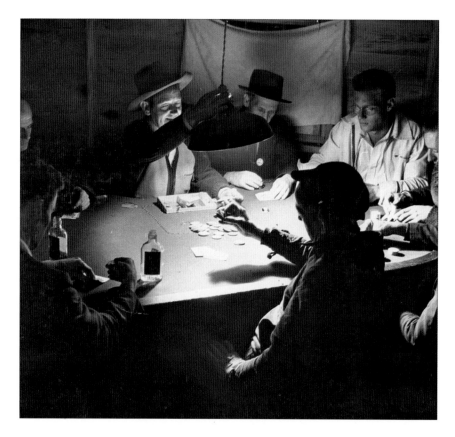

player's five cards. Since a hand this strong may not materialize until fifth street, the prospect of having to survive three rounds of volatile betting in order to achieve it underlines why hands of such magnitude are seen so infrequently. By contrast, it is difficult to capitalize on trips being held in the first three cards dealt, since the open pair that must be apparent compromises the chances of keeping enough opponents involved in the pot to make the hand pay off.

Third street

The receipt of the third card – third street – marks the decisive point for most five-card stud hands. Good players will rarely consider going beyond this stage if their hand is outranked by an opponent's visible face-up board cards in play. They adhere to the primary rule, which is that any player who cannot beat the board should fold as a matter of course. An example occurs when an open pair appears, the recommendation being, for any player not yet holding a pair, to fold. Having cards that rank higher than an opponents' cards on the board – also known as 'overcards' – might seem worth playing, but pairing one of these could prove inadequate, especially if several other players stay involved. Sometimes, the opponent showing a pair will already have three of a kind and anyone in this position will happily entertain speculative calls from the unwary.

Sensible third-street play precludes betting in support of causes that may already be lost. This applies to hands such as three-card straights and flushes that are virtually worthless. To underline this, anyone holding As, 10s, 8s, may calculate that they have a slightly better-than-even chance of completing the flush in a six-player game. But these odds only apply if all players stay to the showdown and no other spades appear amid their up cards, a scenario that is unrealistic even in the least competitive of games.

Right: A player takes a look at his hole card to confirm possession of three kings now that the final card has been dealt to those still in the game. Securing three of a kind in five cards will happen, on average, around once in every 35 deals. As in this instance, however, a player may have to wait until the final card to make the hand, meaning that three possibly costly betting rounds will have already been negotiated.

PLAYABLE HANDS

HOLE CARDS	BOARD CARDS

PLAYER A

PLAYER B

PLAYER C

PLAYER D

Above: Knowing which hands to play and which to fold on third street is crucial to solid poker. A player with a pair of kings with an A kicker (the highest unpaired side card in his hand) is in a strong position. If no open pairs are visible, this hand will open the betting on third street, allowing the player to control the action. Similarly, having an A to support a hidden pair of jacks will intimidate opponents showing a K or a Q. Even if they have a hidden pair, the A will make them wary of calling a bet. Players holding three-card straights and flushes should fold on third street should any opponent bet. The chance of completing the hand is usually too remote to justify a call.

143

Effective strategies

The fact that most guidance on how to play five-card stud tends to advocate caution highlights how difficult it is, in limit poker particularly, to manipulate the betting and win large pots. On many occasions, the strength of a player's hand will be clearly apparent from the board cards, making it unlikely that an opponent will call a serious bet. Anyone with an open pair may double the minimum bet on third street in order to protect the hand, but this has two likely outcomes. Opponents with little chance of overtaking the hand will fold, while anyone who calls, let alone raises, is probably already ahead. Even if an opponent with just one up card higher than the open pair bets in the second round, then it is best to assume they have it beaten.

Pairing a mid-ranking hole card is not much better in this situation. For instance, a player who has paired a 9 in the hole with a card dealt face up will feel similarly vulnerable when there are several higher-ranking cards on the board. Any bet from an opponent showing A, Q, for example, will suggest that a third 9 is required to win. In a six-player game, a player will have seen a maximum of 13 cards – their three plus the ten other up cards, assuming everyone is still competing. Provided no other nines have appeared as yet, the chance of making trip nines in the next two rounds is never better than 8 to 1. Added to the fact that an opponent's hand might also improve, most players will fold rather than call in this situation, thus removing the temptation to commit further chips in the later rounds when the minimum bets increase.

Right: Player A cautiously calls the opening bet from player E, because, with two aces on the board already, the chances of either player C or E holding a pair are significantly reduced. The fact that players C and D also decide to call rather than raise is read as indicating neither has a pair as yet.

THE DEAL

PLAYER A
Hole card

Above: In this 25/50 fixed-limit game, player A is dealt a pair of threes, which is useful, but no more than that, at present, given the high cards on the table. However, since it is 16 to 1 against any player being dealt a pair in the first two cards, there is a good chance that the pair of threes is currently leading.

OPENING BETTING ROUND

Bluffing

Opportunities to bluff in five-card stud do not arise very often in a fixed-limit game, since the cost of calling a bet is rarely prohibitive enough to force all opponents to fold. For a true bluff to be successful, each opponent must relinquish their claim on the pot. In games that involve ten players, there are usually enough cards in circulation to make bluffing with a weak hand on third street a risky proposition, in any case. Any player who has a reputation for tight play might capitalize on this image to perpetrate the occasional bluff, but then all experienced five-card stud players have a tendency to be extremely conservative in their approach. When playing against such opponents, a bluff on third street might be all that is needed to steal a small pot, but this is a manoeuvre best reserved for games with five or fewer players. Those players who wish to promote more bluffing in five-card stud are usually advised to play it as a pot-limit or no-limit game. The larger bets that are allowed have greater potential to intimidate opponents, which makes bluffing a much more viable prospect.

THIRD STREET

160

POT TOTAL

Above: The third card for each player brings no open pairs, but player A's chances of being dealt another 3 are compromised when the 3d is dealt to player C, there now being just one remaining unseen. If, as suspected, players C and E do not have pocket aces, then they may be reluctant to call a bet. But player D still has two overcards – cards higher than player A's threes – and probably represents the biggest danger given the possibility that he has a pocket K or 10 for a higher pair.

Right: Executing a bluff in five-card stud is more likely to succeed when the game is played with a no-limit or pot-limit betting structure. Since larger bets are permitted, it is easier to intimidate opponents into folding when possessing a hand such as the one illustrated here.

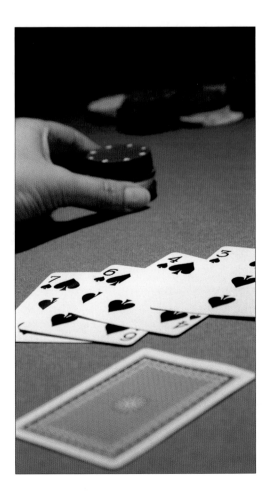

TIMING A BLUFF
♦ ♣ ♥ ♠

Bluffing is more prevalent in pot-limit and no-limit games because of the greater freedom for players to make large bets. This increases the risk of sacrificing more chips on bluffs that fail, so a player needs to time the move correctly in order to lend any bluff credibility. For example if the opener shows an A after the deal, but is raised by a player whose door card is a lowly 6, then the bet suggests a pair is held. If the raise is big enough, it might take the pot uncontested, but, if not, any improvement in the hand – ideally another 6 – will reinforce the bluff and could persuade anyone holding a high pair to fold in the face of another large bet. Should one or other of the remaining sixes later be dealt to an opponent, the integrity of the bluff may quickly unravel. Players should therefore pay attention to the up cards at each stage, to determine whether the hand they are trying to represent has been compromised by events.

Fourth street

A typical game between six or more reasonable players is likely to feature a maximum of three or four contesting fourth street, and will probably only see a couple continue to the final round. Whichever betting structure is in operation, patience and due caution remain the recommended characteristics to exhibit during play. Players with poor chances of winning usually fold prior to fourth street, when the minimum bet routinely doubles for the remaining two betting rounds. Those who continue in the game can therefore be assumed to have the leading hand or one that has a fair chance of improving to be the best. Each remaining player will have three up cards showing at this stage, which makes an assessment of their ultimate hand's value quite simple

In terms of strategy, any player who is clearly ahead should capitalize on the situation by betting. Should everyone else fold, the player can take the pot, but any opponents who call, evidently do so in the belief that one or more cards in the deck may yet help them win. Offering the chance of a free card by checking in this situation represents poor play no matter how remote the opposition's chances of winning.

At the other end of the spectrum, a player with a trailing hand must realistically compare the pot odds with the odds against drawing a winning card. If the risk is unjustified, as is often the case, a player should fold in response to any bet, remembering that the bettor's hand may also improve. Players who harbour any doubts at all about the merit of their hand after four cards should check, when possible, whether first to act or not. Adopting a cautious approach such as this does, however, present the chance for players acting in late position to try stealing the occasional pot with a bluff.

THIRD-STREET BETTING

PLAYER A
Hole card

Above: When player E checks, player A takes it as a sign of weakness and bets, in order to test the strength of opponents' hands. Player C folds, obviously having no pair, but player D, with two overcards, calls the bet, perhaps slow-playing a bigger pair.

FOURTH STREET

Above: After player E decided to call the second-round bets, fourth street brings player A trip (three) threes and the option to bet first with a pair of threes showing. Knowing the hand is definitely leading, player A rightly bets, forcing those who may still have a winning opportunity to pay for their final card. Player D may make higher trips if holding a pair, but has given no positive indication yet that a K or 10 is held. It might be assumed, therefore, that player D's hole card is another high-ranking spade such as a Q or J. Player E folds, evidently having no pair and, as player A knows for certain, no chance of drawing to a straight.

Reading the cards

Accurately reading the cards is crucial when forming any betting strategy on fourth street. By recalling the up cards previously folded and turned face down during play, as well as the various bets made by opponents in preceding rounds, a player has all the information needed to gauge the actual and potential strength of opposing hands. A player showing Ac, Jd, 9h, for instance, could have a pair of aces, with the possibility of making three of a kind if another A comes on fifth street. But if an A has already appeared among up cards that were folded earlier, the chances of the player fulfilling that potential are obviously reduced. Also, any opponent who does hold a pocket A will know for certain that, with only one remaining A unaccounted for, the player cannot have more than a pair of aces at present. If that is the case, then two pairs are the best the player can achieve, should a J or 9 appear on fifth street. If not, then the best possible hand the player showing Ac, Jd, 9h can hit is three jacks, assuming that the Jd is the only one of that rank to have appeared during the game. Deductive reasoning of this nature should guide betting decisions at this stage of play.

Fifth street

Once the final card has been dealt, there is little mystery concerning the competing hands, since, with only the hole cards obscured from view, their potential value can be quickly estimated. Typically, it is rare for more than two players to reach fifth street, which reduces final-round strategy to a couple of simple rules. A player who has possession of the winning hand should always bet at the first opportunity, in the hope that an opponent will call or even raise, thus boosting the size of the pot. By checking in this situation, a

FIFTH STREET

| PLAYER D | PLAYER A |
| Hole card | Hole card |

Above: On fifth street, player D bets in support of the pair of tens, inferring that this has made two pairs or, more credibly, trip tens, which would be enough to win. This is a tough call for player A, who could be second best, but sticks to the earlier reasoning that if player D has a pocket 10, a raise on third street might have been expected in view of the hesitancy exhibited by those holding the aces. Also, if player D has a busted flush, then only a bluff can secure the pot. Player A therefore calls and wins with trip threes as player D's bluff, the hole being a 9s, is revealed.

player invites opponents to check, too, and so runs the risk of missing out on additional chips. Should a player be unsure of holding the winning hand, then a check is the best policy. Whether first to act or not, a bet may prompt an opponent to raise, at which point the player either forfeits the additional chips unnecessarily put into the pot or calls, uncomfortably, with what is probably a beaten hand.

Left: A player considers his next move at the table although, in five-card stud, the strategy to be adopted on fifth street is usually straightforward. If it is evident from the board cards that an opponent possesses a weaker hand, a player should bet and hope for a call.

Seven-card Stud

Seven-card stud starts with each player contributing an ante to the pot prior to the deal. Cards are then dealt one at a time until everyone has three cards, two face down, variously described as hidden, pocket or hole cards, and one face up, known as the door card. The player with the lowest door card opens the betting, typically by making a compulsory bet for a sum less than the usual minimum bet permitted. After the first round, those still in the game each receive a fourth card, face up, prior to the next round of betting. From this point, the first player to act is the one now showing the best visible hand. In this (the second) and subsequent rounds there is no obligation to bet and players may check. Players receive a fifth and sixth card face up, and a seventh card face down with the deal of each punctuated by additional rounds of betting. Players still in the game at the showdown have seven cards from which to make a five-card poker hand, four face up and three face down. The winner is the player who either makes an uncalled bet or who displays the best five-card poker hand once the fifth and final betting round has concluded.

The game of seven-card stud developed from the five-card variation and became popular during the years leading up to World War II. Having travelled the world with the US military, seven-card stud emerged afterwards as the most widely played form of poker and dominated the commercial scene in both Las Vegas and Europe for nearly 40 years. Indeed, up until the 1980s a couple of the more famous Las Vegas casinos offered only seven-card stud in their poker rooms.

Though challenged by Texas Hold 'em for contemporary favouritism, seven-card stud remains a very challenging game which draws upon the whole gamut of any poker player's skills in order to prove rewarding. The five betting rounds help to generate sizeable pots, relative to the stake-levels in operation, and the exposed cards offer a great deal of information as a hand progresses. Yet the fact that players who sustain interest to the showdown will have three of their cards face down still leaves room for doubt in the minds of opposition over the composition of anyone's hand. This creates the opportunity for some imaginative play and leaves the way open for players to consider the occasional bluff, especially in the pot-limit version of

LIKELY WINNING HANDS
FIG 1: TWO PAIRS

HOLE CARDS

UP CARDS

SEVENTH STREET

FIG 2: THREE OF A KIND

HOLE CARDS

UP CARDS

SEVENTH STREET

Above: The quality of hand required to win at the showdown will be dictated by the nature of the game and the stakes for which players are competing. In high-stakes fixed-limit games, particularly those incorporating the use of substantial antes, players with good starting hands are prone to bet aggressively right away. Such games are therefore likely to see just two or three players involved at any showdown with hands such as two high pairs or three of a kind often proving good enough to win. Fig 1 features two pairs of aces and kings, a hand completed by the 9 kicker (the highest unpaired side card in that player's hand) which could prove decisive in the unlikely event that an opponent also has aces and kings. Fig 2 shows a hand comprising three jacks, the discounted cards in this case being the 3c and 4c.

Below: This figurative representation highlights the fact that, in seven-card stud, a player must count five cards from the seven ultimately available in order to make a viable poker hand. Here, the 8h and 5d are redundant since the player will count the remaining five cards to make a full house of aces over kings.

COST OF INFORMATION

Before the cards are dealt, it must be understood that the level of the antes and bring-in bets may vary from one poker room to another, irrespective of betting limits. Games featuring low antes tend to encourage loose play and can provide rich pickings for a tight, conservative player who is prepared to wait for a strong hand before committing chips to the pot. Players who enjoy being regularly involved in the action should probably play with higher antes as this helps to inflate the pot and capitalize on their good hands, offsetting the losses which come from contesting a high proportion of pots. Many guides to seven-card stud focus on high-stakes games in which tight but aggressive play is the norm. In these, players who are not disciplined enough to fold opening hands may be drawn into situations where their hands improve but still trail that of the aggressor who has two aims in mind. The first is to reduce the field to maybe one opponent, the second is to ensure that players with inferior starting hands pay the maximum amount for the chance to improve. When playing such opponents, calling for a couple of rounds in the expectation of help from the deck can soon reduce a player's chip stack. In social games, the betting is quite restrained with players often content to wait until fifth street before deciding whether to play or fold. The key factor in both types of game is that the betting levels rise on fifth street for the final three rounds, when any player who wants to see extra cards will inevitably pay more for the privilege.

the game. However, this betting structure is most popular among experienced players and those who prefer low-stakes, social poker are more inclined to play fixed- or spread-limit stud.

Early considerations

At the beginning of the game, every player is dealt three cards, the first two are face down and the third – the door card – face up. In common with all poker variations, the decision on which of these opening hands might be worth playing should be determined by an understanding of what is likely to prove to be a winning hand at the showdown. This, in turn, is affected by the culture of the game and whether it is a volatile, low-stakes contest, between loose players, or a tight game between experienced players.

Ordinarily, at least two pairs, probably including aces, will be required to claim victory and three of a kind is often good enough. However, if the cost of betting is not too restrictive, then the likelihood of players chasing straights or better is much greater and could render the average winning hand of two pairs extremely vulnerable. In a low-stakes game, even a player in possession of three eights by fourth street, for example, may not be able to bet a sufficiently large amount to dissuade opponents from calling with inferior hands that still hold the potential for substantial improvement. It is therefore worth remembering that when four or five players stay to see a fifth card, the rank of the winning hand will quite often be higher than two pairs or three of a kind.

Below: A restrained low-stakes game which features little in the way of forceful betting prior to fifth street could easily see several players willing to continue to the showdown. When the betting is light, more players tend to remain involved and this leads to hands that initially looked unpromising being given the chance to develop into probable winners. Strong hands such as straights, flushes and full houses are therefore much more likely to occur, although sometimes a solitary pair will still be sufficient to win.

BETTER THAN AVERAGE HANDS
ACE-HIGH STRAIGHT

HOLE CARDS

UP CARDS

SEVENTH STREET

ACE-HIGH FLUSH

HOLE CARDS

UP CARDS

SEVENTH STREET

FULL HOUSE – SEVENS OVER KINGS

HOLE CARDS

UP CARDS

SEVENTH STREET

Starting hands

Assessing the value of the first three cards received will very much depend on the style of game. In a tight game, featuring first-round raises and plenty of folding, only the very best starting hands may warrant support, although this may reduce a player's participation to around one in five hands on average. Social games are likely to feature much more leeway regarding which hands to play, but this does not disguise the fact that it is advantageous to start with any one of five key combinations.

The best possible starting hand is three of a kind, or trips, with high pairs of aces, kings or queens are also highly prized. A starting hand featuring a low pocket pair and a high-value door card (the player's first exposed or 'up' card) such as an A or K may also be worth playing as are three-card flushes and open-ended three-card straights.

Being dealt these combinations does not guarantee victory and players must observe the up cards held by opponents as the game unfolds. This is why players bet aggressively with strong hands when the antes are high in order to end the contest quickly and rake in the chips, winning these small pots being crucial to keeping the cost of the antes at bay.

Rolled-up trips

There are 22,100 possible three-card combinations available from the standard 52-card deck and the best of these, naturally, is trip aces which will materialize only once in every 5,525 deals on average. Although such a hand is very powerful, the fact is that any three of a kind may well win even without improvement, and the probability of being dealt 'rolled-up trips' – three of a kind in the first three cards – is rated at 424 to 1. The great benefit of seeing such a hand is that its strength is hidden during the early part of the game,

ROLLED-UP TRIPS

HOLE CARDS   **HOLE CARDS**   **HOLE CARDS**

DOOR CARD   **DOOR CARD**   **DOOR CARD**

Above: Being dealt any three of a kind presents a player with a huge advantage since the hand will often prove good enough to win on its own while also having an excellent chance of improving to a full house. However, the odds against receiving any three of a kind in the first three cards are 424 to 1, while finding a pair of aces in the hole to match the door card for trip aces will happen, on average, about once in every 5,525 deals. When a player holds such a starting hand, the strength of which is concealed, a winning outcome should be expected with the main concern being to manage the pot for the maximum possible gain.

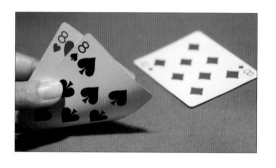

Left: An example of 'rolled-up trips' as this player finds a pair of eights in the hole to match the door card 8. Hands such as these are very rare and highly likely to win the pot even if the remaining cards do not bring improvement.

HIDDEN PAIRS

HOLE CARDS   **HOLE CARDS**   **HOLE CARDS**

DOOR CARD   **DOOR CARD**   **DOOR CARD**

Above: Any pair dealt in the first three cards is helpful but holding a high pair – aces or kings – is more likely to give a player an early advantage. Having the pair concealed enhances that advantage as it allows a player to bet in a fashion that disguises the strength of the hand. Someone holding pocket aces and showing a 7 can justifiably call any first-round bet or raise by an opponent and should certainly be willing to make the first raise if acting from an early betting position. Opponents may suspect the hand is better than a pair of sevens but they will be wary of other possibilities. It is this uncertainty that a player must aim to exploit as the hand progresses.

although playing low trips can be problematic. A player in possession of three threes may well bring in the betting and find that a couple of opponents showing a K and an A respectively both put in a raise. Since they have to be credited with at least a high pair each, a further raise with just a 3 showing will alert them to danger and even a call will put them on their guard.

In most cases, professionals advocate supporting a strong opening hand with maximum bets since underplaying it to keep opponents involved can backfire. However, on rare occasions when rolled-up trips materialize, players can usually afford to bet the minimum and keep opponents involved in the action until the time is right to strike with a large bet. Although opposition hands may improve sufficiently to threaten the early advantage obtained from holding trips, the odds against this hand itself improving to a full house with four cards still to come are only just over two to one. Given that it may also improve to something higher than a full house, it is almost certain that a player dealt trips in the first three cards is going to play to the showdown unless there is strong evidence to suggest an opponent has a higher-ranking full house or better.

SPLIT PAIRS

HOLE CARDS	HOLE CARDS	HOLE CARDS
DOOR CARD	DOOR CARD	DOOR CARD

Above: Players can expect a pair in their first three cards from around one deal in every five. On many occasions this will feature the door card matching a hole card for a 'split pair' which, although still beneficial in the case of high pairs, obviously makes disguising the hand very difficult. Ordinarily, any first-round bet from a player showing an A, K or Q is almost bound to be interpreted as representing a pair, allowing some scope for the occasional bluff when a player holds just a high card and no pair. By contrast, a player who does hold a split pair of aces but simply calls the bring-in from an early betting position may lull opponents into sensing weakness. Should one of them subsequently raise the betting, a subsequent call or re-raise from the player holding the door card A will probably dispel that notion immediately.

Right: Another decent starting hand in the shape of a split pair, a K in the hole being matched with a door-card K. If no other kings are showing amid opponents' door cards and aces are also absent from the board, a solid bet in the first round is certainly justifiable.

PAIRS

♦ ♣ ♥ ♠

The chances of being dealt a pair among the first three cards in seven-card stud are fractionally less than 5 to 1, although it is around 25 to 1 against receiving jacks or better. While they offer potential for improvement, players must weigh up the merits of holding a hidden pair or a split pair, the former meaning that both paired cards are dealt face down while a split pair, as the name suggests, is one in which the door card matches a hole card. Obviously, it is easier to play deceptively when holding pocket aces and showing a 7 than it is if one of the aces is a door card. Opponents will expect a bet in support of the A on display and will be wary of becoming too involved given the potential for it to be paired with a hole card. In this situation, it can be assumed that any opponents who do call to see fourth street are holding reasonable hands. Nevertheless, they could only be leading a pair of aces and a 7 kicker, in this instance, if holding three of a kind or the other pair of aces with a higher-ranking odd card. A maximum bet when the aces are hidden and the 7 is showing might flush out those opponents holding decent hands without them having a clear idea of the strength truly represented by the first-round bet.

Three-card straights

Open-ended three-card straights, such as 7, 8, 9 or J, Q, K, offer attractive potential as starting hands as the chances of converting them into a full straight are around 6 to 1. Players can expect to see three cards to a straight regularly, maybe as often as one in six deals, making them appealing hands to play in a restrained betting game which regularly features four or five players paying for a fifth card.

In an eight-handed game, each player can see ten cards following the deal, these being their own three cards and the seven door cards in front of their opponents. If holding the 7, 8, 9 combination, for example, any 5, 6, 10 or J on fourth street immediately increases a player's chances of making the straight. Improvement is also ensured if a 7, 8 or 9 is dealt to make a pair which means that up to 25 cards in the deck have the potential to help the hand. However, several of those cards could already be visible on the table and this is the key factor in deciding how far to proceed in a bid to complete the straight. If an opponent with a 10 showing chooses to raise the betting, it would be realistic to assume at least a pair of tens is being

THREE-CARD STRAIGHTS

HOLE CARDS   **HOLE CARDS**   **HOLE CARDS**

DOOR CARD   **DOOR CARD**   **DOOR CARD**

Above: Opening hands of three cards to a straight often occur and an open-ended combination such as a 10, J, Q offers multiple chances for improvement, with the odds for a straight being completed after seven cards of around 6 to 1. Higher-ranking three-card combinations of 10 and above offer the potential for an A-high straight. Pairing any of these with subsequent cards could allow a player to take the pot long before a showdown. This is less likely when a player holds low-ranking cards such as 4, 5, 6 and makes one or even two low pairs. More importantly, should a straight come by fifth street, perhaps with a 7 and a 3, the hand may still be a poor betting option if an opponent seems to be drawing to a higher-ranking straight or even a flush. If fourth and fifth street bring no improvement to a hand such as this, it is probably best to fold at the first sign of a large bet.

Left: Three suited picture cards such as the K, Q, J are generally worth support, especially if the game features little in the way of aggressive betting in the early rounds. The combination is such that half the remaining cards in the deck offer the potential to improve the hand. This is usually enough of an incentive to bet for at least a couple of rounds.

LOW PAIRS, BIG KICKERS

Though they can be more dangerous to play, medium or low pocket pairs still have the same potential for improvement as pairs of aces or kings. The problem is that a player holding the low pair must improve when up against such cards, a prospect made easier if the kicker (the highest-value unpaired card in their hand) is of a high rank. For example an opening bet from an opponent showing a K, and so probably representing a pair, is worth calling if a player holds pocket tens with an A kicker. Such a call implies possession of a reasonable hand, possibly a pair of aces, and could enable the player to see another card or two quite cheaply against the probable pair of kings. Should an A materialize on fourth street to provide an open pair, the player will act first while the opponent holding kings ponders whether any bet indicates trip aces, and not just the pair on display. If a 10 is dealt instead, then a well-disguised three of a kind is secured along with an opportunity to dominate the betting, provided the opponent has not been dealt another K. As with the three-card flush and straight examples, deciding whether to support an opening hand with a small pair is generally based on the possibility of catching a good card on fourth street. If this fails to happen and opponents' hands clearly improve, it is wiser to fold than to continue betting. This helps to avoid the disastrous possibility of improving sufficiently to play to the showdown with what remains the second-best hand.

represented. Immediately, this reduces the prospects of making anything better than a 9-high straight since half the tens in the deck could already be out. On top of that, even pairing a 7, 8 or 9 on fourth street will still leave the player trailing and would make further participation in the hand inadvisable.

Three-card flushes

Flushes outrank straights and the chances of being dealt three assorted cards of the same suit are correspondingly longer at around 24 to 1. Though a flush is a likely winner, disguising a flush draw can be more difficult with each round making it vital that, in pursuing the hand, a player is well aware how many cards of the relevant suit are already in play.

A player holding Kh, 10h, 6h, for instance, has a 5 to 1 chance of making the flush, an appealing prospect after the deal though these odds assume no knowledge of the opposition's cards. If there are hearts among the door cards on the table, then the odds against completing the hand obviously lengthen. As with the straight draw, there are four rounds in which to hit the two hearts that will make the hand but, if missing them on fourth and fifth street, the rising cost of trying to catch them could become prohibitive. For this reason, though three-card flushes have a fair chance of developing into winning hands, they are rarely worth pursuing beyond fourth street in the face of aggressive betting from an opponent.

Drawing hands such as flushes and straights are generally played cautiously, with solid players recognizing that support should be confined to those comprising high-ranking cards only. These provide insurance since pairing aces, kings or queens when drawing to flushes and straights can offer another route to victory should the initial promise of the hand not be realized.

THREE-CARD FLUSHES

HOLE CARDS   **HOLE CARDS**   **HOLE CARDS**

DOOR CARD   **DOOR CARD**   **DOOR CARD**

Above: Holding three cards to a flush after the deal offers scope for staying in a hand, though a player will hope to draw the cards needed to complete the flush cheaply. Calling an opponent's first-round raise is justified if a player holds an A, but help must materialize quickly in the face of aggressive betting to warrant further participation. If two or more cards of the relevant suit are among the opposition's door cards, any attempt to pursue the flush draw should be entertained with caution. High cards are of more value because they present alternative chances to win if the flush draw is derailed.

LOW PAIRS WITH BIG KICKER

HOLE CARDS   **HOLE CARDS**   **HOLE CARDS**

DOOR CARD   **DOOR CARD**   **DOOR CARD**

Above: Though not without potential, starting hands that feature both hidden and split low pairs are immediately vulnerable and will usually need a helpful card on fourth street to encourage a player to continue in all but the lightest of betting heats. To this end, having a high-ranking kicker – ideally an A – to supplement the pair is preferable since pairing the kicker for two pairs could transform a modest hand into a likely winner. For example should a player with a split pair of threes and an A in the hole catch another A on fourth street, the hand could already be strong enough to win while its true value can be disguised if betting remains light. Slow-playing the hand is possible though a raise should be considered if any open pairs lower than aces are visible after four cards.

Third-street strategy

A common mistake players frequently make is to overestimate the value of their starting hands, following which they bet modestly to keep several opponents involved in the game to help swell the pot. There are so many possibilities at work in seven-card stud that opponents with the weakest of hands can improve past, for example, a high-value opening pair. Consequently, players who are dealt a premium hand of a high pair, and possibly even three high cards offering powerful straight and flush potential, should bet aggressively in the opening round to advertise strength and encourage opponents to fold. The exception to this is when a player holds trips since the time to exert pressure in this case is on fifth street, when the betting levels rise and opponents with drawing hands may feel they are committed to the pot. For example a player who is dealt three nines when there are two or three higher up cards visible should sit tight and just call any opening-round bets whenever possible. Raising in the opening round may be justified from a late betting position if opponents possessing higher door cards – their first exposed or 'up' cards – have so far been content to call. They may think the raise represents an attempt to steal the pot with a pair of nines, in which case their higher-ranking up cards could tempt them into staying for another round or two. However, if an opponent showing an A, for example, has already raised the betting, a re-raise will be read as confirmation of trip nines. This may be enough to take the pot, but calling the raise is a better option in this situation since the meaning behind the bet is more difficult to interpret. By generating an element of doubt in the minds of opponents, the player is more likely to maximize the profit on a probable winning hand.

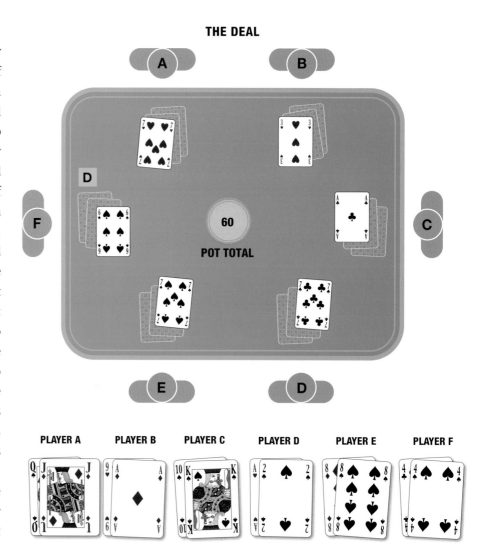

THE DEAL

Above: The scene following the deal in a 50/100 fixed-limit seven-card stud game, with the pot already comprising an ante of 10 chips from each player. Player E's pocket eights is the best hand at present while player F also has a pair in the hole, although the fours are clearly weak. Player C, with high-ranking cards to support the A on display, is in a good position to pressurize opponents given the lack of any door cards higher than his 10 in the hole.

ALL-IN
♦ ♣ ♥ ♠

One of the key elements of table-stakes poker is that players can never be priced out of a hand when they have insufficient chips to call an opponent's bet. In this situation, players may push all their chips into the pot and declare that they are 'all-in' or, if preferred, 'tapped-out'. Should they hold the winning hand at the showdown, they may only claim from their opponents a sum equal to that which they have staked. So a player calling all-in for 100 chips when the bet is 200 may only claim 100 chips from each of those who made the full bet. The rest of the chips constitute a side pot that is contested by the other players. In no-limit poker, the all-in bet can be a powerful tactical ploy, since players are permitted, at their turn, to bet all their chips at any stage of the game.

Door cards

Assessing the potential of any three-card starting hand is the most crucial factor in deciding whether to take part after the deal. To this end, knowing which hands are likely to secure an early advantage is important, but there are, as always, other factors to bear in mind. The most obvious source of these comes in the value of the opponents' door cards since these must always have an influence on any player's strategy.

Holding a concealed pair of aces with a J as the door card is a good opening hand, but its potential for improvement would obviously be compromised if the two remaining aces in the deck were visible among the opposition's up cards. Possession of the top pair at the outset normally confers an advantage and offers a player the chance to bet aggressively to reduce the competition. The danger in not doing so is that more picture cards will be dealt to opponents in subsequent rounds, perhaps creating an open pair or two, at which point a reassessment of the strength of the pair of aces will be needed. By fifth street, it may be clear that two pairs will not be enough to win and that the chances of catching the K, Q and 10 needed for a straight have all but evaporated.

Again, it is worth stressing that players must keep a watchful eye on the up cards as they are dealt, remember any that have been folded, and constantly re-calculate the changing value of the cards in their possession.

DISGUISING A HAND
♦ ♣ ♥ ♠

One of the better drawing hands to be dealt is a three-card flush which features a low-ranking door card with two higher cards in the hole, particularly when one of those is the A. Pairing the A in this instance could be the springboard for further investment in the hand since it gives insurance against the flush itself not materializing by offering another chance to secure the pot. If there are any cards of the relevant suit already on the board then the flush draw becomes less likely, but the potential for disguising the merit of the hand is high when no other cards of that suit are visible. For instance, with the Ac, Kc in the hole and the 8c as a door card, calling a raise in the opening round from an opponent showing a lower door card than an A or K gives away few clues regarding the hand held, most opponents being likely to credit the player with a pair of eights at best. Indeed, a re-raise at this point could have opponents thinking that a high pocket pair is held, rather than two other clubs, such that another club on fourth street could seem quite innocuous.

Should this happen, the chances of converting the four-card flush into a five-card hand are about even money which will normally be enough to persuade a player to stay to the showdown, provided the flush still appears to be a probable winner.

FIRST-ROUND BETTING

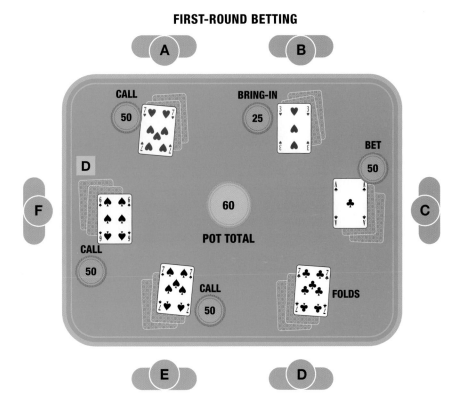

Right: Player B makes the compulsory – or forced – bet known as the bring-in by virtue of holding the lowest door card. To offset this obligation, the bring-in is set at 25 chips, not 50. Player C immediately 'completes the bet' by betting 50 chips and raising the level to the accepted minimum for the first two betting rounds. Player D folds because with one A and two sevens already in play, his own hand of A, 2, 7 is rendered worthless. The remainder all call, including player B who contributes the additional 25 chips to make up the betting.

Fourth street

The arrival of fourth street sees another card dealt face up to those players still in the game while the opening bet in this round, and all subsequent rounds, is the preserve of the player showing the best hand. Importantly, the player in this position is not obliged to bet and may check if desired, a privilege not extended to the holder of the low card in the previous betting round.

In terms of strategy, how to respond to events after the fourth card is dealt depends on the nature of the game. Tight but aggressive opponents assumedly have a promising hand and if fourth street brings them obvious mprovement, they are likely to press home the advantage with a bet or, when in late position, a raise. Defending against such strong play in a serious-money game is only advised with a hand that is either already powerful or, as in the case of a flush draw, has multiple opportunities to become a winner with any one of several cards.

In a similar vein, although more liberties are taken by players in low-stakes games regarding which hands to play as far as fifth street, they must still consider their chances of making a better-than-average hand. Since more players are

Above: Fourth street brings help in the shape of a pair for both players B and C and, with no pair on the board at present, they may feel this has given them an advantage. In player C's case, the K provides the top pair and a good opportunity to exert more pressure on opponents given the apparent lack of danger represented among the other cards visible on the table. For those holding the pocket pairs there may be just enough incentive to see a fifth card, but player A is definitely in trouble.

Right: Holding a hand such as this open-ended straight-flush draw on fourth street will tempt most players to continue betting given that any club will make a flush while any 9 or 4 will complete a straight, and possibly even a straight flush. These all have the potential to emerge as winning hands at the showdown.

likely to continue to the showdown, when players remaining in the hand reveal their cards to determine the winner, the opportunity for back-door straights and flushes to develop increases, meaning that even two pairs will not be good enough on many occasions.

Premium hands

Identifying the most promising hands on fourth street logically follows the same criteria as that applied after the deal. Anyone holding three of a kind – trips – of whatever rank is in a strong position, although this may be weakened from a betting perspective if an open pair on fourth street matches a player's hole card. A player with an open pair of kings who raised the betting in the previous round, for example, will alert the opposition to the likely presence of trip kings, a very powerful hand. An opening bet is likely to win the pot immediately, thus reducing the profitability of the hand, while exercising the option to check will typically result in everyone else checking since they will, quite rightly, suspect a trap is being set. Though trip kings is still likely to be the leading hand after five cards and will usually go on to win, this tactic does offer a chance for opponents to improve at no cost, which rarely constitutes good poker.

SECOND-ROUND BETTING

Above: Player C duly opens the betting and is called by player E who has the pair of eights and is hoping to find some help on fifth street for the minimum cost. However, with several cards that may complete a low-ranking straight already in play, this is a questionable decision. Realistically, only an 8 for three of a kind will instil any confidence in player E's hand.

Holding any two pairs on fourth street is another good position to be in although, once again, it is better to have two up cards of different rank matching the two in the hole. This conceals the strength of the hand while having an open pair combined with a hidden pair is evidently much more revealing. Other hands that almost demand to be played are high-ranking four-card flushes and open-ended straights, along with three-card flushes and straights that are supplemented by a high pair.

CONTROLLED AGGRESSION
♦ ♣ ♥ ♠

When holding well-disguised high-ranking trips on fourth street, or two high pairs including aces, the key to maximizing the advantage comes from keeping opponents involved in the pot. Because the strength of the hand is concealed, a player can normally afford to check the betting and offer a free card, or make a minimum bet to induce others to call. Controlling the urge to raise on fourth street paves the way for more aggressive betting in the later rounds when the stakes rise. One or two opponents may have improved sufficiently by then to feel committed to the pot with drawing hands that would still not be good enough to win even if completed. By contrast, players who hold low-ranking trips or two pairs usually cannot afford to exercise such restraint on fourth street and are generally advised to bet or raise the maximum when the chance comes. In this situation, the objective is to force opponents with drawing hands to fold, particularly those with high-ranking but, as yet, unpaired door cards.

Strategic ploys

For the most part, the strategies applied in the opening betting rounds of a seven-card stud game are similar to those in other poker variations. Players who believe they have the lead should bet accordingly and force opponents to pay more for a chance to take the pot.

The exception to this policy comes when a player holds a distinctly powerful hand that is likely to win without progress. Chances such as this do not arise very often, so players need to exercise a degree of flexibility when betting on fourth street. This is unavoidable since the number of cards in play and the permutations that result prevent any dogmatic approach to the game beyond this stage.

Most guides to seven-card stud highlight a range of hands that, by fourth street, have the potential to become winners. Apart from some of the examples already described, even a hand comprising three cards ranked 10 or higher, but with no pair, is sometimes worth playing. The decision on whether to do so, however, will be dictated by the betting patterns exhibited and the number of open cards already seen. Holding 4s, 10c, Jd, Kh, for example, can only be appealing if there are few cards of the same rank or higher in play. If an array of different picture cards is on display and the betting is heavy, then the value of the hand is considerably diminished since a flush is already impossible and a straight may be very unlikely. This highlights the importance of interpreting the information on offer at the table, rather than relying on a rigid concept of which hands to play.

Right: A hand such as this has limited potential to improve with two cards needed for a straight and a flush already impossible by virtue of possessing a card in each suit. Only if the betting is very light and the opposition's face-up cards are of medium-to-low rank should a player persevere. If fifth street then brings no help, ideally via a Q to provide the open-ended straight possibility, then a decision to fold would probably be wise.

RAISING IN LATE POSITION

A · B

FOLDS · RAISE 100

D

F · 310 POT TOTAL · BET 50 · C

CALL 50

CALL 50

E · D

Above: As the second-round betting continues, player F also makes a poor decision by calling given that player E has been dealt a 4, one of the few cards that could immediately improve player F's hand. The pot continues to grow, however, making it difficult to resist taking a chance on another card. Player A's hand is folded but player B makes a raise in late position with the pair of nines. The suggestion that two pairs or possibly three nines have been secured is designed to test the character of the opposition.

PLAYER A	PLAYER B	PLAYER C	PLAYER E	PLAYER F

Stealing the pot

In low-stakes fixed-limit games, the chances of stealing the pot on fourth street with a raise are limited. It is usually not possible to bet a sufficient amount to force everyone else to fold. Pot-limit stud, however, offers players a little more leeway when making such a move. This is because a pot-sized bet is hard to call, even at this stage, for opponents holding marginal hands such as small pairs, or three-card flushes and straights. Trying a bluff along these lines is best when in a late betting position and the action has been checked around the table, inferring no one has great faith in their cards. If successful, it enables a player to cover the cost of the antes for several more rounds.

If the bluff is uncovered, this is far from disastrous as it shows a willingness to take a chance with a weak hand which may bring reward later. A bet in a similar situation when holding a strong hand is more likely to be called by opponents who have seen a player's tendency to bluff. Such hands have a greater chance of being paid off by opponents too suspicious to take the hint.

FREE CARDS
♦ ♣ ♥ ♠

Securing more cards as cheaply as possible is vital when holding a viable hand. One way to do this is to raise the betting on fourth street with a hand that is trailing but has potential. Assuming the bet is called but nobody has any obvious help on fifth street, the opposition could warily check the betting around and allow sixth street to be dealt for free. The extra bet on fourth street, which amounts to a semi-bluff, will have saved the player from making a bet at the increased level in the next round. The winning chance of the hand can then be re-assessed with just one more card to come and two further betting rounds to negotiate.

BUILDING THE POT

FOLDS

RAISE 100

D

CALL 50

BET 50

F

310
POT TOTAL

C

CALL 50

CALL 50

50 CALL

50 CALL

E

D

Above: Following player B's raise, player C could re-raise to try driving players E and F out of the pot but, respectful of the bet from player B, decides that the call is a better option. This allows players E and F to follow suit with a call, ensuring that the pot continues to grow and presenting the first player to act in the next round with immediate pot odds of a tempting 7 to 1.

Above: Player B pairs the pocket 9 on fourth street and, acting last, decides to raise given the lack of aggression exhibited in the second round of betting. Although three opponents call the raise, a move such as this is enough to keep them on their guard since they will be aware it could signify three nines are already held.

Fifth street

When playing seven-card stud there are two critical points at which a player must decide whether to participate in a hand, these being after the deal and then again on fifth street. Being able to distinguish a promising opening hand from a poor one is essential, but such promise usually needs to show signs of fulfilment by fifth street for a player to consider any further betting. Since the minimum bet doubles from the third round onwards, players still needing to draw cards for a probable winning hand can expect to pay dearly when trying to catch them. An experienced opponent with a leading hand will certainly ensure this is the case.

Assuming a player has a pair of aces and a four-card straight, holding Ac, Qc in the hole and Kc, Js, Ad on the board, the decision on whether to proceed or not will depend on the strength of hand it is possible to achieve and the likelihood of it occurring. If the four tens, several picture cards and a handful of clubs remain unseen, then the number of live cards available to improve the hand beyond a pair of aces makes participation on fifth street highly likely.

However, these possibilities will be of less interest should an opponent who raised in the opening round with a 7 showing now possess a board comprising trip sevens. If the remaining 7 is in play, a pocket pair is the obvious inference to be drawn from the original raise meaning that a full house must now be suspected. The player holding the pair of aces, expecting the straight and flush draws to be redundant, would need to draw live cards on sixth and seventh streets to improve, though the odds against hitting a full house are 39 to 1. Obtaining a royal flush or four of a kind under these circumstances is highly improbable even if the relevant cards have yet to appear on the table.

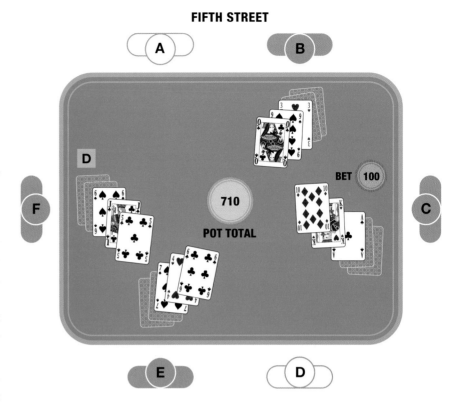

FIFTH STREET

710

POT TOTAL

BET 100

Above: Once the fifth card has been dealt, the betting levels rise making this the critical moment in the game. Anyone who bets at this point is likely to continue to the showdown, especially when a fixed-limit betting structure is in operation, as in this example. The size of the pot often becomes too big to resist if players can see they have a chance, however remote, of making the winning hand. Player C acts first once more here with the best hand showing – still the A-high – with the two high pairs of kings and tens well disguised.

PLAYER B   PLAYER C   PLAYER E   PLAYER F

Below: On the face of it this appears to be an attractive hand on fifth street since the pair of aces is supplemented by high-ranking cards. Any 10 will complete a straight while pairing the K, Q or J for two high pairs might just prove enough. But whether to bet or not at this stage will very much depend on how many of these key cards have already been seen in play during the hand.

Promising positions

Although it is possible that a lowly pair of twos on fifth street could blossom into four of a kind by the time of the showdown, there are many more promising positions to be in at this point in the game. The general consensus among poker critics is that any hand of aces up or better has to be played, with disguised high pairs and trips remaining very strong hands. Players who have already completed straights will obviously expect to continue in the hand unless an opponent's up cards and betting suggest that a higher straight or a flush is likely to be held. Finding such a hand in five cards will normally guarantee the lead but it can still be difficult to fend off speculative opponents with drawing hands in a low-stakes, fixed-limit game.

The escalating size of the pot, relative to the cost of a bet, will often encourage opponents to call in the third round even though they know they are trailing. In pot-limit stud, by contrast, a player with a made straight can advertise the fact with a pot-sized raise, thus making it much more expensive to call for those opponents still needing additional cards to win.

Below: Any player holding two medium or low pairs on fifth street, like the eights and fours shown here, could easily be leading and yet remains vulnerable if unable to force opponents to fold in the face of a bet. This is particularly true in fixed-limit poker when the size of the maximum permitted bet may not be intimidating enough to prevent several of them from calling.

CALLING THE OPENER

Above: The 6c presents player E with a small chance of hitting a straight although the 5 dealt to player F does not help. A raise now might be enough to suggest to opponents that the straight is already made but, with so many chips already in the pot, player E realizes that even a bet of 200 will be unlikely to dissuade them from calling. Consequently, player E simply calls for 100.

COMPROMISING SITUATIONS
♦ ♣ ♥ ♠

As might be expected, there is a wide variety of hands that can prove tempting for a player to support from fifth street onwards, the most dangerous being leading hands that are still likely to need improvement in order to prevail. A player holding two medium or low pairs, perhaps holding 9c, 8s, 4h, 8d, 4c, will not feel secure unless dealt another 8 or 4, the chances of which depend upon how many of those remaining are still live. Opponents with higher open pairs or who have previously represented possession of a concealed high pair, could easily have several cards in play that will win them the pot.

A solitary pair of aces is another hand that could frequently be leading after five cards, and most players will probably pursue it to the river – the seventh and final card dealt – if the board suggests no obvious threat. When up against four or five opponents, however, a high pair will rarely be enough to win on its own, though the odds of improvement to two pairs are good at less than 2 to 1. Hitting three of a kind is a 14 to 1 chance which, in itself, is probably less significant in determining whether to bet than the size of the pot and the amount a player has already contributed to it.

Winning positions

Having a strong hand after five cards obviously helps a player to determine how best to play the remaining three betting rounds. Anyone holding a high-ranking straight, a flush or possibly even a full house will not only be in a strong position to win but can escalate the betting if necessary to ward off potentially dangerous opposition.

The typical strategy to adopt when in this situation is to check, if opening the betting, or call, if this privilege falls to an opponent who decides to bet. This move is used to keep other opponents active in the game such that they will be more likely to call a big bet or raise on sixth street even if, by now, they know they are trailing. By delaying a big bet when holding a made hand, it is possible that an opponent's hand will improve sufficiently to win. On the whole, however, provided a player's assessment of developments throughout play is sound, such occurrences will be rare enough that slow-playing a hand in this way will regularly prove profitable.

Vulnerable leading hands

To be in possession of an invulnerable five-card hand on fifth street is unusual in the extreme. A more likely situation is that a player who currently leads will see plenty of evidence to suggest that this advantage could be temporary. Under these circumstances, an aggressive betting posture is generally advised in a bid to eliminate potentially dangerous opponents. For instance, a player with Ac, Jd in the hole and Jh, 8c, As on the board could easily be leading with two

Above: A player holding two pairs, aces and jacks, can expect to be in a very competitive position on fifth street with a hand that might prove good enough to win at the showdown. An aggressive betting posture is recommended unless there is any reason to suspect that an opponent may have the hand beaten already. Someone showing an open pair, for example, just might have a third card of the same rank for three of a kind.

A COSTLY DECISION?

Above: The third betting round now sees player F call for 100, a decision which could easily prove costly given the improvement surely needed to win. By avoiding any aggressive betting moves so far, player F is advertising no strength at all and must be aware by now that a pair of fours is not enough. A flush might yet come good but this requires two of the remaining six unseen clubs in the deck (remember, player D folded the 7c earlier) on sixth and seventh street.

| PLAYER B | PLAYER C | PLAYER E | PLAYER F |

high pairs if the opposition's up cards reveal no obvious threat. Though a maximum bet is advised, any raise from an opponent would have to be taken very seriously and would call for a re-evaluation of the situation.

Unless the hand improves on sixth street, a more cautious approach will then be required since another maximum bet could trigger the same response from the opponent who is, at the very least, likely to call anyway with one card to come. Though the opponent may be bluffing with a weaker hand than that implied by the raise on fifth street, the warning signs are there to suggest that the player may need an A or J to win. In order to draw a relevant card, the player will want to keep the cost of doing so as cheap as possible, which means checking if in an early betting position and just calling if the opponent bets first.

Two cards to come

Assuming a player has identified that any drawing hand still has the chance to win with two cards to come, the strategy from fifth street onwards is to see those cards for the minimum outlay. Opponents will be attempting to make this as difficult as possible, a tactic that is much easier to achieve in pot-limit stud than in the fixed-limit game. Nevertheless, even when the likely cost of continuing to the showdown can be readily calculated, playing a drawing hand presents a challenge if there are several opponents still in contention. In these circumstances the best policy is to check or call but definitely not raise, particularly when in an early betting position. The danger of being drawn into a protracted betting war with the worst hand is far too great when in this situation and can result in the size of the pot tempting a player to continue unjustifiably in relation to the chances of actually winning.

STILL IN CONTENTION

Above: After the exploratory raise in the previous round, player B just calls on this occasion, first because the Q has brought no improvement to the hand and, second, because the other three players seem intent on remaining involved. Perhaps of more importance is the fact that, even if player B pairs the A on sixth street, this could still prove inadequate given that player C could have paired the A and a higher card than a 9.

DRAWING DEAD
♦ ♣ ♥ ♠

All players strive to avoid persevering with a hand after fifth street when no available cards can improve it sufficiently to win – a situation known as 'drawing dead'. The number of hidden cards and a subtle betting strategy can help opponents to lay traps for the unwary. Novices often fail to spot the potential difficulty ahead when chasing drawing hands that, even if completed, could fall short of the mark. For example a player might continue betting on a straight draw, needing just one card to complete the hand, when an opponent with three diamonds showing has bet. A call may see the straight completed on sixth street and tempt the player into staying to the showdown where it will too often be beaten by the opponent's made flush or an equally successful draw for an even stronger hand.

Left: An open-ended straight draw after five cards is the type of hand that might lure a player into drawing dead. Though a K or an 8 will complete the straight, it may not be worth pursuing if an opponent has three diamonds showing and has bet to infer at least one hole card is also a diamond. The merit in receiving a K on sixth street is devalued if the opponent is then dealt a fourth diamond since the flush is almost certainly now complete.

Sixth street

Even in a fairly loose fixed-limit game it is unusual for there to be many more than three players still contesting the pot on sixth street. A combination of the cards on display and the inferences drawn from the betting is generally enough to have caused anyone without a realistic chance of winning to fold beforehand.

Those at the table will have a fair idea of the quality of hands still in play and, for the players remaining in contention, the considerations are quite simple. A player who possesses what is clearly a winning, if not unbeatable, hand will be aiming to extract as many chips as possible from opponents who are now likely to stay to the showdown. Betting in a bid to eliminate them is extremely difficult at this stage, even in pot-limit stud where a sizeable bet may be interpreted as a bluff. Conversely, a player who holds a good hand but is uncertain whether it is strong enough to take the pot will hope to see seventh street for the minimum cost. This is only worthwhile if the cards that can improve a hand into a likely winner are available. This calculation is reasonably simple given that between a third and half the deck may, by now, have been exposed during play.

SIXTH STREET

1110

POT TOTAL

Above: After persisting with by far the worst hand, player F now takes the lead on sixth street with trip fours and just one card to come. Player B, meanwhile, has now found two pairs but knows that nines and threes, with four players competing, is unlikely to be good enough at the showdown. Players C and E both draw blanks.

| PLAYER B | PLAYER C | PLAYER E | PLAYER F |

Extra bets

In fixed-limit stud there is little likelihood that a player can bet strongly enough to prevent any opponents on sixth street from calling for the final card. Anyone still taking part at this stage will have a reasonably accurate idea of the quality of hands apparently in opposition. As such, they will be more concerned with how their sixth card improves their prospects than with deciphering the subtleties of any betting move.

A player who is confident of leading on sixth street should bet, or raise if appropriate, in the expectation of being called. Checking not only offers opponents a free opportunity to form a better hand, but also reduces the potential winnings on those occasions when the leading hand on sixth street retains its status at the showdown. The whole strategy for a player who is confident of being ahead is to try to induce as many extra bets from opponents as possible.

Checking and then raising a subsequent bet made by an opponent, a tactic known as 'checkraising', is sometimes worth considering but only if the player with the leading hand is confident that one or more opponents will bet on the strength of their cards. If so, then the player who initially checked can raise in the knowledge that anyone who has bet on sixth street will probably call the raise, rather than fold, even if they now suspect they are behind. The size of the pot relative to the amount required to call almost ensures this eventuality and satisfies the raiser's strategic aim of generating extra bets to maximize the profit on winning hands.

Seventh street

By seventh street a player's strategy in a fixed-limit game will be influenced by the number of opponents still involved and the player's position in the betting sequence. The final betting round will often be contested heads-up by just two players, in which case there is limited scope for subtle betting moves.

A player who is confident of victory and is set to act first should always bet to pressurize an opponent into calling with a beaten hand. Most opponents will do so in this situation provided there is still the slimmest of chances they might win, if only to indicate that they cannot be bluffed out of a pot at the end. When the player acting first harbours serious doubts about holding a successful hand, then a check is the only viable decision. There is nothing to be gained by betting since an opponent will fold if clearly beaten, but will probably raise if ahead, leading to the likely but unnecessary loss of additional chips when the player feels obliged to call.

In the same scenario against two or more opponents, a check is advised. Any bet with a weak hand is likely to be wasted since a caller will probably have a better hand. Also, there is always the risk that the bet could be raised and even re-raised. Then the player either folds, losing one bet, or calls with a good chance of losing even more last-round bets.

By checking first instead of betting, opponents may fear a checkraise move and might also check, so the showdown would come at no further cost. Likewise, any unraised bet in the final round might make a call justified in this position to trigger the showdown because the potential loss would be limited to a single additional bet. This provides a timely reminder that minimizing losses in poker is as important to long-term success as consistently winning large pots during a session.

FIRST TO ACT

Above: In the fourth round of betting player B is first to act because of the pair of threes showing and he checks, hoping to see seventh street for free. If the others remember player B's raise on fourth street and think it represented three nines, they might be reluctant to bet now for fear that player B is planning a checkraise with a full house. Irrespective of this, player C ploughs on by betting in support of the two pairs, kings and tens, although the K dealt to player E has reduced the chance of player C improving to a full house. Player E also calls.

MORE AGGRESSION

Above: Player F now takes the chance to show some aggression by raising in support of the trip fours, a move that could represent to the opposition that the 4d has helped to complete a straight rather than three of a kind. Player B is now thinking that a full house is probably required to win, meaning that any of the nines and threes that are among the 31 cards he has yet to see must come on seventh street. The odds against this are about 7 to 1, making a call now almost obligatory as the pot odds are roughly the same.

Tournament play

Many poker players remain puzzled that despite its immense popularity, seven-card stud was passed over in favour of Texas Hold 'em as the game played for the WSOP world championship in the early 1970s. While the latter has come to dominate the tournament scene ever since, its rise to prominence owes much to the predilections of the professionals who contested those early contests. Their preference for the game is thought to have influenced Benny Binion's decision to adopt it for the WSOP.

However, pot-limit and fixed-limit seven-card stud tournaments soon became a fixture of the month-long WSOP event, while Europe's annual Poker EM, held in Vienna, is one of the most prestigious seven-card stud tournaments outside America. Pot-limit seven-card stud events are popular with experienced players, making them a risky prospect for the novice. For those considering a fixed-limit tournament, here are a few basic guidelines that may prove helpful.

Early stages

At the start of a multi-table tournament with seven or eight players per table, a cautious approach in support of only the best opening hands is the typical strategy. Anyone holding a strong hand will bet aggressively in the first round to capitalize on the early advantage by encouraging opponents to fold. To counter such aggression, only playing the best starting hands and drawing hands is therefore advisable to protect one's chip stack.

Any player holding a high pair after three cards is almost bound to continue to at least fifth street before re-assessing the situation, and will likely continue to bet aggressively until this stage to whittle away the opposition. With this in mind, only drawing hands featuring high-value cards should be considered an alternative since they offer

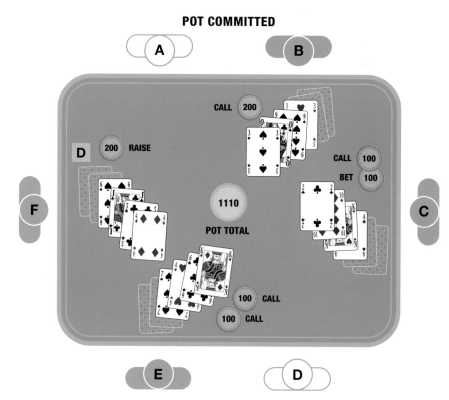

POT COMMITTED

Above: The fourth round of betting is completed when players C and E call for the additional 100 chips. Both are under the impression that player F may well have formed a small straight and that they are likely to need help from the final card to emerge victorious. For player C, this means that only a K or a 10 will help while player E cannot be sure that a 5 will provide a straight good enough to win. However, having come this far, player E feels 'pot committed' and will obviously be reluctant to fold at this point for the sake of a few more chips with so much already invested in the pot.

SEVENTH STREET

Above: Player B retains the honour to bet first in the final round but checks once again, convinced that the two pairs are not enough. Player C, by contrast, bets 100 in support of the full house of kings over tens which is confidently expected to prove the winner. For players E and F the moment of reckoning has arrived. Although both have improved their initial low pairs into three of a kind, the questionable decision to keep calling in the earlier rounds has now come back to haunt them. They call, and so too does player B, prior to the showdown.

other chances to win. A player holding As, Ks, 8s, for example, is justified in calling a raise from an opponent who has a Q showing and is representing a high pair since pairing the A or K may be enough to win, even if the flush does not materialize. Players must be wary of pursuing drawing hands blindly during the early stages of a tournament risking a regular loss of chips when survival is of most importance.

Middle stages

A tricky element of tournament play is that participants have no knowledge of their opponents' abilities or playing styles, so conservative play is sensible during the early stages. At a table of very conservative opponents, a player may be able to adopt a loose style by supporting marginal hands. For example a raise in late position to represent a large pocket pair when showing a 9 on third street could set up a winning bet on fourth street if another 9 or a picture card is dealt. A cautious opponent will suspect two pairs or three of a kind and will probably fold in the face of a possible full house developing unless there is a realistic chance of beating such a hand. Similarly, if there is plenty of action at the table with several players staying until fifth street, then it is wise to restrict one's involvement to hands which offer the most winning potential.

Apart from gauging the opponents' strength, another key factor governing strategy at this stage of the tournament will be the size of a player's chip stack. If low on chips, opponents are likely to raise with lesser hands than usual as they try to fashion a heads-up scenario that may eliminate the player from the event. Despite the pressure of being short on chips, having the patience to wait for a prime starting hand before committing oneself to a pot offers the best chance of surviving to the later stages.

SHOWDOWN

2310 POT TOTAL

Above: The showdown confirms that player C has won with the full house to claim the pot of 2,310 chips. This example shows the quality of hands that can occur in seven-card stud, especially when several players stay to the showdown. Two pairs and three of a kind are often good enough to win, but the chances of these hands holding up is greater if the field is substantially reduced by fifth street, something that did not occur here.

| PLAYER B | PLAYER C | PLAYER E | PLAYER F |

THE FINAL TABLE
♠ ♣ ♥ ♠

Stack size at the final table is the crucial in determining strategy. During the tournament, players in the leading chip positions can avoid getting involved in hands, while short-stacked opponents try to claw their way back into contention. Players with just enough chips for a handful of bets need to be similarly selective in which hands they play. The difference is that when dealt a reasonable hand, they must bet aggressively straight away. A player has a better chance of winning when all-in on third street against one rival than betting all-in on fifth street against two or three. By the time the tournament is down to the last three or four players, the average value of the winning hand will drop while play is likely to be more aggressive. Stealing the antes with the first raise is a typical ploy and more bluffing is apparent, especially when a player's board cards suggest a strong hand.

The key to success at this stage lies in a player's ability to judge the situation and the opposition as much as the quality of hand to support.

TEXAS HOLD 'EM

Texas Hold 'em begins with the first player to the left of the dealer making a compulsory bet known as the small blind, after which the next player bets the big blind, usually set at the same level of the minimum bet for the first round, while the small blind is generally half this sum. The cards are dealt one at a time, face down, until each player has two cards which are referred to as their hole or pocket cards. A round of betting follows before the dealer reveals three cards, face up, on the table. This is called the 'flop'. Following the flop, a second betting round takes place and then a fourth card – the 'turn' – is dealt face up next to the flop, after which there is further betting, with the minimum bet permitted typically doubling at this point. The fifth and final face-up card, known as the 'river', is revealed by the dealer prior to the last round of betting. The objective is for players to make the best five-card poker hand possible from their two hole cards and the five community cards revealed on the table. Players may, if they wish, discount their hole cards entirely when finalizing their hand, in which case they are said to be 'playing the board', their hand comprising all five community cards.

If there is one poker variation that has contributed to the recent resurgence of interest in the game, it is without doubt Texas Hold 'em, often referred to simply as Hold 'em. The game is thought to have originated in Robstown, Texas, early in the 20th century, and was widespread in the southern states of America, although it was eclipsed in terms of popularity by seven-card stud. This state of affairs existed until Benny Binion decided to employ Texas Hold 'em as the variation to decide the WSOP World Champion in the early 1970s. The publicity surrounding the event created a demand for more poker tournaments and Texas Hold 'em established itself as the game of choice for such knockout events.

The most popular game

The legendary Johnny Moss once said that "chess is to checkers what Hold 'em is to draw or stud", underlining the complexities of the game that have made it so appealing to millions of players worldwide. Although the basic concepts of Texas Hold 'em are simple enough to grasp, playing it well takes courage, cunning and skill, particularly in pot-limit games (where maximum bets can be no higher than the total in the pot) or no-limit games (where players can bet all their chips at any time during play). These are the favoured betting structures for Texas Hold 'em tournaments, which have helped the game establish itself as a cultural phenomenon in the 21st century.

Television coverage of the tournament circuit and patronage from the stars of show business and sport has generated a stylish and fashionable image for the game that is attracting ever more interest. Consequently, Texas Hold 'em has acquired the status given to chess and bridge, with a wealth of books, feature articles and websites offering serious analytical appraisals of the game and how best to play it. In short, Texas Hold 'em is big business, while at the recreational level, it has revived interest in forming card schools and poker clubs, as newcomers to the game aim to discover the secrets behind its popularity.

Left: The late Johnny Moss, the first WSOP world champion and the man whose lengthy poker battle with Nicholas 'Nick the Greek' Dandolos in 1949 stimulated Benny Binion's desire to initiate the WSOP. Moss always considered Texas Hold 'em to be a much more complex game than either draw or stud poker.

Online impact

Draw poker is traditionally the game to which beginners are exposed first, but in the Internet age, this situation is rapidly changing. Media coverage of Texas Hold 'em, together with the upsurge of interest that ensued, has coincided with the growth, since 1998, of online gaming sites that have been perfectly placed to meet the demand for ready access to poker. Texas Hold 'em attracts more players than any other online poker variation, and the ubiquitous nature of the game at present makes it likely that the next generation of poker players will cut their teeth on this game rather than on draw or stud.

Not all players appreciate the impact of the medium on the game itself, believing it to encourage poor poker habits in line with the speed at which decisions are made. Turbo tournaments, in which the blinds – the compulsory bets made by the two players to the immediate left of the dealer – are raised every two or three minutes, are popular at the lower-stake levels and will often be completed within the hour. However, the suggestion is that much of that popularity comes from the greater propensity for luck, rather than skill, to play a part. Bad calls do win on occasions and a poor player may need to be lucky just once with an all-in call in order to eliminate someone whose reading of the game is superior. For online players, the key point is that they should be open-minded in their analysis and not misread a lucky winning streak as evidence of skill.

Above: Behind the scenes at the TV production room during the *Ladbrokes Poker Million Masters* in 2004. Broadcast by Sky Sports in the UK, the event has become an integral part of the TV company's schedule since its inception in 2002. Each player's hand is always visible on camera, allowing the director to piece the action together in a suitably dramatic fashion to enhance a viewer's interest.

TELEVISED TOURNAMENTS

After enthusiastic but limited attempts to convey the WSOP to a television audience during the 1970s, poker truly made its mark on the TV schedules from the late 1990s onwards. Cameras beneath the table enabled viewers to see the players' cards and, since tournaments almost invariably feature Texas Hold 'em, the game quickly became part of the mainstream consciousness. The enthusiasm for online gaming sites to sponsor tournaments staged for television has seen interest expand to the point where there are channels solely dedicated to broadcasting poker. Texas Hold 'em is the principal poker variation driving this interest, inspiring more viewers to play and improve their poker skills.

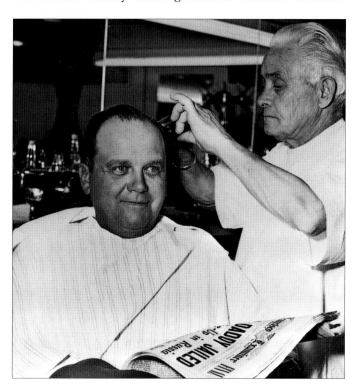

Left: Benny Binion, getting his hair cut for his court appearance, is the founder of legendary Binion's Horseshoe Casino, where all WSOP events were held up until 2005. In 1964, he regained control of the Horseshoe Casino after selling his interest to cover his legal costs defending himself from tax evasion and other charges. As a convicted criminal, Benny was no longer allowed to hold a licence to run a gambling establishment. His sons Jack and Ted took over the daily operation of the casino. Benny remained on the payroll as a consultant.

Starting hands

In Texas Hold 'em, players are dealt just two cards at the start of play, yet even with so little initial information upon which to base a betting decision, this is still perhaps the most crucial moment of the game. Successful cash game players will probably see less than a third of all flops, and maybe as few as a fifth if they are strict in their choice of starting hands. Poorer players are usually much less disciplined in which hole cards they support, trusting in possibilities rather than probabilities. To an extent, this approach is conditioned by the factors motivating them to play; by definition, recreational or social players are keener to take part in the action and to view losses as the price paid for their entertainment.

Which of the 169 potential two-card combinations are worth playing depends on the likely value of the winning hand, as in all forms of poker. In Texas Hold 'em, a single high pair will often win the pot and hands such as two pairs or three of a kind (trips) are highly likely to do so, especially when the hand incorporates both hole cards. A player who holds pocket eights when a third 8 appears on the flop, the moment when the first three community cards are revealed, is in a powerful position due to the concealed strength of the hand. This is an obvious advantage compared to holding a pocket 8 that matches two eights on the flop when the implication behind any bet is much more easily read by opponents.

A straight or better will usually be good enough to win, but many hands of such potential are folded before they have a chance to be realized. This happens because unless the flop brings immediate promise of making the hand, the cost of drawing the cards for a straight or a flush, for example, can be made prohibitively expensive, relative to the odds against success.

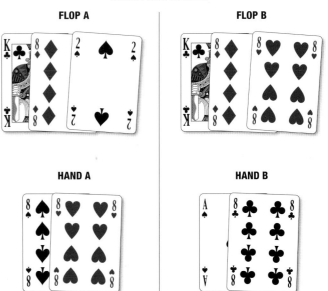

STARTING HANDS

FLOP A   FLOP B

HAND A   HAND B

Above: Making three of a kind – trips – on the flop using a pocket pair and one board card, as here in hand A, puts a player in a better position than when making a similar hand with a pair on the board, as is shown in hand B. In the first example, only a player holding a pair of kings could be any threat, but an opponent holding A, K may bet in the belief that the top pair is leading. Whether a call or raise should follow depends on the willingness of the player holding trips to allow any opponents a chance to improve their hands before making a maximum bet. While making trips using just one pocket card is generally strong, any bet in support of the hand immediately suggests possession of either a K or an 8, which will normally be enough to end the hand.

Above: This hand of 7, 2 offsuit is popularly regarded as the worst possible two-card starting hand to be dealt in Texas Hold 'em and most players in receipt of these cards fold immediately. If dealt them while in the big blind, a player might choose to see the flop provided the betting has not been raised. Only if the flop then brings a minimum of two pairs could the player contemplate becoming seriously involved in any subsequent betting.

POCKET PAIRS

Pocket pairs

A pair will often be enough to take the pot, so being dealt a pair in the first two cards is advantageous, but players must beware of becoming too attached to the hand. Some pocket pairs are more valuable than others, with tens and above seen as playable wherever a player is sat in relation to the dealer. Pairs ranked 9 and below will usually need help from the board in the form of a matching card to prove successful, with the odds against making trips on the flop in the region of 8 to 1 against. This could justify calling a bet to see a cheap flop, but anyone with a pair lower than tens may find calling an opponent's raise much more difficult.

A raise is typically indicative of high cards being held, if not paired, meaning that any A, K, Q, J or 10 on the flop – any one of 20 cards – could immediately leave a player with pocket nines, for instance, trailing to a bigger pair. By contrast, a player who has pocket aces or kings has the chance to raise or re-raise any first-round bets, to defeat opponents and consolidate the early advantage.

This is crucial, since, while a pair of aces is the best possible hand before the flop, occurring once in every 220 deals, the board could supply a mixture of cards to help opponents. The more players who see the flop, the more card combinations are in play to blend with the board and render the aces second best. This is why most players advocate playing premium pocket pairs, such as aces, kings and queens, as aggressively as possible arguing that opponents must be made to bet heavily for a shot at beating them.

TOUCHING CARDS

Two cards that are consecutive in rank – 'touching cards' – are valuable in Texas Hold 'em because, on 80 per cent of occasions, the board will contain at least three cards that could help form a straight, which, if held, is often good enough to win the pot. Two touching cards such as J, 10, for example, will fit with four different three-card combinations to form a straight, these being A, K, Q; K, Q, 9; Q, 9, 8 and 9, 8, 7. By comparison, even a hand such as A, 10 can only make a straight if K, Q, J appears on the board. Hands such as A, K and K, Q, although offering reduced chances of making the straight, are compensated by their potential for making the high pair, which is often enough to win at the showdown. Lower down the scale, hands such as 10, 9 and 5, 4 are generally regarded as poor starting hands and players who choose to play them usually do so when pre-flop betting is light. The inherent problem in playing low connecting cards is that when they do make straights, they may be at the wrong end of the spectrum. If the board contains 6, 7, 8, for example, then the player holding the 5, 4 has the low or 'ignorant end' of the straight and is outranked by anyone with 10, 9 or 9, 5. Similarly, K, Q, J on the board provides a straight for a player with 10, 9, but a holding of A, 10 will prove superior.

Above: Hands that feature touching cards offer straight opportunities and are often worth considering given that the five board cards will include three cards to a straight 80 per cent of the time. A hand such as the A, K can only make a straight with the Q, J, 10 on the board but has the added benefits that come from simply holding high-ranking cards. The 9, 8 combination, however, will blend with four different three-card combinations to make a straight, although there is always the potential for it to be second best. The Q, J, 10 combination to form one possible straight could easily form a higher example for a player holding A, K or K, 9.

Suited cards

Holding two suited cards after the deal offers a player possibilities of a flush, although these are best realized when just three cards of the relevant suit are on the board, rather than four. Holding Ks, Qs is much more beneficial if the board reads Ad, 9s, 8s, 6d, 4s, rather than Ad, 9s, 8s, 6s, 4s. In the first instance, it is plausible that an opponent contesting the pot holds the As and a card of a different suit, thus the resulting flush represents the best hand. But with four spades on the board, an opponent with the As would obviously take the pot. This underlines another benefit in holding the A in any suit, and highlights the possibilities of playing any A-suited combination, although the A, 9; A, 8; A, 7 and A, 6 hands are weaker. They do not offer the added benefit of blending with a three-card combination on the board to make a straight.

Flushes are strong hands in Texas Hold 'em, but they have to be played with a degree of caution, since players will often have to see the turn and the river card in order to fill them. A flush draw can be expensive for a player to pursue when an opponent has read the hand correctly. Although there is a 40 per cent chance that the five board cards will feature at least three of the same suit, there are four suits, reducing the relevant chances of any suited pairing matching the board to 1 in 10. Furthermore, the chances of a flush being made on the flop when in possession of suited hole cards are fractionally less than 1 per cent but, although such a hand is powerful, exploiting it to the full can be testing, especially without the A. Betting with such a hand will usually win the pot, making a small profit, however slow-playing it always runs the risk of someone else securing a higher-value flush or, if the board subsequently pairs, a full house.

FILLING A FLUSH

FLOP	TURN	RIVER

EXAMPLE 1

EXAMPLE 2

PLAYER'S HAND **OPPONENT'S HAND**

Above: This illustration highlights the potential problems that arise when holding suited pocket cards but not the A. In the first example, the player holding Ks, Qs has two chances to hit a winning spade although the opponent, who holds the leading hand on the flop and the turn with a pair of aces, could make it expensive to stay in the game. In the second example, the turn card puts the player in front with a flush but even an all-in bet might not persuade the opponent holding the As to fold, with potentially disastrous consequences if the river brings a fourth spade.

Above: An opening hand of K, 9, often referred to as 'Lassie' or 'Rin-Tin-Tin'. The hand is more valuable when suited, as in this example, but it can be tricky to play it well. Doyle Brunson is one professional who dislikes it because too many of the cards that might help it develop into a strong hand are likely to do the same for an opponent. Pairing the K, for instance, is of no help if someone else holds a K with a higher kicker, which is a very plausible prospect.

PLAYING MEDIUM PAIRS
FLOP A

FLOP B   FLOP C

Left: A medium pair is worth the occasional call before the flop when the pot is unraised, since there is around an 8 to 1 chance to secure trips immediately, as in example A. However, if the flop consists of three higher cards, an underpair has little value and should be folded if an opponent bets. Occasionally, as in example C, the hand will not directly improve but will generate additional potential to help make a strong hand. Indeed, a post-flop bet or raise may be enough to win the pot, such are the visible threats apparent.

Marginal hands

The dubious potential of mid-ranking pairs has already been explained, as they can too often become impotent after the flop. A hand such as a pair of sevens can be played when in the big blind since, if nobody raises, a player in that position can check the betting and see the flop at no further cost having already committed the required chips in the pot. If there is no help from the flop in the shape of a 7 or a low straight-draw possibility, the hand should probably be folded in the face of the first bet.

Touching cards ranked J or lower, even if suited, pose similar problems. Whether to play them will depend on the opposition and the situation in a game, but they are rarely powerful enough to call

any pre-flop raise. The flops that can help marginal hands are less likely to appear and the danger is that when they do, an opponent's hand may improve even more.

Poor prospects

More than half the possible two-card combinations are simply never worth playing by anyone with pretensions to being a profitable player. Picture cards with unsuited low cards such as Kh, 2d or Js, 6c have little merit when one considers the composition of the board. They need very specific flops to fall in order to warrant continued support. For example a player holding Kh, 2d when the flop is Kd, 10s, 7c has a top pair but with a very weak kicker. If an opponent bets, the obvious conclusion is that a pair of kings is being represented, it being unusual for a player, holding 9s, 8d for instance, to open the betting in pursuit of a straight draw. This is terminal for the K, 2 since any opponent holding a K cannot hold a kicker lower than 2 and so cannot be losing, making it difficult to withstand any aggressive move. Similar comments apply to a pair of twos that can only be confidently supported after the flop should another 2 be dealt.

POTENTIAL DANGER

FLOP A   FLOP B

FLOP C   PLAYER'S HAND

Above: A weak hand such as K, 2 offsuit needs too much help from the board to be seriously competitive. Flop A offers two pairs, which could warrant a maximum post-flop bet to dissuade any callers who may fear trips. Yet it could still be losing to another poor starting hand of K, 7. Flop B is more dangerous because holding a top pair with such a weak kicker is inviting trouble. Any opponent who holds a K with a better kicker is immediately in front, and K, J offsuit, a very playable hand, could easily be in opposition. In extreme cases, even making trips as shown in flop C could see the K, 2 up against an opponent holding the final K with any higher kicker.

Before the flop

Having assessed the promise of their opening two cards, players have to consider the other factors at work when deciding whether to bet or fold before the flop. Of these, the number of opponents, their position relative to the dealer, and the nature of the game will be the most vital.

A restrained, low-stakes fixed-limit game between ten players may well see five or six calling to see the flop if it is habitually unraised. By contrast, pot-limit and no-limit Texas Hold 'em could see sizeable raises before the flop, as players try to test the resolve of their opponents and reduce the competition. Only by understanding the context of a particular game can a player form a strategy for the hand in progress.

When betting to see the flop, players should be clear on what they need in order to win, while retaining the discipline to fold if the flop brings no encouragement. Loose players are inclined to see too many flops with poor or marginal hands, the likely result of this indiscriminate policy being a steady reduction in their chips as the game unfolds.

Early betting decisions

How to proceed once the cards are dealt will depend on the character of the players and their motives. This underlines the value of observing, to build up a picture of the hands opponents play and the betting moves they make. In a tight game featuring plenty of folding before the flop, it can pay to be flexible regarding which starting hands to support. A raise before the flop, with a marginal hand, may even be enough to steal the blinds occasionally in a game where opponents are reluctant to play with anything less than excellent cards. They are more likely to respect a pre-flop raise and assume it indicates a high pair or A, K until it is proved otherwise.

In a hectic game where several players routinely see the flop, a more patient strategy is prudent. Playing only the stronger starting hands would conserve chips for those times when a player wishes to maximize the return on investment, having found a winner. Opponents who are preoccupied with their own game may not notice the implications behind a cautious player's participation in the hand until it is too late.

PLAYER A	PLAYER B	PLAYER C	PLAYER D	PLAYER E	PLAYER F

Right: In this example, the game is 100/200 fixed-limit Texas Hold 'em and the players have just been dealt their cards. Assessing the starting hand and considering how to play it in relation to one's betting position are crucial. Player A has a good hand, but is first to act after the deal and is in mid-position, so a call, not a raise, is probably advisable. Players B and C both have pairs, although the kings represent a premium starting hand and easily justify a raise. Player D has two suited connectors and would like the betting to remain unraised in order to see the flop. Players E and F both have poor hands and are likely to fold if there is any significant move by an opponent.

STARTING HANDS

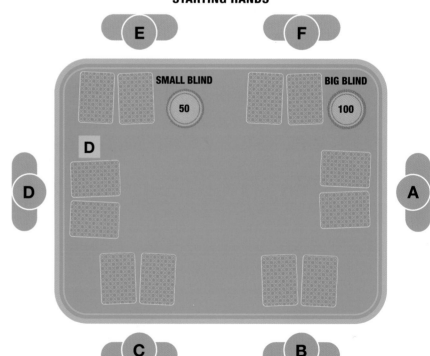

Positional play

In Texas Hold 'em, a player's position during the betting round is more significant than in any other poker game. The earlier a player has to act, the more difficult it is to control the betting given the lack of information upon which to base any decision. This affects the quality of the starting hand a player can expect to support before the flop, with hands that are virtually unplayable in an early betting position becoming much more attractive when on the dealer button. The dealer is always last to act in the betting rounds that succeed the flop and so has much more information from opponents regarding the quality of their hands. For example, when holding K, J offsuit and seated next to the big blind (who is in second position, clockwise from the dealer), a call might seem reasonable, but the player is vulnerable to subsequent raises from opponents. Since the initial reaction would be to assume such opponents hold a high pair or an A with a good kicker – A, K; A, Q; A, J, for example – the potential of the K, J is immediately devalued. The decision is whether to fold for the loss of a single bet or risk another bet in the knowledge that the hand is probably already losing. The problem in doing this is that cards that may help on the flop could easily improve an opponent's hand as well in this situation. Pair the K alone and an opponent with A, K or K, Q is still ahead, while a flop of K, J, 10 for two pairs could be losing to someone with A, Q for a straight.

Holding the same hand on the dealer button, however, offers much more scope, since, if nobody raises, a call will probably be enough to see the flop. This allows the player to gauge the inferences behind opponents' post-flop bets without having to risk any further chips. Premium hands such as the high pairs and A, K can be played in any position, almost without exception. As a general rule, the earlier a player's position relative to the dealer, the stronger the starting hand is normally required to be.

Below: A pair of twos, sometimes referred to as deuces or ducks. While being dealt a pair in Hold 'em is generally regarded as advantageous, a pair of twos should normally be played as inexpensively as possible given that making trips on the flop is the likeliest route to victory. Calling a pre-flop raise with them is rarely wise and, if failing to hit three of a kind on the flop, the hand is almost certain to prove worthless.

PRE-FLOP BETTING

Right: Player A's decision to err on the side of caution by calling encourages player B to call with the pair of fours, although a raise from player A might well have seen the small pair folded instead. Player C has the chance to raise but decides instead to disguise the strength of the hand with a call. This is a questionable move since it could easily allow one of the weaker hands to improve past it. Player D now has the chance to call as well and player F checks on the big blind, leaving five players to see the flop. Player E's hand is too poor to be worth calling for the extra 50 chips and is folded.

Playing the flop

Although deciding which starting hands to play is crucial, it is the flop that defines whether or not such decisions were justified. Strong two-card holdings can easily be compromised while poor hands will, on occasion, become unbeatable, given the right flop. When each player can see five of the seven cards from which they will ultimately form their hand, they can quickly deduce the best that they can achieve and, most importantly, whether that will be enough to win the pot. However, it is rare for a player to hold the nuts at this stage, from which it can be understood that leading hands may yet be beaten, while weak hands could still improve sufficiently to win.

This volatility is what makes Texas Hold 'em such an appealing and challenging game to play. In terms of strategy, factors such as position, the betting structure in use and the playing styles of opponents are still of paramount importance. But with more information now available in the form of the flop, players are able to calculate how many of the cards

remaining unseen might help or hamper their chances of victory. Any post-flop strategy, therefore, should always begin with an assessment of the probabilities that emerge from the cards in play. Only then can the actions of opponents be viewed from the proper perspective as each player attempts to outwit the others and secure the pot.

Strong play

Each deal offers a completely different scenario, so knowing how best to exploit any given situation depends on a player's ability to assimilate all the information available and act accordingly. Skilful players are better able to strike a balance between aggression and caution after the flop and choose a strategy that fits the specific situation. In this regard, strong play may involve folding a good hand in response to a large bet as much as managing the pot when holding a guaranteed winner. For example a player holding pocket kings who raised before the flop and elicited one caller will be extremely wary if the

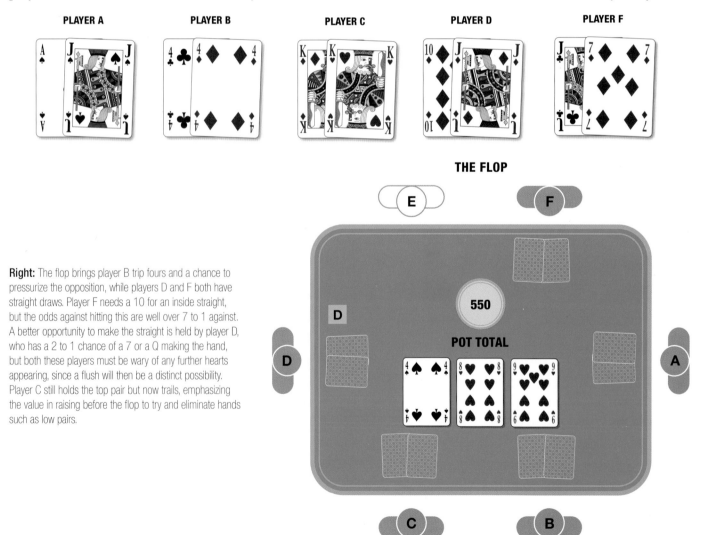

Right: The flop brings player B trip fours and a chance to pressurize the opposition, while players D and F both have straight draws. Player F needs a 10 for an inside straight, but the odds against hitting this are well over 7 to 1 against. A better opportunity to make the straight is held by player D, who has a 2 to 1 chance of a 7 or a Q making the hand, but both these players must be wary of any further hearts appearing, since a flush will then be a distinct possibility. Player C still holds the top pair but now trails, emphasizing the value in raising before the flop to try and eliminate hands such as low pairs.

flop shows an A but no K. Any bet from the opponent surely indicates possession of an A and good players will fold the kings there and then. However appealing the hand was after the deal, it is no stronger in this situation than any other pocket pair lower than aces.

Conversely, raising before the flop to represent an A and then putting in a big bet when one materializes on the flop is powerful play, particularly if opponents are known to call pre-flop raises with marginal hands. Unless they can beat a pair of aces, calling a bet in this situation is extremely difficult for anyone without an A, even if they have the potential to improve their hand. Given that the typical policy in Texas Hold 'em is to bet with leading hands and force opponents to pay for the cards that may win them the pot, the occasional bluff representing an A can be a positive move when used sparingly.

Weak play

Instances of weak play are not always restricted to players in possession of poor hands, either before or after the flop. Most experts would advocate raising before the flop with a pair of aces in a ten-player game, for example, since to enable several opponents the opportunity to see the flop cheaply decreases the hand's effectiveness. Any pair on the flop could easily provide an opponent with three of a kind and render the aces impotent. This highlights one of the guiding principles of Texas Hold 'em, which determines that players should never become emotionally attached to a powerful starting hand that is diminished in strength after the flop.

On the whole, however, weak play generally consists of players making the wrong decision in relation to the current state of their hand. Those who decide not to bet when in a leading position always run the risk of allowing an opponent to overtake them at negligible cost. Nevertheless, the poorest betting strategy is to continue calling opponents' bets when the possibility of obtaining the card or cards required to win simply does not justify remaining involved in the hand. Pots that are won on the occasions when a player is lucky enough to draw the relevant cards will very rarely compensate for the amount of money lost in similar circumstances during the game.

Above: A pair of aces in the hole, sometimes called 'pocket rockets', is the best starting hand available in Texas Hold 'em. Despite the initial advantage enjoyed when holding pocket aces, success cannot be guaranteed which is why most players dealt the hand will raise before the flop as with any other high-ranking pair.

Right: Player F is first to act and checks, as does player A, who has two overcards to the flop but little encouragement to pursue the hand further. Any significant betting might be enough to prompt a fold, given the straight and flush draws made possible by the flop. Player B bets with the three fours, but knows this may still not be enough to force opponents out of the game. Were this a pot-limit or no-limit game, then a much bigger bet would be possible to drive out any drawing hands, but, as it stands, player C is able to call, in the belief that the pair of kings could still be winning. This also allows player D to call, since the current pot odds of over 7 to 1 exceed the 3 to 1 against drawing one of the six cards that will make the straight, these being the Q and 7 in any suit but hearts.

POST-FLOP BETTING

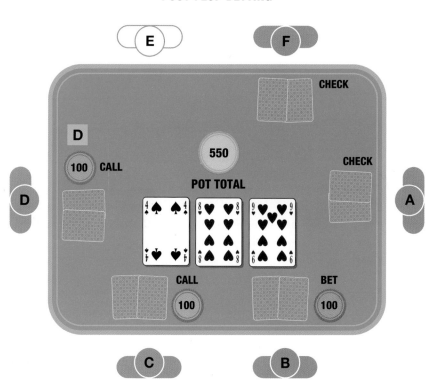

Assessing chances

The three community cards on the flop provide the most immediate opportunity for a player to evaluate the chances of success prior to the beginning of the second betting round. Those players who are in the later positions have time to factor their opponents' betting decisions into the equation once the action is under way, but the cards themselves provide the earliest clues regarding whether to play or not.

On occasions where the flop offers no help at all, the usual recommendation is to fold at the first sign of any betting. A hand of 9d, 9s, for instance, is unlikely to withstand a flop of Ad, Kh, 10c when an opponent bets to indicate possession of at least a high pair. Apart from the possibility of someone holding another A, K or 10 (constituting nine cards), the appearance of a Q or J on the board (a further eight cards) would simply enhance the possibility of a straight being made. In this situation, while the pair of nines may be winning, it is highly unlikely with so many cards in the deck working unfavourably. Only seeing nines on the turn and river – when the fourth and fifth and final community cards are dealt respectively – can guarantee victory and the odds against this are 1,000 to 1, so the rational decision would be to fold. This example illustrates that a player should always be assessing the probability of a hand improving enough to win the pot, rather than for it merely to improve.

Calculating outs

On the vast majority of occasions, the flop will not furnish a player with the nuts, and, when it does, the board cards will probably nullify any attempt to capitalize on the hand. To take an extreme example, a player holding a pair of queens when the flop is Q, Q, 7 faces an obvious problem in persuading opponents to call a bet. Consequently, players will typically have to calculate the number of outs – cards that can help them keep or obtain the winning hand – available in the deck. For the most part, players who require help from the board will typically be seeking just one of several cards on either the turn or the river.

The more cards that help, the better the opportunities with the tipping point being 13 or 14 cards, since having this many working in a player's favour offers an even-money chance of success. Those drawing to flushes or open-ended straights usually have eight or nine cards that will make the hand, the odds against which are 2 to 1. Any player with 14 or more unseen cards in the deck that will help secure victory is favourite to win.

Below: While player F folded, the escalating size of the pot tempted player A to call on the flop and the turn card – Ks – now offers the chance of an unlikely winning flush. It also illustrates the dynamic nature of Texas Hold 'em, with the lead changing hands once again, as well as highlighting the need for players with leading hands to bet aggressively in an effort to eradicate such potential threats. Player C is now in a very strong position, but may still not be able to bet enough to induce the others to fold.

THE TURN

PLAYER A PLAYER B

PLAYER C PLAYER D

POT TOTAL 950

Common errors

Mistakes made by players after the flop tend to fall into two categories. They either overvalue their hands and call optimistically despite their poor chance of winning, or they simply pay too little attention to the betting and fail to grasp the implications behind it. This can befall those with leading hands as well as those who need cards to win. Anyone holding Jc, Jd when the flop reads As, Jh, 9c, for example, may be inclined to slow-play the hand, since trip jacks is very strong and would be second only to a player with pocket aces. However, should any K, Q, 10, 8 or 7 be seen on the turn, then an opponent could conceivably make a straight. That is a total of 20 unseen cards that could beat the hand, while any A could do the same if an opponent has an A with the remaining J for a bigger full house.

With so many cards promising potential danger, a maximum bet is advised to force opponents out of the pot. Waiting until the turn card before betting could prove too late to have any effect, by which time the promise of the trip jacks has dissolved.

Above: The scene after the flop as a player hits three Js. Despite the apparent strength of the hand, any one of 20 cards on the turn could conceivably provide an opponent with a straight. In recognition of this, it would be best for the player holding the jacks to bet the maximum now to encourage opponents with straight draws to fold. If the bet is big enough, even players who have paired the A on the flop may think twice before calling.

BETTING ON THE TURN

Right: Undeterred by the calls in the previous round, player B bets 200, this being the minimum for the final two rounds, but is raised by player C, whose bet indicates that the K has proved helpful. For player D, the cost of calling is too prohibitive, since the pot is now offering less than 4 to 1 when the chance of hitting a winning card on the river has risen to over 10 to 1 against. This is because only four cards – the Q and 7 in clubs and diamonds – can now secure a potential winning hand without filling a flush. Player A, however, has a 4 to 1 chance of catching another spade for the nut flush, but must be concerned that, with two evidently strong hands in play, a call of 400 chips may yet be raised again by players B and C.

Leading hands

Holding a leading hand after the flop is obviously advantageous, but playing the hand correctly in order to realize its winning potential is still a challenging proposition. On the occasions when a player makes a powerful hand on the flop, such as a full house or a straight flush, the objective is to manage the pot and extract as much as possible from opponents. In this case, checking on the flop, and perhaps on the turn card, is often the only way to induce a bet from opponents, who, if their hands have improved, might assume that the board has not helped other players at all.

Making an unbeatable hand – the nuts – on the flop is a rare occurrence, and most leading hands, no matter how strong, remain vulnerable to defeat. A player with Kc, Qs, for instance, will probably be leading if the flop cards are Kd, 8d, 7s, but if several opponents call a bet advertising the pair of kings, then it is likely that straight and flush draws are being pursued at least. If so, the high pair could be beaten by any one of 29 cards that could complete an opponent's straight or flush, added to which any A, 8 or 7 in suits other than diamonds could also threaten defeat. With up to 80 per cent of the cards working against the pair of kings, the likelihood is that the hand will lose in a showdown. If some aggressive betting on the flop cannot eliminate all opposition under these circumstances, then caution is definitely advocated as the game progresses.

Drawing hands

Whether in possession of a leading hand or one that is trailing, requiring one of several cards to bring about certain victory after the flop is an integral part of Texas Hold 'em. The term 'drawing hands', however, is usually associated with those players who need one card on the turn or river in order to improve sufficiently past a leading hand to win. Players holding suited or connecting cards repeatedly encounter this situation as they try to draw the one card needed to complete a flush or a straight.

In general, the strategy behind playing such hands is to remain in the game as cheaply as possible, since, with two chances to hit the required card, there are obviously two more possibly expensive betting rounds to negotiate. Yet the potential for straights and flushes and full houses when there is a pair on the flop, is all too apparent to those with leading hands. Opponents currently holding the best hand can be expected to try forcing out the drawing hands by betting, so a keen eye on the existing and implied pot odds is advisable when in this situation.

By way of warning, it should be emphasized that more chips are lost by players fruitlessly pursuing drawing hands than in any other aspect of the game. This covers not just hands that fail to improve, but those that do realize their potential, only to secure the runner-up position.

Right: In the event, both players A and B call the raised bet of 400 chips, the former still hoping the flush draw will materialize while the latter is working on the assumption that player C has made no more than two pairs. The river gives player A the nuts since the A-high flush in spades is the best possible hand now available given the board cards, the chances against which were 24 to 1 against occurring when the flop was revealed. Now a bet from player A is absolutely essential, since it is the only way of tempting opponents into putting more chips into a pot they cannot win. Checking in the hope of being able to re-raise later runs the risk of seeing everyone do the same; the pot will still be won, but the profit will be reduced.

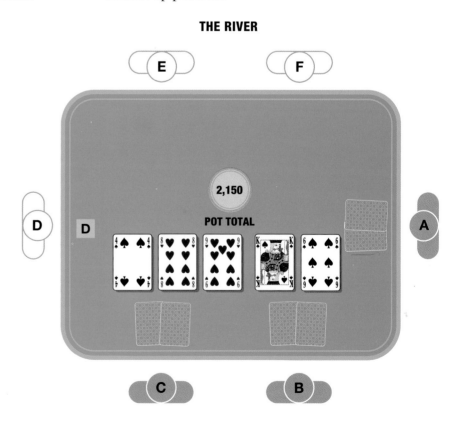

THE RIVER

PLAYER A   PLAYER B

Chasing hands

Hands that need two cards to realize their potential – chasing hands – should ordinarily be folded unless everyone checks on the flop. Expecting two cards to fall conveniently on the turn and river is extremely optimistic and players in such situations should usually fold if there is any significant betting. A player holding Qh, Jh when the flop is Kd, 5s, 6h, for example, would be ill-advised to pursue the flush, since there is only a four per cent chance of the next two cards bringing running hearts. Odds of 24 to 1 against this occurring virtually guarantee that the pot odds will never justify supporting a chasing hand.

When they do win, it is usually in a light betting heat in which all players have poor hands. An example would be when a player holds Kc, 9c and the flop reads Qs, 4c, 8d. Should nobody bet on the flop and the turn card is the Jc, then the player has a 4 to 1 chance of seeing another club on the river for the flush, odds which might justify a third-round call if the pot odds are appealing.

Above: An example of a typical chasing hand with the player holding Q, J suited realistically needing help on both the turn and the river cards to offer a possible winning opportunity. Two more hearts will provide a flush while an A and 10 or 10 and 9 will complete a straight, and these are hands that could easily prove best. Unless there is little or no betting after the flop, chasing two cards for a winning hand is rarely worthwhile since the pot odds rarely justify it.

THE CONCLUSION

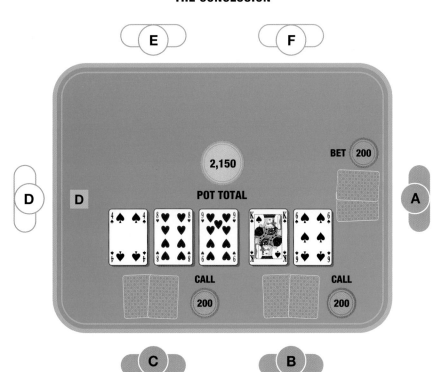

Left: Player A bets with impunity, knowing that players B and C must have reasonably strong hands and might call just to be certain a bluff is not being executed. Both are aware that player A initially checked on the flop and the turn but later called the bets made in both rounds, indicating that a flush could now be held. However, with both of them holding trips, they decide to call, with player C, particularly, regretting that the earlier advantage could not be pressed home. Had the game been a no-limit contest, an all-in move by player C after the K appeared on the turn may well have forced player A out of the hand.

PLAYER C

Post-flop strategies

Players who are sufficiently enamoured of their cards to consider betting will visualize the potential for winning. To achieve this, players will require their visions to be coloured by some strategic thinking concerning the probability of various outcomes during play. Although an assessment of the cards on display is important, the style and betting structure of the game, as well as the quality of the opposition will also influence any viable strategy.

Irrespective of the cards and probabilities in play, it is always easier to call a bet from a serial bluffer in a fixed-limit game than it is to call a raise by someone who normally folds nine hands in every ten while playing pot-limit Texas Hold 'em. For champion Doyle Brunson, the key elements in any post-flop strategy are the intangible qualities of patience and self-discipline, particularly when playing fixed-limit Texas Hold 'em. The pot-limit and no-limit games do permit greater licence to prosecute bold post-flop play via large raises and credible bluffs, but having the patience to wait – for the right cards against the right opponent and when in the right position – remains an asset.

Varying approaches

The fluid and volatile nature of Texas Hold 'em provides enough uncertainty over the outcome of most hands that players need to adopt a range of varied strategic approaches when playing the flop. In early position with the leading hand, the recommendation is generally to bet. Allowing opponents free cards is only advisable when a player is confident they can do little damage. If the flop offers a probable winning hand, however, a checkraise after the flop may be in order when one or two opponents can confidently be expected to bet. If they fold after the raise, the pot is won, but

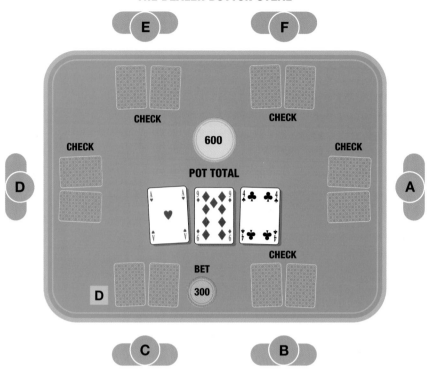

THE DEALER BUTTON STEAL

PLAYER C

Above: When a pot is unraised before the flop and the action is checked around to the dealer afterwards, it will often mean that the flop has helped nobody much at all. Should opponents show weakness in this way, a bet from player C, in this instance, could be enough to take the pot. By representing an A in the hole to make the high pair, opponents who have no A and no help from the flop will find it immensely difficult to justify calling. Such a move is more likely to succeed when the player can bet substantially in order to underline the threat, making this a more viable tactic in pot-limit or no-limit Texas Hold 'em.

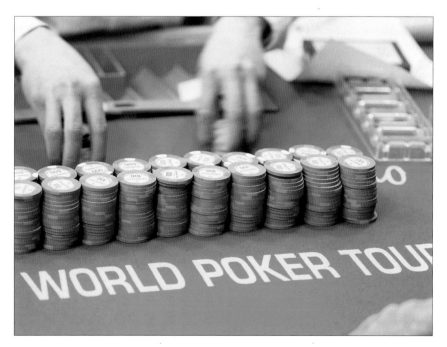

Above: A cashier at the Commerce Casino in Los Angeles counts out an equal number of chips for each player participating in the World Poker Tour Invitational event. Exposure to the styles and techniques of the top professionals via televised events such as this has helped confirm Texas Hold 'em as the poker game of choice for most players.

should the motive behind the raise be doubted, they will probably call and may well feel committed to the pot thereafter, despite the chance of drawing to a beaten hand.

In later positions, players have the opportunity to take a few liberties on occasions, especially when betting is light. Should the action be checked around the table, for example, the player on the dealer button may be able to steal the pot with a finely judged bet. If a flop of Ah, 9d, 4c invokes no response from others, then a bet to represent an A in the hole for the top pair is perfectly reasonable, provided nobody had raised before the flop. Here, a 'feeler' bet will win the pot or expose the fact that any caller probably has an A, which, if combined with a weak kicker, could explain the previous reluctance to bet.

The key to which strategy or betting style to adopt lies in closely observing the opposition. In a game featuring several cautious players, a little loose play can reap benefits by playing on their fears. Equally, in a game with inexperienced or loose players inclined to call at every opportunity, a more conservative and studied approach is recommended.

BLUFFING IN THE BIG BLIND

PLAYER D

Above: When Texas Hold 'em is played as a pot-limit or no-limit game, the chance to make bigger bets can help to make bluffs more likely to be respected than in the fixed-limit variation. Here, everyone has called the minimum bet of 100 chips before the flop. A check from player C when the flop is revealed could allow player D to infer possession of a strong hand such as trips or two pairs. Having paid the big blind and been allowed to see the flop for no extra cost, the other players know that player D could have any two cards. A hand such as 8, 5 or 5, 2, which would ordinarily have been folded, could have made two pairs, while 3, 4 – another poor hand – could make an open-ended straight draw. Players holding an A could easily believe that pairing it on the turn might also fill a straight for their opponent in the big blind.

BLUFFING OPPORTUNITIES
♦ ♣ ♥ ♠

As mentioned previously, bluffing on the flop in a fixed-limit game is hampered by the inability of players to bet sufficient amounts to intimidate opponents into laying down their hands. In this respect, carving out a reputation as someone who only raises with a top-quality hand can help a player to sneak through an occasional bluff, perhaps, when the risk of being called is generally high. Other betting structures, however, do improve the chances of bluffs being successful, since larger bets are permitted – the impact of this is twofold. First, any pot-sized bet after the flop makes the cost of calling more expensive, and second, the pot odds facing anyone wishing to call are immediately rendered much less attractive. Since a bet from a player in early position usually advertises strength, a pot-sized bluff by the player in the big blind becomes a possibility. Assuming there were no pre-flop raises, a forceful bet from the big blind when the flop reads 8c, 5h, 2s, for example, could easily persuade opponents with high cards to fold. Having already paid the obligatory bet to see the flop, but no more, opponents know that the player could have made a pair or even two pairs with cards that ordinarily would have been folded, such as 8, 5 or 5, 2. Even someone holding an overpair to the board will be wary of calling, given that any 8, 5 or 2 on the turn just might provide the big blind with three of a kind. Opportunities such as this may be rare, but there are times when they can be exploited, especially when opponents are betting timidly.

The art of deception

The ability to deceive opponents is an integral part of the game, which is why bluffing and varying one's betting style is so vital. The aim is to create doubt in the minds of opponents regarding the meaning behind any bet. If a bluff fails, opponents may consider it the tactic of a loose and reckless player, an image that may be exploited later when a strong hand develops.

In Texas Hold 'em, the capacity for the flop to offer potential to several players generates many opportunities to practise the art of deception. For example a flop of Ad, 3d, 10s presents the chance of a high straight, a low straight or a flush being realized, added to which anyone matching the board with their hole cards for a pair of aces, two pairs or three of a kind will almost certainly be keen to see the turn. Representing any one of these hands with a call or even a small raise could lay the foundations for success. Should any A, 10 or 3 be dealt on the turn, then a large bet would signal three of a kind or a full house has been made, making it difficult for those still needing a card to call. If the card is the 10d specifically, even someone with a made flush might baulk if having to call a large bet against a possible full house, while any opponents still drawing to a straight will definitely think they are beaten.

Using the flop in this way enables players to pick up pots occasionally, without necessarily having the cards to win. The one danger lies in representing a hand that is already held by an opponent, since betting as though holding pocket aces, for example, will prove costly should an opponent actually have pocket aces.

Right: Marlon Brando shuffles the deck prior to another game in the 1951 film *A Streetcar Named Desire*. Adapted from the play by Tennessee Williams, the film features several scenes in which Stanley Kowalski (Brando) and his friends play poker.

CHECKRAISING OPPORTUNITIES

PLAYER E

Above: By checking in early position after the flop, player E with a K-high straight has induced a bet and two calls from opponents and can now consider a raise with what is currently the best possible hand. Should everyone then fold, the manoeuvre will have successfully obtained a few more chips than might have been the case if player E had bet in turn. Alternatively, anyone who subsequently calls the raise will still be trailing and will need further help from the board, leaving player E in a strong position to manage the pot. The checkraise can also be a viable bluffing tactic if the board cards offer the credible threat of a made hand.

Checkraising

While many players deem checkraising, or 'sandbagging' – the latter a tactic of slow-playing a strong hand, perhaps by checkraising – to be an underhand ploy, the fact remains that it is a perfectly legitimate ploy in a game premised, after all, on deception. As an aid to pot management, it allows a player who holds a strong hand in an early position to lure opponents into betting more than intended. Should a check be followed by a bet and a couple of calls from others at the table, a raise might be enough to win straight away. At the very least it might persuade one or two opponents to fold, thus reducing the field and leaving the checkraiser in good shape for the turn, with probably the best hand.

In pot-limit and no-limit Texas Hold 'em, the checkraise is a more powerful bluffing tool than in the fixed-limit game, but players have to be sure that conditions are right. The potential offered by the flop must act as a guide, for it is the board cards that a player must use to engender fear in opponents. For instance, players in late positions will frequently try to pick up the pot if the action has been checked to them, even with a modest hand. If the flop suggests the potential for a much better hand to exist, a checkraise in early position may be sufficient to convince opponents that it is already held. A flop of Qs, 9h, 8c, for example, would make a straight for someone holding J, 10 but, if the betting is checked around, anyone holding a hand such as A, Q or A, 9 may bet in the belief they are leading. By checking and then raising with a large bet to imply possession of the straight, opponents with such hands are instantly put onto the back foot. Even if the bluff is called, any K, J or 10 on the turn followed by a large bet can reinforce belief in the opponents' minds that the straight has definitely been achieved.

SLOW-PLAYING A HAND

PLAYER F

Above: Deceiving opponents is an essential element of Texas Hold 'em, so being able to disguise the strength of a hand is a tactical move that can pay dividends. In this example, player F resisted the urge to raise before the flop with the pair of kings and has generated a family pot in which everybody remains involved. By checking on the flop, the hope is that others will sense weakness and bet with hands far inferior to the trip kings. Slow-playing the hand in this fashion, therefore, is a tactic that can increase its profitability as opponents inflate the pot with little or no chance of winning.

Left: A pocket pair of jacks which is best regarded as a medium pair only. Notoriously tricky to play, pocket jacks can be played aggressively from late position if nobody is keen to raise the pot. Calling with a pair of jacks when an opponent has already raised is much more testing, though, since any A, K or Q on the flop will often have made a higher pair.

SLOW-PLAYING A HAND
♦ ♣ ♥ ♠

When holding an exceptionally strong hand on the flop, players are best advised to slow-play it by simply checking or calling as needed to keep opponents involved. A flop of Kh, 6d, 4c when holding pocket kings, for example, is unlikely to have helped many opponents given that the cards needed for a straight draw are so low. Here, the player with trip kings can probably allow opponents to see the turn card cheaply and reserve bigger bets for the last two betting rounds. While an opponent may strike lucky, there remains a 30 per cent chance that the trip kings could still improve to a full house or four of a kind, which would be highly unlikely to lose.

The turn

The revealing of the turn card, or 'fourth street' as it sometimes known, clarifies the situation even more, as players face the same considerations as on the flop. The difference lies in the fact that with just one card to come, assessing one's own hand and comparing it with the best that might result on the river, the last card, is much simpler.

Equally, calculating the pot odds when considering whether to bet or not is a straightforward task. Crucially, it must be remembered that any card that helps one player may improve an opponent's hand as well. The danger in this situation is that, having survived as far as the turn card, it is very easy to become committed to the pot and see the hand through to the showdown. Despite believing it is a probable loser, the amount in the pot and the proximity to claiming it can all too easily prompt a player into casting good money after bad.

Playing the turn

As ever, discipline and realism are needed at this point in the game, irrespective of how many chips a player has already contributed to the pot. The fact that the minimum bet on the turn and the river is double that of the previous two rounds should encourage players to be circumspect regarding their chances.

Once again, how to play the turn is dependent on a player's position, the number of opponents and the betting that has already occurred. A maximum bet when clearly leading is advisable, to put pressure on opponents with drawing hands who, although tempted by the pot odds on offer, will need to improve on the river to win. In most cases, some doubt will remain over the ultimate result. For instance, if a flop of 4h, Ac, Jh is supplemented with the 6h on the turn, then a player holding Ah, Js is in a reasonable position with the

TRAPPING AN OPPONENT

♦ ♣ ♥ ♠

Opportunities to trap opponents by inducing them to place a bet when they are already losing do not occur very frequently, so it is essential to take advantage of such opportunities when they arise. For the most part, this will involve sitting tight on a winning hand in the hope that an opponent improves sufficiently to risk making a bet. A player seated in early position who checks on the flop with Ks, Qh when the board displays 10s, Kd, Kc ideally wants an opponent to possess As, Jd, for example, to complete a straight should the Qc appear on the turn. By indicating weakness with another check, anyone who has made a straight could well be tempted to walk into the trap by betting. If that is the case, a call will suffice to see the river card, following which a bet is recommended, in the hope that the opponent with the straight has misread the situation and calls, or raises, suspecting a bluff.

PLAYING THE TURN

FLOP	TURN

PLAYER'S CARDS (a)	LIKELY DANGER

PLAYER'S CARDS (b)	LIKELY DANGER

Above: Although the quality of a hand may be defined by the flop, doubt over the final outcome could still exist once the turn card is revealed. The A, J offsuit for the top two pairs and the nut flush draw is still vulnerable if a bet on the flop is called, indicating that an opponent may already have two hearts. The possibility of a flush draw having been made on the turn is high, but the player holding A, J still has 11 cards that can win the pot, with the aces, jacks and remaining hearts all helping.

top two pairs and odds of about 3 to 1 against making the nut flush or a full house. Only an opponent who has already made a flush – which could yet be beaten – is likely to call, or more likely raise, any bet in this situation.

By contrast, if the player holds Ah, 6s instead, given the same board cards, then the options are less promising, especially if the betting on the flop indicated that one opponent may also have an A while another was drawing to the flush. Now only another heart on the river can guarantee success, since an A, 6 or a J could give an opponent a better full house. Therefore, choosing whether to bet in this situation must be guided by the inferences drawn from earlier play.

Reading the betting

While players are naturally inclined to focus on their own prospects of winning, the clues on offer from the betting of opponents are ignored only by the foolhardy. Whatever the standard of the game, players bet for a reason and deducing the rationale behind their strategy is all part of the challenge presented by Texas Hold 'em. For example if a flop of 10s, 2c, 5c generated only light betting, but a player in early position bets after the turn card is revealed as the 4c, then a flush is surely indicated.

Should that player hold Ac, Jc for the nut flush and be raised by an opponent, then the natural conclusion, however unlikely, is that a straight flush has been secured with pocket cards of 6c, 3c. An opponent with a lower-ranking flush may have called, but would probably credit the player with possession of the Ac for a flush draw at least, making the hand vulnerable.

Any player trying to draw to the flush without the Ac, meanwhile, is likely to fold. The danger for the player

Above: A sizeable pot develops as the game unfolds. In a fairly loose Texas Hold 'em game that features several players regularly paying to see the turn card, substantial pots can develop. As the minimum bet doubles after the turn, players must be certain in their own minds that contributing more chips to the pot is justified by the strength of their cards, not merely the size of the pot on offer.

READING THE BETTING

PLAYER'S CARDS	FLOP	TURN

POSSIBLE DANGERS

Above: Clues to the strength of an opponent's hand will usually arise from the betting and, on occasions, players have to accept that the improbable can happen. A player holding Ac, Jc, for example, would normally expect to take the pot if a third club should appear on the turn. But if the betting up to this point has been light, players with weak starting hands could still be in contention. Should a bet supporting the A-high flush be called, it is possible that an opponent could be drawing to a full house. However, a raise from an opponent would logically indicate that an unlikely straight flush has been achieved with the 3c, 6c.

with the Ac, Jc in this example comes from calling the raise while potentially already losing, only to see the 3c, 6c, 7c or 8c on the river. Judging by the betting, a straight flush for the opponent would then seem highly likely, not just possible.

The river

Typically, it is rare for more than three players to be contesting the pot by the time the river card is dealt, whichever betting structure is in place. Players should expect that anyone still in opposition at this stage must like something about the board cards, even if to win they may yet need to execute an impressive bluff.

Once the final card is revealed, players are able to see exactly what their hand comprises and also the potential hands available to opponents. Yet the best hand may still not win depending on the perceived threats held by the board cards and the nature of the betting throughout play. Unless holding the nuts, calling a large bet with a hand that is a potential but not guaranteed winner can test the nerves of even the most experienced player. Whether such a call would be justified depends on the likelihood of the hand proving the best and, as usual, whether the pot odds favour a call even if it is likely to lose. Clues are available from the cards and the previous betting rounds, and play on the river often hinges upon a correct reading of the game. In this regard, knowledge of opponents' playing styles is often crucial, although sitting in on a game with total strangers, as when playing online, understandably makes this more difficult.

Available options

There are not too many options available on the river. A player holding what seems to be a winning hand must concentrate on pot management by doing what it takes to encourage opponents to contribute more chips. In early position during a pot-limit or no-limit game, a small bet relative to those of previous rounds might be enough to goad an opponent into calling, just to prove that the hand represented is actually

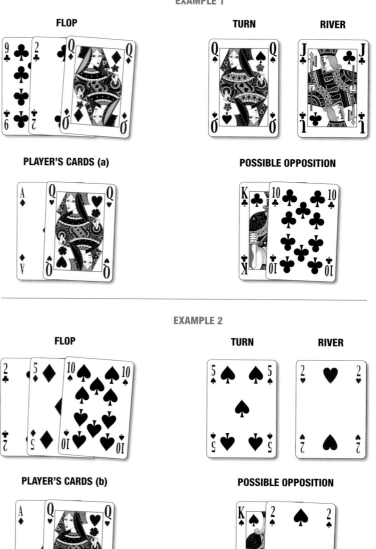

AVAILABLE OPTIONS

EXAMPLE 1

FLOP / TURN / RIVER

PLAYER'S CARDS (a)

POSSIBLE OPPOSITION

EXAMPLE 2

FLOP / TURN / RIVER

PLAYER'S CARDS (b)

POSSIBLE OPPOSITION

Above: Clues from the previous betting rounds will help to make a decision on the river, especially when a strong hand may have been beaten on the river. In example 1, the player holding three queens would have to fear that an opponent had completed a flush if the opponent had previously called a large bet after the turn card. In example 2, holding the A in a light betting heat may be enough to win when the board reveals two low pairs and a medium kicker. But a lack of earlier betting action may ensure the final round is contested by several players, any of which could hold a vital low card such as a 2 to make an unlikely full house.

> ### FISH, GEESE AND SHEEP
> ♦ ♣ ♥ ♠
>
> Those unable to read a game are considered weak players with 'fish', 'geese' and 'sheep' being just a few of the common terms used by experienced players to refer to them. The challenge for novices is to improve with experience, to avoid continually making the right move at the wrong time. Competent amateur players may be regarded as 'fish' when they move up to a higher level and start competing with the sharks of the professional poker world.

JUDGEMENT CALLS

Playing the river when not holding the best possible hand is a common experience for all Texas Hold 'em players, although this is often due to the inclination of many to keep calling bets from the flop onwards with hands that improve just enough to put them in further trouble. A player holding Ad, 3d, for instance, may have stayed to the end, having seen the board cards revealed as As, 8s, Kh, 6c and finally 3s. But if an opponent has matched bets all the way, it is unsafe to assume that two pairs of aces and threes will be enough to win. If the betting has been at the minimum level throughout, then the opponent probably has an A, could already have two higher pairs and might conceivably have played for the flush draw holding Ks, Qs. Sometimes, however, the river card may simply complete a nondescript board, which makes it possible for a player with, perhaps, just an A-high, to steal the pot by betting first. Judging whether to try this move will depend on how confident a player is that small bets and checks in previous rounds confirm that nobody has a hand good enough to call such a bet.

held. A bet is advised in a fixed-limit game, as there is no point in allowing opponents to check and thus miss the chance of winning a few more chips.

When in a later position, playing the leading hand is more straightforward, since a bet or raise can always be made in confidence. Hands that are made on or before the river but could easily be beaten are more difficult to play. Having three of a kind by the turn when the river card puts a third club on the board, for example, is an awkward position to be in if it is plausible an opponent has pursued the flush all along.

Similarly, a board of two pairs and a low kicker will sometimes generate little action and be won by a player holding an A. It is difficult to call a large bet with the highest kicker when the prospect of encountering a slow-played full house looms. Players will then sometimes have to rely on their instincts concerning the opposition as much as the odds at work.

The river card will often signal the failure of some players to draw the card needed for a straight or a flush. Folding is the usual option here, unless the board holds the promise of a bluff. These are more likely to succeed in games that permit large bets, since, in fixed-limit Texas Hold 'em, the cost of calling is simply not enough to force opponents to surrender the chips already bet.

Left: Once the river card has been dealt to the board, a player who holds the nuts should definitely bet, the real test being to stake just enough that opponents with inferior hands are tempted to call for fear of being bluffed. If the bet is too big, the opposition may well fold leaving the winner of the hand with a smaller profit than might have been the case.

JUDGEMENT CALLS

FLOP	TURN	RIVER

PLAYER'S CARDS   **POSSIBLE OPPOSITION**

Above: This example illustrates the problems that can result by the river when playing an A with a low kicker. The A on the flop for a high pair offered promise, but if any bet on the flop or the turn was called, then any one of several credible hands could be in opposition. An opponent with an A and a higher kicker could easily have made two better pairs, while a flush is equally possible. In this instance, the improvement for the A, 3 could lead to a player calling a bet with a beaten hand.

Know your opponents

Successful Texas Hold 'em players are obviously aware of the opportunities presented by various starting hands and the board cards as they are revealed. What separates the excellent players from those of average ability, however, is their aptitude for quickly gauging an opponent's playing style and reacting accordingly. Indeed, the very best players will alternate their style throughout a session to confuse and unsettle opponents, many of whom are prone to make predictable moves governed by their personality. Such players generally fall into one of four recognizable categories, irrespective of the stake level at which they normally play poker.

Know your solid players

Solid players, often known as 'rocks', are those who have the discipline and patience to fold the majority of hands and cautiously wait for an unbeatable hand – the nuts – or something very close to it, before committing too many chips to the pot. Conscious of their playing position at all times and the chip stacks in front of their opponents, they have a tendency to play only the highest-ranking starting hands and support them vigorously unless there are enough loose players at the table to justify setting a trap. In fixed-limit games, such players will play the percentages and seize upon mistakes.

Know your tight-aggressive players

At high-stakes tournament level, most solid players will adopt a tight-aggressive mode of play, folding anything but the best starting hands and pressurizing opponents with large pre-flop raises that leave little doubt as to the strength of their pocket cards. On those occasions when their strategy backfires, however, such players will still retain the discipline to fold rather than chase their losses.

KNOW YOUR OPPONENTS

SOLID PLAYER

LOOSE PLAYER

E

F

SMALL BLIND 100

BIG BLIND 200

D

RAISE 500

D

1,000 CALL

A

FISH

LOOSE PLAYER

RAISE 1,000

CALL 500

C

B

TIGHT-AGGRESSIVE PLAYER

CALLING STATION

Above: Each individual's style of play has a profound bearing on the shape of any game. After the deal in this no-limit Texas Hold 'em contest, player A raises out of position with a low pair, in keeping with an enterprising approach to the game, while player B cannot resist calling, because of a desire to be involved in the action. Player C, holding a premium hand, takes advantage by raising again with the pair of queens, only to be called by player D, who, through inexperience, is unable to read the implications behind the previous bets. A solid player like player E will be prepared to fold the A, 9 suited for the loss of the small blind, but a loose player on the big blind could easily call the further 800 chips for the chance, however remote, of claiming a large pot.

PLAYER A

PLAYER B

PLAYER C

PLAYER D

PLAYER E

PLAYER F

Know your loose players

Those who play poker for social rather than financial reasons are likely to indulge in a much looser style of play. A desire to stay in the action characterizes such players, and their enthusiasm for Texas Hold 'em will make them likely to call a raise when holding a small pair or 8, 7 suited in the small blind, for example, after which they may disregard the pot odds for an outside chance of winning.

Other examples of loose play include raising repeatedly when out of position and calling in contradiction of the evidence on display when needing cards to win. Such players tend to have volatile periods of good and bad fortune, and their hands are difficult to read, making them dangerous opponents.

Know your calling stations

For a player with pretensions to winning, knowing the 'calling stations' – these being players who repeatedly call other players' bets, irrespective of their chances of winning – is crucial. These players will frequently upset the odds by drawing unlikely winning hands. Being suspicious by nature, they find it difficult to release any chance of winning a pot, even in the face of particularly antagonistic betting. No matter how big the raise or how unlikely their chances of winning, calling stations will play sheriff as they insist on verifying that the raiser has the hand being represented.

The tendency to call, irrespective of the pot odds or inferences on offer during play, is very common among novices. They are often insufficiently familiar with the nuances of the game to understand the inferences behind a bet, which makes them very difficult to bluff. Should a good player not realize soon enough that an opponent is unable to interpret the meaning behind large bets, valuable chips could quickly change ownership when bluffs are repeatedly called.

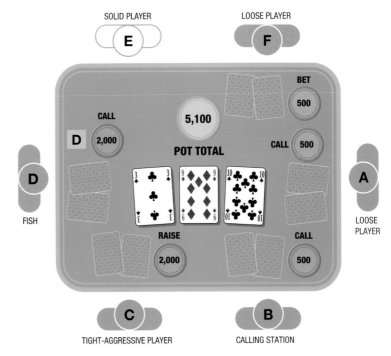

IMPACT ON THE BETTING

Above: After the flop, the loose players in early position press their case by betting in defiance of the pre-flop raise by player C who again tries to force the opposition out of the pot. However, player D sees a possible straight materializing and calls another big raise, unaware that the pot odds are vastly inferior to the chances of catching a J, one of which – Jc – could make someone else a flush. With over 10,000 chips in the pot, players F, A and B may yet contribute more, as the potential rewards for winning override their concerns at being beaten.

SAME HANDS, DIFFERENT APPROACH

Above: By way of contrast with the first two examples, here the same pre-flop situation is replicated, but in a game between solid and experienced players. A flat call from player A with the low pair is raised by player C, who, content to pick up the pot right now, presses home the early advantage with the pair of queens. Player D reads this as indicative of a high pair and knows that if player C has kings or queens, then any chance of improvement is compromised. Similarly, player E will fear that player C has an A with a bigger kicker, thus undermining the A, 9 suited. Both players fold, as does player F, at which point player A faces a difficult call for 800 chips with a hand that should probably be folded in the face of such aggression from an astute opponent.

Betting structures

Although much of the expert guidance available on how to play Texas Hold 'em is relevant, whichever betting structure is in place, each has sufficient impact on the culture of the game to warrant consideration. The stakes are important too, emphasizing that anyone buying in to a game ought to play at a stake level commensurate with their financial means. Players who participate in games for money that they cannot afford to lose are rarely able to focus entirely on their poker and run the risk of compounding their error with poor play. Contrasting betting structures were devised to satisfy the tastes of different players and their various gambling preferences, with three in particular emerging as the most popular.

Fixed-limit

This is the betting structure favoured by the majority of recreational cash game players, although there are numerous professionals who grind out a living playing fixed-limit Texas Hold 'em in the casinos and card rooms of the world. In the resort casinos of Las Vegas and Atlantic City, the small-stakes limit games are frequently populated by 'rounders' – itinerant gamblers who play only premium hands and sit patiently waiting for the tourists to make mistakes.

Therein lies a clue as to the best way to play fixed-limit Texas Hold 'em, which is a game of position, and percentages. It favours conservative players who are reluctant to gamble wildly, since the scale of any betting during a hand is easier to predict. This helps players to calculate the upper limit of any possible losses while devising their betting strategy.

Right: In no-limit Texas Hold 'em the daunting prospect of throwing away all of one's chips in a single hand is always present.

FIXED-LIMIT EXAMPLE

Above: Raising before the flop with A, K offsuit is a perfectly legitimate tactic, whichever betting structure is in place, but the difficulties of pressing home the advantage in a fixed-limit game are illustrated here. Player B only has to call twice the minimum bet to stay in the game, while those players in the blinds could well call, even with mediocre hands, to see if the flop brings any help. Player A's attempt to reduce the field to perhaps one opponent, over whom the A, K will probably be a favourite to win, is thus hampered by the limit on the size of raise permitted.

In general, players are advised to apply rigid standards to the quality of hands they play, relative to their betting position. Pre-flop raises are less common in this form of the game, since it is difficult to force up to nine opponents to fold for the cost of a single bet. Following the flop, a checkraise in early position may suggest enough threat to cause opponents to fold, but bluffing in this position is rather hazardous. Indeed, bluffing is best kept to a minimum, as players are restricted from betting the sums needed to intimidate the opposition.

Pot-limit

Popular with both professionals and amateurs, pot-limit Texas Hold 'em allows the freedom for players to bet more aggressively in support of their strong hands, to reduce the opposition and improve their chances of winning. Pots can quickly escalate in size, but a typical game with blinds set at a nominal level often features several players willing to see the flop. Making a pre-flop raise may encourage some opponents to fold, but the serious action normally begins after the flop has been revealed, since this is when most players are able to define their chances. If they are good, then the betting can be expected to increase, although it may not be until the turn card is dealt that the pot-sized bets start to appear.

So, while the cost of seeing the flop may be relatively small, players are often happy to call with modest hands because the prospect of picking up a very large pot when the flop fits is that much greater than in the fixed-limit game.

Left: A player bets all-in before the flop having decided that, with just a few chips remaining, the hole cards justify taking the risk. Most often seen in no-limit games where making an all-in bet can be an aggressive tactic, players may still find themselves going all-in during fixed-limit games when they have fewer chips than required to make the minimum bet.

NO-LIMIT EXAMPLE

E   F

BIG BLIND 200   FOLDS

BET 1,000

SMALL BLIND

D   100   A

FOLDS   FOLDS

D

C   B

Above: By way of contrast, when there is no limit on the maximum bet, player A is better able to represent strength in an effort to dissuade opponents from calling. Player B's 10, 9 suited may have been worth a call of 400 chips in the fixed-limit example, but calling a pre-flop bet of 1,000 chips is much more difficult with the same hand. Unless the players in the blinds have at least a medium pair, they will probably surrender the pot, enabling player A to pick up the blinds with this aggressive move.

PLAYER B

NO-LIMIT TEXAS HOLD 'EM
♦ ♣ ♥ ♠

No-limit Texas Hold 'em is the most prominent of all tournament poker games and is regarded by many professionals as the most challenging variation currently being played. While it obviously suits the tournament format, the fact that players only ever stand to lose what may be a modest entry fee can disguise the inherent difficulties of playing it well as a cash game. For anyone hoping to make a modest bankroll stretch over several hours, buying in to a no-limit Texas Hold 'em game promises only anxiety and tension when an entire stack of chips could be lost in one hand. A tight or aggressive style is regarded as the most effective in the long term, which requires folding the majority of hands and betting aggressively, perhaps with a pre-flop raise, when holding premium cards. Having the patience to withstand such aggression from opponents while hoping to see cheap flops and light betting could lead to plenty of inactivity. Yet aggression is definitely an asset in the no-limit game, meaning that anyone who is not prepared to risk their entire chip stack on one hand is probably better suited to fixed-limit Texas Hold 'em.

Tournament play

Prior to the inception of the WSOP in 1970, tournament poker was virtually unknown, but this situation has changed dramatically. The success of the knockout format and the concept of the winner taking all permeated Las Vegas casinos and soon spread to the rest of the world. By the end of the 20th century, television had realized the potential for tournament poker to offer keen entertainment. No-limit Texas Hold 'em has since emerged as the most widespread tournament game, but fixed-limit and pot-limit Texas Hold 'em tournaments are also a key part of the professional circuit, as well as being popular in poker rooms, both real and online.

A new challenge

Although the basic concepts behind sound Texas Hold 'em play are relevant to tournaments, players must adjust their strategic thinking, to take account of the different context. The search for a definitive winner and the systematic increases in the blinds force players into taking a few more risks than might be the case in a cash game. The ebbs and flows of competition, and the corresponding impact on a player's chip stack, trigger many decisive confrontations as competitors try to keep themselves in contention for a share of the prize money.

Critics consider that luck plays too big a part in tournament poker and that the public's affection for knockout games owes much to a desire for quick and decisive results. For cash game devotees who take a long-term view of their work, constantly raising the blinds in order to provoke the inevitable confrontations is anathema, because hands that would ordinarily be folded, frequently have to be played during a tournament. Some players are highly skilled at both forms of the game, and there are enough successful tournament professionals who consistently finish in the money to suggest that, at the highest level at least, luck remains no substitute for skill and experience.

Choosing a tournament

The phenomenal success of world-class tournaments, is partly because anyone who wishes to enter usually has only to pay the required entry fee. This could run into thousands of dollars since many of the events cost upwards of US$1,000, with the fee for entering the WSOP world championship game currently set at US$10,000. That does not prevent the tournament from attracting up to 8,000 players for a competition that takes the best part of a week to complete.

TYPICAL TOURNAMENT SET-UP

Right: This represents the typical scene at the beginning of a tournament, with up to ten players seated at the table and each starting with, in this case, 5,000 chips. A single-table tournament would feature a maximum of ten players, but a multi-table tournament featuring one hundred entrants would see this scene replicated on nine other tables as play commences. The dealer button (D), which is moved clockwise round the table after each deal, indicates that player B will be the nominal dealer for the first hand. Card rooms will often employ a professional dealer to conduct proceedings, leaving the players free to concentrate on play.

PRIZE STRUCTURES

The prize structure in the formative years of tournament play was often a simple case of the winner taking all. Gradually, as tournament poker grew in popularity, the prize pools on offer led to a more equitable distribution of cash prizes, with the top 10 per cent of entrants now likely to win sufficient to cover their entry fee at least. To claim the more substantial prizes, however, still requires a player to finish in the top three or four per cent which is, understandably, a major challenge. The breakdown of the prize pool varies according to the numbers involved, the winner often claiming 50 per cent in events comprising less than 50 players, but only 25 per cent in those featuring 200 players or more. Although obviously more difficult to win, it is the prospect of turning a few dollars into a few thousand that makes large-scale, multi-table tournaments so appealing.

At a lower level, regular tournaments for players with tighter budgets exist, with online poker rooms offering the tournament experience for pocket-money entrance fees. The tournaments are varied in terms of style and structure. Daily or weekly competitions in real and online card rooms are supplemented by sit 'n' go tournaments, satellites, freerolls, qualifiers, turbo tournaments and single-table or multi-table events. There are also freeze-out or rebuy tournaments, meaning that, in terms of consumer choice, there is likely to be a tournament structure to suit every Texas Hold 'em player. Deciding which one to play will depend on a player's own personal tastes and financial means.

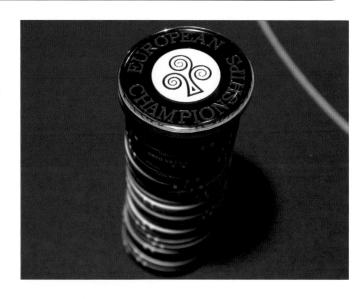

Above: A stack of chips as used in the European Poker Championships. Specifically branded chips are common in casinos and the idea extends to tournament events as well. Apart from the obvious promotional aspects associated with such branding, there is a practical purpose behind the use of exclusive chips since it prevents players from introducing chips from one establishment into a game at another.

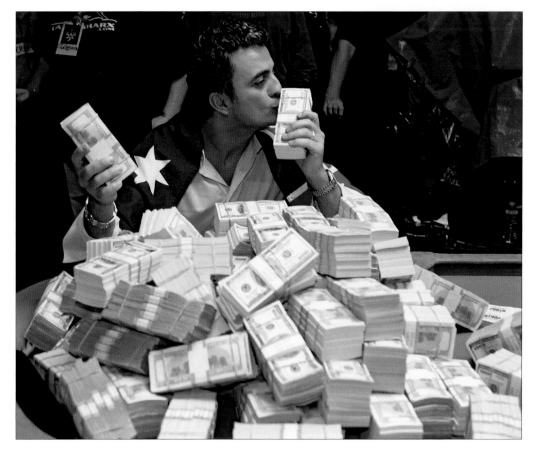

Left: Joe Hachem from Melbourne, Australia, kisses a stack of US$100 bills having won the first prize of US$7.5 million at the WSOP world championship in 2005. Entries for the event have increased massively over the last decade, fuelled by thousands of online qualifiers, leading to a corresponding increase in the top prize. After the US clampdown on online gaming in late 2006, it remains to be seen whether entries for the WSOP will be reduced as a result.

Early stages

Since no-limit Texas Hold 'em is the most popular tournament game, the general considerations detailed here will focus on the situations encountered in such an event, although many of the comments will apply equally well to pot-limit and fixed-limit contests. Also, any reference to cash sums will be in US dollars, this being the common currency of poker the world over.

The entry fees involved have an impact, with it being likely that players will play more loosely in a freeroll tournament in which there is no entry fee at all than they would having paid US$1,000 for the privilege of competing. In a similar vein, tournaments that offer the chance to rebuy chips during the first hour or two of play also invite players to take chances early on in the game. A successful all-in bet could double or triple a player's chip stack to secure an advantage, which is a tempting move, given that immediate elimination from the tournament is not at stake.

Freeze-out tournaments, the main focus of attention here, are generally characterized by most players easing themselves into the game as they assess their opponents. However, even these will include a minority of players who play aggressively from the start.

Stealing the blinds

The difference between cash games and tournaments is that the blinds will rise at specified intervals of anything between two minutes and a couple of hours. Players who sit waiting for a perfect hand to materialize risk being anted away before having a chance to act. Irrespective of whether playing in a single or multi-table tournament, the need to put in the occasional pre-flop raise to steal the blinds must be considered. Successful moves such as this, whether they are bluffs or not, help to keep a player's chip stack intact while covering the cost of the compulsory bets as the deal moves round the table.

While the blinds are modest at the start, the need to pressurize the blinds when there is little interest before the flop is a recurring theme during play as they increase in scale. Since this tactic is common, combating such a move when in the big blind, for example, usually needs possession of a good starting hand to justify a call. If one opponent repeatedly targets a specific player in this situation, a substantial re-raise might put them off doing so for a while. In tournament play, timing is everything, since one wrong move can devastate a player's chip stack, if not guarantee elimination.

EARLY STAGES

Right: This shows the situation in a typical tournament after the betting has already risen through a couple of levels. The total number of chips currently held by each player is indicated, all having started the tournament with 5,000 chips. The player in seat D has been eliminated, with player E having profited from the early action. Player C is under the most pressure, because, with the blinds having risen from 25 (small) and 50 (big) to 100 and 200, for example, the minimum bet represents more than one-twelfth of the player's total chip count. As players are eliminated during a multi-table tournament, others are moved from adjoining tables to occupy vacated seats. This keeps the ratio of players per table consistent and enables the organizers to gradually reduce the number of tables in operation.

Survival of the fittest

At the beginning of a tournament, each player receives an equal number of chips, the objective being to amass the total in play by eliminating all opposition. Events in which the blind levels are raised every 15 minutes or less do not provide much scope for players to remain patient. However, while some aggression is required, players should still be wary of fighting early betting wars when dealt only fair starting hands. Those who are intent on pursuing a death-or-glory policy can usually be left to eliminate each other as the tournament settles into its rhythm.

No tournament is ever won within the first few hands, so surviving until the later stages of the game should be uppermost in players' minds. This is certainly true in events with much longer intervals between the increased betting levels. The general advice is for players to monitor the level of the average chip stack and stay ahead of that figure. In online tournaments, such information is updated after each hand, but at a multi-table event in a real card room, a quick glance at the other tables for an assessment of the opposition's chip standing might be necessary. There is no suggestion that a player holding a premium hand should never

consider betting aggressively. Good opportunities to double-up with an all-in bet will occur, but only by exercising a high degree of selectivity over which hands to play – and when – will a player maintain interest in a competition.

Above: Jeff Williams, the American student who won the 2006 EPT Grand Final in Monte Carlo having qualified via satellite tournaments on the PokerStars online site. Though experienced tournament professionals often have the edge in big events, the proliferation of online poker tournaments means that Internet players can rapidly develop the skills required to be competitive at the highest level.

STEALING THE BLINDS

PLAYER H

Left: As the tournament develops, the need to accumulate chips to meet the demands of the ever-increasing blinds prompts players to exert pressure when they can. Here, the action has been folded around to player H, who, with A, Q offsuit, makes a large bet, hoping to pick up the 300 chips on offer from the blinds without a contest.

Middle stages

As the tournament nears its middle stages, with as many as half the original starters already eliminated, the strategy to adopt very much depends on how many chips a player still holds. Being the chip leader is obviously beneficial, but holding a better-than-average chip position should at least help a player fend off the pressure of the ever-increasing blinds.

By now, the big blind could easily be as much as a fifth of the original starting stack, emphasizing the need to keep picking up pots on a regular basis. A run of poor cards in the face of aggressive betting can make this prospect exceedingly difficult, so making a few bluffs is almost unavoidable.

Under normal circumstances, many of the loose and reckless players will have been knocked out by this stage. As a result, the more astute players who are left may be more susceptible to a credible bluff, since they have a sharper awareness of the inferences behind any bet. Also, as the possibility of claiming a prize draws closer for those managing to avoid elimination, players are sometimes prone to becoming more defensive, which presents another situation to be exploited.

Chip count

From the middle stages onwards, it becomes essential for players to monitor their opponents' chip positions as well as their own. Assuming that to finish in the prizes means making the final table, a keen eye on the chip counts will help guide a player's tactical and strategic thinking as the number of opponents dwindles. Anyone in the top third has the chance to fold a succession of hands and avoid confrontations, while short-stacked opponents battle against each other. Also, the possibility of intimidating opponents with the occasional large raise to force them all-in if they call is another available tactic.

Short-stacked players can expect to be pressurized all the time as the blinds eat into their reserves. In this position there may not be time to wait for a large

PLAYER B   **PLAYER C**   **PLAYER D**

PLAYER A

Right: The ability to change gear during the middle stages of a tournament is a major asset. This means that players may start to bet with lower-ranking starting hands than usual when they have an above-average chip count and the advantage of position. For those low on chips, pressure will come from all quarters and they may have little option but to go all-in with a poor hand. Here, for example, player J makes a substantial raise that threatens each of those still to act with elimination in this hand, given that there are three further betting rounds to negotiate. Player B, in particular, has a limited number of opportunities to survive, given the big blind is approaching, but decides to fold the J, 8 offsuit on this occasion. The action now is on player D, who has an uncomfortable decision to make with the pair of sevens.

MIDDLE STAGES

pair or A, K before pushing all the remaining chips into the pot, so opportunities with lesser hands have to be taken. Certainly, when a player is down to no more than five times the big blind, every hand must be considered in terms of its all-in potential, although the need to double-up one's stack may arise sooner than that. Another point to bear in mind is that the chip leaders may also fold in the face of aggression from mid-ranking players, since they could well be reluctant to sacrifice valuable chips with a place at the final table beckoning.

Changing gear

The ability to vary one's style of play is an asset in any form of poker, but being able to change gear during a tournament can help improve or stabilize a player's chip position. A burst of aggressive play featuring pre-flop and post-flop raises may be enough to win a few blinds and reluctant calls from opponents locked into a tight, conservative pattern. Winning enough to cover the blinds for another three or four circuits of the table will typically give a player 30 or more additional hands to consider and time to see more opponents eliminated.

This strategy is more effective when implemented by someone who has previously exhibited all the traits of a sound but cautious player. When short-stacked, such a ploy may smack of desperation, but for those within reach of the prize-money spots, it offers the chance to exploit any timidity in opponents, regardless of their chip position. It does mean being less selective over which starting hands to play, bringing with it the risk of being caught out by a strong hand. However, if the strategy is unsuccessful but still leaves a player with a manageable chip stack, consolidating for a while by reverting to caution once more remains an option.

As the tournament moves towards its conclusion, the value of a player's hole cards may be less significant to any betting strategy than the current chip positions of opponents. If three short-stacked opponents go all-in before the flop, even a large pair such as kings or aces may be worth folding. Competing against several opponents with a high pair simply increases the combined chances that one of them will beat the hand. Winning the pot could mean knocking out three opponents, but losing it could see just two of them eliminated, while the other emerges with a more substantial chip stack than need have been the case.

TACTICAL DECISIONS

PLAYER J

Left: As the pressure mounts, the need for discipline from those within touching distance of the final table increases. In this separate example, ordinarily player J would consider the pair of jacks worthy of a bet and, having already bet 3,000 chips in the big blind, a further bet of 11,100 to call player G could establish a chance to knock out three players in one hand. But a win for player G would see the pair of them in a similar chip position. Under the circumstances, a fold may be better, since a win for player G would still leave that opponent trailing player J by over 20,000 chips, which remains a significant advantage. This highlights how the value of the cards themselves may become less important compared to the other strategic concerns that develop throughout the tournament.

The end game

To reach the final table in any regular multi-table tournament, a player is likely to have prospered on several different tables, for a number of hours, against up to nine opponents at a time. Despite the fact that luck may well have played a part at some stage of the competition, it is the players with the skill to capitalize upon their fortune rather than relying on luck alone who will usually reach the prize-money spots. The difference between first place and tenth, however, will still be represented by a huge variation in the prizes available. Having successfully made it to the final table, plotting a strategy towards ultimate victory will again be dependent on the chips at a player's disposal.

Players who have short stacks will be highly aware that every hand could be their last and should bet all-in while they have enough chips to make the risk worthwhile. By allowing the stack to dwindle, a player might be faced with having to win a succession of all-in bets to find a way back into the game and, since many such confrontations provide no better than an even-money chance of winning, achieving this is exceedingly difficult.

Changing fortunes

Players with medium-sized chip stacks still need to exercise caution as the tournament reaches its final stages. Should the chip leader start bullying opponents with aggressive raises, it is best to avoid confrontations for as long as possible in the hope that those with shorter stacks succumb to the pressure. Raising a bet from an opponent with many more chips can only be confidently considered while holding an excellent hand.

As the eliminations continue and the number of players falls to four or five, the increased blinds will circulate the table much quicker. Players in the blinds can expect opponents to try stealing them with ever-larger bets, although judging what cards they hold becomes more of a challenge. With fewer players, the value of the average winning hand decreases and more risks are therefore taken with marginal starting hands.

Large pots contested by two players will develop repeatedly and fortunes can change rapidly. Having half as many chips as the leader when in an all-in battle will see the players swap positions should the low stack triumph, underlining that a tournament is never won until the final opponent has been eliminated.

THE FINAL TABLE

Right: Reaching the final table of a large multi-table tournament will usually ensure a prize, but the differential between first and tenth is still quite substantial. This example shows that there are eight players left in the event, but, with the big blind now 10,000 chips, five of those in contention effectively have less than four bets each. For players A, C and I, the best policy may be to play passively for the next few hands while those with the low stacks eliminate each other.

Heads-up

When there are only two players left competing heads-up at the table both will be assured of a prize usually well in excess of their entry fee. To secure victory, however, requires each player to pressurize the other with large bets, frequent bluffs and the willingness to support some weak starting hands.

Against one opponent, J, 7 offsuit represents the average hand and will win on half the occasions it is played. Holding a card higher than a J therefore offers a decent opportunity, while being dealt an A or any pair could easily warrant an all-in bet, whether having the majority or minority of chips.

Aggression is very important, since the blinds by this stage are usually so high that folding on two or three successive occasions can seriously weaken a player's chip position. Even when holding a substantial lead, with perhaps 80 per cent of the chips, a player cannot afford to fold too often, while losing to an all-in bet from an opponent on two successive occasions will see the lead change hands.

Generally, good heads-up play involves pressing home any perceived advantage as forcefully as possible in what amounts to an archetypal poker confrontation. Practising heads-up play is advisable, since there is no doubt that some players respond to the challenge of one-to-one combat much better than others. Ultimately, with almost every hand being contested, the conclusion to several hours of intense competition could be swift, with the winning hand often ranked lower than a pair. This may seem a little anti-climactic, given the quality of hands that will have been played to reach the last two, but both winner and runner-up will have successfully shown a consummate range of poker skills to be contesting the concluding hand of the tournament.

HEADS-UP

Above: When just two players are left, a heads-up situation exists, with the size of the blinds ensuring that almost every pot is worth contesting, irrespective of the cards held by each player. Ordinarily, a player either raises before the flop, or folds, since merely calling a bet invites an aggressive move from the opponent. This is the point at which a player's nerve is tested to the full.

RAPIDLY CHANGING FORTUNES

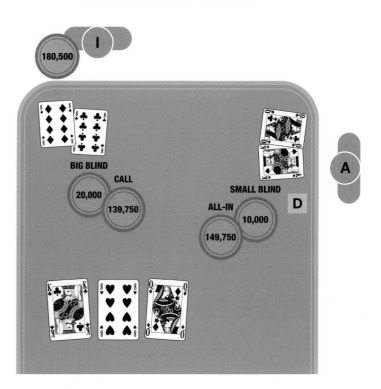

Above: Even a substantial chip lead at this stage of the game can soon be eradicated, with player I on the verge of winning here, having called player A's all-in bet from the small blind. Both have above-average hands and the flop, although favouring the chip leader, still provides player A with an outside chance to double up and take the lead. Any of the four remaining kings and queens in the deck will make a better full house and prompt another deal, and another potentially decisive confrontation.

OMAHA

In Omaha, the action begins with the small blind and big blind being posted by the players to the dealer's left, just as in Texas Hold 'em. The dealer deals the cards one at a time to each player, clockwise around the table until everyone has four cards face down prior to the first betting round. Once the first-round betting is complete, the dealer reveals the flop which consists of three cards face up on the table which all players can use towards finalizing their hand. A second betting round takes place after which the turn card is dealt. Betting limits usually double at this stage of the game and, after a third betting round, the river card is revealed. This acts as a prelude to the final round of betting. The winner is the player who either makes an unmatched bet during the game or who holds the best poker hand at the showdown, of two hole cards and three from the board.

Below: When assessing which starting hands to play, consideration must be given to the likely possibilities presented by the board cards when they are all revealed. Half of the time, at least one pair will be present, as in the first example, making four of a kind a possibility and a full house almost certain. Players will usually need at least a straight to win and ample opportunities exist, since, as in the second example, three cards or more to a straight will appear on four out of every five occasions. However, flushes are regular winners, too, with three or more cards to a flush on the board occurring 40 per cent of the time as shown in the third example.

WHAT TO EXPECT FROM THE BOARD

FLOP   TURN   RIVER

EXAMPLE 1

EXAMPLE 2

EXAMPLE 3

Almost unheard of before the 1980s, Omaha – Omaha Hold 'em if preferred – is one of the most popular games played at home and online, and is firmly rooted on the professional circuit. Omaha tournaments reflect the most common betting structures applied to the game, though they are often played for high stakes. The pot-limit variation allows players room to manoeuvre, since the capacity to make pot-sized bets and raises creates bluffing opportunities. Fixed-limit Omaha tends to reward knowledgeable and often conservative players in the long run.

The game shares the same basic structure as Texas Hold 'em, with players receiving four hole cards, not two, prior to the five board cards being revealed. Also, their hands must comprise two hole cards and three from the board. These differences completely change the nature of the game and the strategies that should be applied in the search for success. The major factors to consider are reading the cards, understanding the odds and observing opponents. Acknowledging the impact of the betting structure – pot-limit or fixed-limit – on a player's strategic thinking is also important and this will be reflected in the following analysis of the game.

Crucial considerations

The starting point when considering any poker strategy is to contemplate the end of the game in order to understand the quality of hand that is likely to prevail. In draw poker or five-card stud, this may be as little as a pair of queens, while in Texas Hold 'em, two pairs and three of a kind are frequent winners. This is prone to confuse even experienced Texas Hold 'em players who are new to Omaha, a game in which a hand such as trip aces will very rarely prove good enough.

The minimum hand normally required to win at Omaha is a straight, but flushes and full houses are so frequent that even a straight is quite weak. Generally, it will win only when the board cards make a full house or flush impossible to achieve. Before assessing the relative merits of any starting hand, it is pertinent to consider the likely outcome on the board once the five community cards – the widow – have been revealed.

There are three key issues to remember, beginning with the fact that half the time at least one pair will appear, making a full house very likely. Second, at least

Above: Players receive four cards in Omaha prior to the first betting round and this represents a fairly good starting hand given that it comprises high-ranking cards and offers chances of a straight. It is, however, compromised by containing four hearts since this obviously reduces the number of available hearts in the deck with which the player could make a flush.

three cards of one suit will be seen in four out of every ten widows, emphasizing the potential for flushes. Third, 80 per cent of the time, three cards that fit a straight will be present, underlining why this is the minimum rank that hand players should be aiming to achieve.

Starting hands

Armed with a knowledge of what hands are likeliest to win at the showdown, players are better able to assess the quality of hand required to justify competing for the pot. After the deal, any four cards that offer realistic chances of full houses, flushes and straights are worth consideration, but Omaha is renowned as a game that is usually won by the best possible hand – the nuts. High-ranking cards, therefore, especially aces, have greater value because they offer players the chance to hit the best straights, flushes and full houses available. Given how often these hands occur, it is always preferable to have the nut flush when there is no pair on the board to indicate a full house might exist.

GOOD STARTING HANDS

Above: A good starting hand in Omaha is one in which all six two-card combinations offer a chance to fit the board cards to make a potential winning hand, with at least a straight usually required. High-ranking pocket cards are best, but their value is not as significant before the flop as in Texas Hold 'em. Both examples here are favoured to fit the highest-value straights, flushes and full houses and should be played almost without exception.

FAIR STARTING HANDS

Above: Any hand that offers four or more viable combinations is certainly worthy of consideration. Here, the Ad, Qh, Qs, 7s offers full house and A-high straight possibilities, although the flush potential of the Qs, 7s combination is relatively weak. Should the board feature three spades not including the A or K, then the Q-high flush is in severe danger of being outranked. The second example has fair straight and full house potential, but both the K, 8 combinations will need plenty of help from the board to contribute to a winning hand.

POOR STARTING HANDS

Above: Opening hands of low-ranking cards or less than three working combinations should normally be folded. A pair of nines may contribute to a full house, but it could easily be second-best, even if a 9 appears. To complete the full house would need a pair on the board and anything higher than a 9 – a pair of kings for example, will lose to anyone with a K and one other card that matches the board. The straight potential of the 4, 3 combination is almost worthless, since a 5, 6, 7 on the board will lose to anyone holding 8, 4 or 9, 8. Similar problems apply to the other featured hand, in which the couplings that do work rank too low to make it anything but weak.

Good starting hands offer the most viable two-card combinations, of which there are six in all; the more of these that might fit any potential widow, the better the prospects of securing a playable hand. For instance, being dealt two pairs, such as Ad, As, 7h, 7c, is good, but holding Kd, Kc, Qd, Qc is arguably better. In the first case, the six combinations offer opportunities for a full house or even four of a kind, but the aces and sevens cannot be combined to make a straight. Having four different suits in the hand also rules out a flush. The second example, however, supplements the full house and four-of-a-kind potential, with the possibilities of high-ranking flushes and straights, offering more chances of success.

Pre-flop strategy

Before taking a closer look at the strategic possibilities that are presented by the first four cards, it is first worth highlighting other aspects of the game of Omaha that will have an influence on a player's betting decisions. In a high-stakes game featuring plenty of aggressive betting, players are far more likely to raise before the flop in an attempt to reduce the opposition. It is therefore a good policy to support only hands that offer multiple possibilities of winning. At a lower level, in fixed-limit home games, for example, pre-flop raises are much less likely, since the majority of players are inclined to call whatever cards are in their possession.

Essentially, this is what makes Omaha such a popular game, since social players enjoy the fact that even the most unpromising combination of hole cards will come good on the odd occasion. However, although players in a typical fixed-limit game will call to see perhaps half of all flops even with marginal hands, this does present them with the temptation of chasing hands that are destined to be second best. Pots can quickly escalate when there are several players involved, and this can encourage some of them to remain in the hand mistakenly pursuing value.

A constant appraisal of the odds and probabilities at work throughout the game remains the foundation for a disciplined approach to Omaha, and enables players to exploit those opponents who are always keen to be involved in the action.

Above: A player commits chips to the pot before the flop even though the hole cards displayed do not offer the greatest promise. Of the six two-card combinations available to the player, only two – the A, K and 6, 6 – have any merit in a hand that cannot make a flush because the cards are of four different suits. Unless the flop fits perfectly, the hand should probably be folded if an opponent bets in the second round.

Left: This example shows a strong starting hand which, because of the high value of the cards, has the potential to blend with a variety of flops to put the player in a good position. If the first three community cards are 9d, Ah, Qd then multiple opportunities open up for the player in the shape of straights, flushes and possibly even a full house.

Right: Irrespective of a player's starting hand, once the flop is dealt it is crucial to understand the immediate implications behind the board cards, and identify what may eventually form the nuts when all five are revealed. Anyone holding 9, 8 in the first example will have the best hand at present, with a straight, but a player with the A, K; A, Q or K, Q of clubs has the nut flush draw and the potential to hit a royal flush. The second example makes a full house highly probable and a player holding pocket kings will feel confident that kings over sixes will be enough, although the nuts at this stage is four sixes. Should nobody hold pocket sixes, then a further 6 on the board, or two aces, could yet see the hand beaten, or counterfeited. Gauging the likelihood of that occurring and whether it will help an opponent should always guide a player's betting strategy.

BE GUIDED BY THE FLOP

EXAMPLE 1

EXAMPLE 2

Seeking the nuts

The safest policy when contemplating Omaha is to remember that, once all the board cards have been shown, the winner in any showdown is likely to possess the nuts. This will not always be the case, but it should be at the forefront of any player's mind when holding a strong but not unbeatable hand and it should also be the guiding principle when assessing the options presented after the deal.

A good hand is one where the first four cards combine to offer six viable two-card hands. Having two high pairs including aces is good since four of a kind and nut full house prospects exist, along with the chance of making a high straight. Flushes are also regular winners, so holding the A plus one other card of a particular suit again guarantees the nut flush if three or more cards of that suit are among the board cards. This is a better position to be in than when dealt four spades, as the reduced number of spades left in the deck makes a flush in that suit less likely. Similarly, when holding four cards in a sequence such as K, Q, J, 10, the hand is always stronger if two cards each from two suits are present to add flush and straight flush potential to that of making a straight.

PROBLEMS WITH MARGINAL HANDS

PLAYER A

PLAYER B

FLOP

Above: Players with marginal hands need to exercise caution when the board cards offer seductive potential. Player A cannot use the K and the pair of fives in the hand simultaneously and has only a pair of kings at present, which is a weak hand on the flop. To make the hand a certain winner requires two kings or two fives in the last two cards; should a K and 5 or K and 4 appear, the full house could still lose to a player holding K, 10.

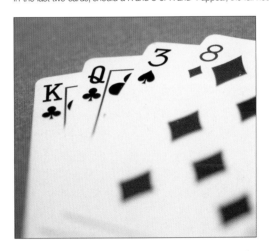

Left: The hole cards shown here represent a poor hand since only the Kc, Qc combination holds any real promise. Nevertheless, if the game features light betting and no pre-flop raises, as is customary when poker is played socially, hands such as these are much more likely to be retained than folded. A pair of eights on the flop, in this case, could then change the complexion of the hand altogether.

MORE COMBINATIONS

Omaha games can feature up to ten players, this being the normal number for a cash game staged by a casino or online poker site. This many participants ensures that 40 cards – almost 80 per cent of the deck – are in play immediately after the deal and with each player forming six two-card combinations from their hole cards, 60 of these exist before the betting begins. This contributes to the typically high value of winning hands and underlines why players should always be trying to attain the best hand possible. However, while hands featuring high pairs, suited cards or connecting cards are favourable, even two-card combinations with modest potential regularly confound expectations. This is particularly true in fixed-limit Omaha games, when players with one decent two-card hand will often call to see the flop and find that their least valuable cards – 'rags' – suddenly become significant. For example a player holding Kc, Qc, 8d, 3s, would realistically expect only the K, Q combination to offer any chance of winning, but if the flop is 8h, 3d, Ks, then nine cards from the unseen 45 in the deck provide the player with a 38 per cent chance of achieving a full house. Any K, 8 or 3 will suffice, along with any two of the remaining three queens, although not all of these necessarily constitute the nuts. Should the turn and river cards be Kd and Ad, a player with a pair of aces or A, K would win, but the example does highlight the impact of having many more two-card combinations in play.

Post-flop strategy

Whatever the potential of a player's hole cards, the flop is the moment in the game when a hand's strength is clarified. Ideally, players will already have a mental picture of the cards they would prefer to see, although the principal consideration at this stage is the same as in Texas Hold 'em. In order to continue in the hand, players need to be confident that they have either the best hand or a realistic chance of achieving it.

This means identifying, first, which hand is likely to constitute the nuts and, second, whether it is possible to obtain it, given the cards at a player's disposal. Careless or inexperienced players are frequently seduced by the merits of a good hand only to discover, to their cost, that it is ultimately not good enough. As ever, a quick assessment of how many cards might make or break a hand, and the odds against them appearing, is crucial in determining whether to bet.

A player already holding the nuts can obviously focus on pot management and do whatever is required to keep opponents interested. They will often have sufficient scope for improvement to feel justified in calling a minimum bet to see the turn card. Loose players may even be prepared to call a raise in a fixed-limit game if they are slow to recognize that the nuts may already have been acquired. On the other hand, a check by the player holding a lock hand, which is essentially a hand that cannot lose, is likely to keep more opponents involved until later in the game, when the betting levels rise.

The aim then is to bet at the higher level and hope that opponents' hands have improved enough to call to see the final card. Should they do so, there is every chance they may call again in the fourth betting round, thus enhancing the profit made by slow-playing the nuts.

Above: Comic actor W.C. Fields keeps his cards close to his chest during a game. During his days in vaudeville in the early 20th century, Fields learned to play poker with some of the hustlers he met while touring, although golf was his preferred gambling medium. He did, however, develop some card tricks to supplement the skills he employed in his juggling act of the time.

COUNTING OUTS

FLOP

PLAYER A	PLAYER B

Above: These contrasting hands show the differing fortunes encountered as players consider the number of 'outs' available, these being the cards that can convert a hand into a winner. Player A has six chances of making a full house on the turn and 8 or 9 chances – depending on whether the turn card is an 8 – of filling it on the river, offering combined odds of just over 2 to 1 against this occurring. Player B has the best hand, but must assume that any pair on the board would be terminal. Of the unseen cards, 36 from the 45 remaining are good, and if the turn card pairs one of player B's hole cards, then 33 from the 44 in the deck are working favourably. Consequently, player B has a 60 per cent chance of surviving both rounds to claim the pot.

Reading the cards

Once the flop has been revealed, players must note the possibilities presented by the three community cards. Any pair that appears will make it extremely likely that a full house or better will ultimately take the pot. Up to a third of all Omaha hands are won by full houses and half of these are likely to have been secured on the flop. Players with trips should therefore be wary of drawing to a full house that will not prove to be the best possible.

A flop featuring three cards of the same suit – Qc, 7c, 2c, for example – will stifle any betting from those who cannot beat a flush. A player holding the nut flush – perhaps Ac, 8c – should bet the maximum, since any caller is bound to be drawing for a full house and must be forced to pay for any of the cards that might complete it. When two cards to a flush appear on the flop, a player with the nut flush draw should also bet and hope for a couple of callers. When the flush is completed, the profits made will compensate for losses that occur when an opponent does hit a full house.

ESTIMATING PROBABILITIES ON THE FLOP

♦ ♣ ♥ ♠

Players are usually able to clarify their position after the flop to the extent that they can quickly calculate how many cards are either beneficial or detrimental to their prospects of winning the pot. Those needing two more cards to complete their hand will normally fold at this point, but players who recognize that any one of several cards will secure victory are more likely to continue. The key to any decision lies in the number of cards available that will confirm a player's hand as the winner. If any one of 13 cards from the unseen 45 will guarantee success, then a player has an even-money chance of taking the pot. Should there be more than 13 cards that will help, then the player is a slight favourite, while having less than 13 cards from which to draw a winner guarantees the player underdog status.

WHO IS FAVOURITE?

THE FLOP   **PLAYER'S HAND**

Above: After the flop, the key number for players to bear in mind is 13, since possessing this many outs for the best possible hand offers an even-money chance of victory. In this example, the player with the A-high straight can be certain of winning if any one of 15 cards appears on the turn or river, making the player a slight favourite to prevail.

Right: The player pictured here in possession of an A-high flush after the flop is in the perfect position to bet. Though holding the best hand, should either the turn or the river bring a card to pair one of those on the flop, it may be beaten by an opponent with a full house. A bet now would make it clear that the nut flush has been obtained which, if not sufficient to take the pot straight away, at least defines any callers as being in pursuit of a full house.

The turn

Since the flop offers so much information to the wary player, anyone still competing for the pot when the turn card is revealed must believe they have a potential winning hand, even if it has only an outside chance of success. After the turn card is dealt, the likely nature of the nuts should be apparent to all those still engaged in the game. This helps keep the basic analysis required to a minimum, since a player would only have three serious questions to consider before deciding whether a bet is warranted at this stage: do I have the best possible hand at the table, is it possible to obtain it, and does someone else already have it?

A player who is already in possession of the nuts should simply try to build the pot, while a player who identifies that the nut hand is still obtainable is justified in calling any opponent's bet when the pot odds are favourable. Meanwhile, those who recognize that their chances of catching a winning card on the river are poor in relation to the pot odds would probably do best to fold.

Above all, players must beware of calling a bet on the turn for a card that will improve their hand but not guarantee the win. Calling in the hope of making a K-high flush, for example, is usually the quickest way to discover an opponent has an A-high flush.

Estimating probabilities on the turn

Allowing the rules of probability to influence one's betting decisions is not always straightforward, even if it is generally advisable. With just one final community card to come, however, calculating the odds against seeing specific cards on the river, when the final community card is dealt, is relatively simple. Players who have leading hands will be considering how many cards might blend with the board to provide an opponent with a winning hand, while those drawing for cards will be making similar calculations regarding their own chances. Each hand represents a different puzzle, so players must be aware of the fluctuating probabilities apparent from one hand to the next. For example a player holding Ah, Kd, 10h, 10s when the board reads 3h, 8h, 4c, 5s has nine hearts remaining to make the nut flush, at odds of 4 to 1 against.

However, this would not be the best possible hand available if either the 4h or 5h completed the flush, because, by pairing the board, they could provide an opponent with a full house. To obtain the nuts and be certain of victory, the player must rely on the other seven hearts, at odds of just over 5 to 1 against. Should the board read 3h, 6h, 4c, 5s instead, then the chances of holding the nut hand if a heart appears on the river are reduced further. Although nine hearts still remain, the 2, 4, 5, and 7 all threaten

PLAYER C

HOLE CARDS

Right: To help visualize some of the strategic thinking that applies to Omaha, this example of a 100/200 fixed-limit game will highlight the betting decisions of player C in the big blind. The starting hand is good, with a high pair, a couple of connecting cards and two spades, offering multiple possibilities.

THE DEAL

danger, since they have the potential to complete a low straight flush, while the full house options still exist. With only five cards that will guarantee the best hand, the player faces odds of 8 to 1 against this occurring.

AIMING STRAIGHT
♦ ♣ ♥ ♠

A straight is the minimum hand normally required to win the pot, although it can be difficult to exploit, given the frequency with which flushes and full houses occur in Omaha. Prior to the flop, the best chance of obtaining the hand arises when a player has a sequence of four consecutive hole cards, since this can complete up to 20 different straights, given the right board cards. A hand such as 9, 8, 7, 6, for instance, can make a Q-high straight with a Q, J, 10, or a 7-high straight with 5, 4, 3, and can work with 18 other three-card combinations to produce straights valued between these examples. On the flop, should there be no pair and no two cards of the same suit, there is an even-money possibility that a straight will ultimately win. However, players should still guard against finishing with anything less than the best possible straight available.

Left: A sequence of middle-ranking cards such as this is certainly worth playing if the pre-flop betting is light. There are 20 possible three-card combinations that could appear on the board to make a straight while the two hearts also offer flush possibilities. Despite the potential for making a strong hand, the low rank of the cards can cause problems. If the flop brought Q, J, 10, for example, the 9, 8 in the hole completes a straight, but this will be outranked by anyone holding K, 9 or A, K.

FIRST-ROUND BETTING

Left: Omaha characteristically features several players calling to see the flop, since even the weakest hand could quickly develop into an almost certain winner. For this reason, pre-flop raising in fixed-limit games is rare since it is unlikely to reduce the field sufficiently to make it worth the extra bet. Here, the remaining players all call the big blind (player C), who decides not to raise the betting further.

Call, bet or raise?

The flop may be the most crucial phase of the game, but the moment the turn card is revealed also prefaces a serious decision for those still contesting the pot. Players who can clearly see they have little chance of winning will probably fold, certainly in a fixed-limit game when it is normally impossible to bet enough to successfully bluff drawing hands out of contention.

Those whose hands still retain realistic prospects of taking the pot, by contrast, face a test of nerve and discipline as the serious betting begins. Not only is the minimum bet doubled on the turn in a typical Omaha game, but the likelihood is that players who bet now are probably committing themselves to further betting on the river. More bets generate bigger pots and this can tempt players into pursuing too many lost causes. Repeatedly finishing as the runner-up in these situations can reduce confidence as well as chip stacks.

In deciding whether to call, bet or even raise after the turn card has been dealt, good players will consider the pot odds on offer in light of the betting patterns throughout the game. Although betting without the best hand is usually ill advised, it is not always certain that an opponent already has it, with the clues behind this assessment coming from bets in the previous rounds. Despite the methodical approach recommended for playing Omaha successfully, being able to read an opponent's hand from the nature of the betting is a clear asset.

Right: As first person to act, hence making a bet from 'under the gun', player B surely indicates either a straight draw, two pairs or perhaps possession of a pocket pair – sevens or nines – that would make three of a kind. If that is the case, then player C's winning full house possibilities are reduced, since the 7 or a 9 that could complete it might now give player B four of a kind. If player B has a Q, 9 or 9, 7, then the odds of 3 to 1 for securing a full house, although not the nuts, may well prompt a bet, too, given the pot odds. Player C's raise is a strong move and will have opponents concentrating their thoughts on what the bet implies. In the event, players F and B call the raise.

THE FLOP

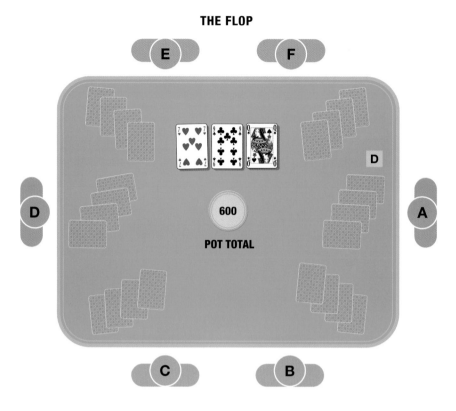

PLAYER C
HOLE CARDS

Above: The flop of 7, 9, Q is almost ideal for player C, who immediately has the best possible hand at present with trip queens, and is just under 2 to 1 to make a full house or 'quads' (four of a kind) come the river card. Since the pot odds currently offer 6 to 1, maintaining interest in the hand is justified and a raise might eliminate a couple of opponents who missed the flop completely. Any 5, 6, 8, 10, J or K – 23 of the remaining 44 cards (player C has a K) – can potentially fill a straight on the turn, however, and an opponent who does so will probably bet to try warding off draws for flushes and full houses.

SECOND BETTING ROUND

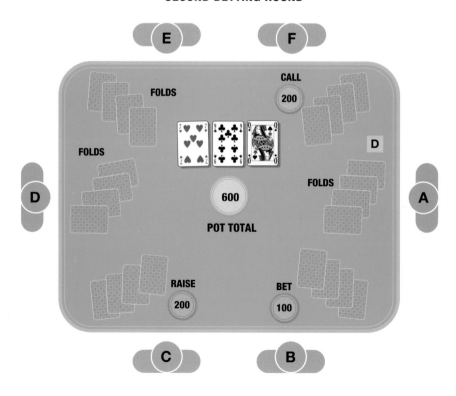

Passive or aggressive?

One of the things that makes Omaha such an enjoyable poker variation is that the many cards in circulation, particularly in a ten-player game, generate plenty of possibilities to make very strong hands. Betting tends to be lighter in the first two rounds, whether the game is fixed- or pot-limit poker, but becomes heavier from the turn onwards.

In pot-limit games, this is when the larger bets materialize, as players try to ward off those who, although possibly behind, still have chances to win. Such bets at this stage shrink the pot odds considerably, making speculative calls less attractive to opponents.

Yet large pots can still develop in fixed-limit poker, even though successful players are usually cautious and pragmatic. A couple of aggressive players who, on occasion, like to buck the odds with an irresponsible raise, can trigger an avalanche of betting in fixed-limit games. Since there are normally three or four raises per round before the betting level is capped, large pots can soon develop if a betting war breaks out. Under such circumstances, the implied pot odds on offer might tempt even the most passive player into calling for the river card if any chance of winning exists.

Simple decisions

Players whose betting on the turn is governed by the probabilities at work can expect to save themselves plenty of chips if they are strictly disciplined in their approach. The key is counting exactly how many of the unseen cards can help them either retain or acquire the winning hand. With four cards on the board and four in the hand, each player knows the value of eight cards. Simply, if half the remaining 44 cards will provide a player with a winning hand, then the chances are evidently even that this will happen, making any bet or call almost obligatory.

THE TURN

Above: The 5h on the turn does not improve player C's hand but can do little either for any opponent holding a pair of nines or sevens in the hole. It does help fulfil a low straight for any opponent holding 8, 6, which is plausible given that these two cards could feature in the hand of someone also holding a high pair such as aces or kings, for example.

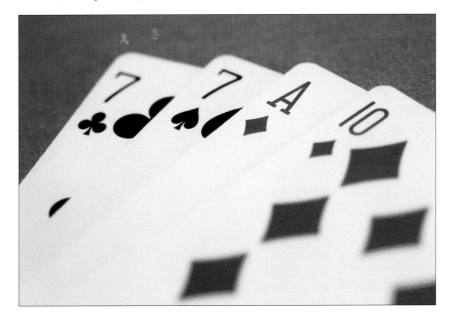

If only 11 cards will confirm the hand as a winner, then the odds against it occurring are 3 to 1, which might discourage a player from calling a bet in a very tight game. Players with fewer than 11 cards working for them should definitely be sure that the pot odds on offer will justify staying for the river, in the face of any bet.

Above: The pair of sevens supplemented by the A, 10 suited represents a fair starting hand and it is just one combination that could plausibly be held by player B in the game illustrated on these pages. From player C's perspective, player B's bet into a flop showing 7, 9, Q could easily be construed as representing trip sevens though this is a hand player C has well covered at present with the trip queens.

The river

The card that completes the deal and removes all doubt regarding the value of a player's hand and how it compares with the best available, is the river card. At this point it is worth reiterating the golden rule of Omaha, which underlines how the game essentially amounts to a search for the nuts. Any player who does not hold the best possible hand available after the river card may safely assume that an opponent probably does.

If the betting patterns suggest exactly that, then there is little sense in a player calling a last-round bet, however modest, in order to confirm what is already suspected. This applies to both fixed- and pot-limit games, although players are more likely to support potentially strong hands on the flop or the turn in pot-limit Omaha with large bets, offering clues to the value of their cards. Having been called as far as the river, a modest final-round bet by a player who had raised in the previous round should create suspicion in the mind of an opponent who has failed to make a lock hand. The possibility exists that the opponent is being trapped into parting with a few more chips by a player with the nuts.

THIRD BETTING ROUND

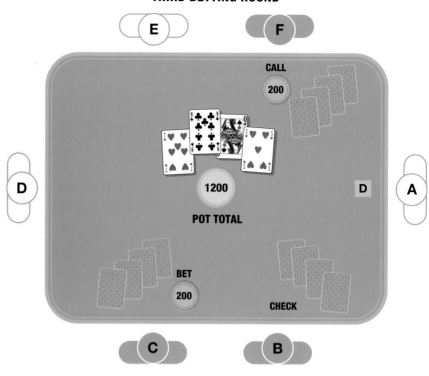

Above: The raise from Player C after the flop causes player B to check this time round after the turn card is dealt, either to re-examine the possibilities presented by the board or, perhaps, to set a trap. Player C bets the minimum, reasoning that player B could be slow-playing a straight by holding an 8 and 6, but that it is still more likely he has three of a kind. If this is the case, then another 7 or 9 on the river could be disastrous for player C since either card could conceivably furnish player B with four of a kind. In the event, players F and B both call, but do not raise, indicating possession of hands that probably still require improvement.

PLAYER C
HOLE CARDS

Right: Three players are still competing as the river card falls, giving player C the nuts with four of a kind. Although opponents may have read the betting patterns correctly and put player C on pocket queens, the pair on the board could have made someone a full house – player B, perhaps – that may induce them to bet. Although four of a kind is not uncommon in Omaha, players find it difficult to fold a hand as good as a full house, even when the signs are ominous. Once player B checks, player C has no option but to bet and hope for a call to swell the pot further. There is no point checking and allowing opponents a free showdown when holding the best hand.

THE RIVER

Reading opponents

Identifying the contrasting levels of players' skills is an essential element of successful poker, as is assessing their motivations. While Omaha strategy involves some inflexible rules, players are still challenged psychologically to decipher the meaning behind any bet after the river card has been dealt.

Having survived three rounds of betting, players hope their efforts have been worthwhile, even when evidence from the cards alone suggests this is unlikely. But the winning hand is not always the best possible, especially when several low cards are featured in the widow. Potential lock hands may have been folded, leaving perhaps the most aggressive players to fight over the spoils with reasonable but not outstanding cards. A player facing an awkward decision on the river should reconsider the scale and timing of previous bets. Players who raised on the flop, for example, may have done so in order to eliminate several dangers to a weak leading hand. If the hand implied by that bet does not appear to have been strengthened by the turn and river cards, the bet could have been a semi-bluff that failed to pay off.

Large bets from players after the turn card ordinarily imply that they hold the nut hand or are strong favourites to do so on the river. But since the inference is easily understood by experienced Omaha players, some may choose to capitalize on this awareness by occasionally prosecuting a bluff.

Pot management

Players lucky enough to have a winning opportunity early in the hand are in prime position to control the betting. They can exercise more choice in whether to raise a pot and eliminate potential threats or conceal the value of their cards by calling along with several opponents. The time for setting a trap may arise later, when an opponent stumbles across a good hand that is destined to lose. For example a player holding Ac, Ah, Jd, 8d will appreciate the promise presented by a flop of 10d, As, 9d. In early position, a check may be in order to see how many opponents also like the flop, with anyone holding trips, two pairs and draws for high flushes likely to bet or call the minimum.

If a call will then suffice to see the turn card, the hand may be underrated by opponents who might have expected a player holding trip aces to have advertised the fact already. Should the turn card be the Ad, prompting a bet from the player now holding four aces, anyone with a full house – by matching a pair of tens, perhaps – may call a bet for fear of being bluffed out of a win. All the time they are drawing dead while the player with the top hand is patiently encouraging them to build the pot. In this position, the player would like to see a 10 or a 9 on the river, since that could give an opponent a lower-ranking four of a kind that would prove very difficult to fold, despite the implications behind the player's betting becoming more clear.

FINAL BETTING ROUND

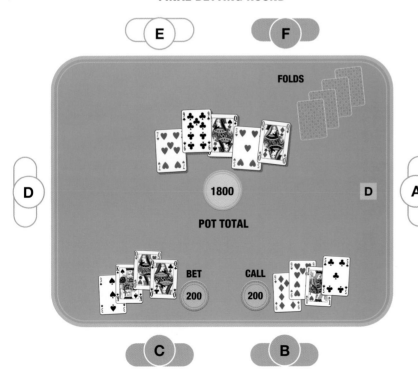

Left: Player C's bet is enough to persuade player F to fold, but player B calls the 200 only to discover that the full house of nines over queens is outranked. This is a common mistake among Omaha players, who are often sufficiently seduced by the size of the pot that they will commit more chips despite knowing they could be beaten. In pot-limit games, players may be more inclined to bluff without the nuts, but, even when suspecting a bluff, calling a large bet with a beatable hand is a tough decision.

ONLINE POKER

The huge surge of interest in poker during the past decade is attributable almost entirely to the increased publicity for the game generated by television and the Internet. As the intricacies of tournament-style Texas Hold 'em entertained and inspired television viewers, so online poker sites emerged to offer convenient and ready access to a game. PlanetPoker started the trend in 1998 and there are now around a thousand poker sites currently generating total revenue estimated at US$2 billion per year. Such sums have attracted many of the world's leading companies from the betting industry and beyond, all establishing their own online poker rooms in their eagerness for a piece of the increasingly lucrative action. However, this rapid growth has understandably brought with it a degree of concern over the morality of gambling online, as well as prompting investigations into its legality. These issues and some basic details regarding the online poker experience are the subject of this chapter.

Right: The upsurge in interest in the game of poker can be squarely placed on the shoulders of rapid developments in the media. As soon as poker tournaments started being televised, the game's legendary players became more widely known and the subsequent inundation of poker guidebooks helped generate even more publicity for the game. The Internet not only offers access to virtually everything there is to know about poker, but also acts as a barometer of poker's global popularity.

THE LAW AND ONLINE POKER

The speed at which online poker has developed as a hugely popular global gambling medium has, to some extent, left the machinations of the law far behind in many countries, and the extensive reach of the Internet has thrown these differences into stark relief.

For the most part, governments of nations in Europe, South America, Asia and around the Caribbean have either adopted a pragmatic approach by legalizing online gambling, or have actively welcomed gaming companies by licensing their operations. However, in America, home to over half of online poker players, the confusion surrounding the legality of Internet betting came to a head in October 2006. Repeated attempts by right-wing Republicans to lobby for an outright ban proved successful when President George W. Bush signed the Safe Port Act, enacting a

law that ostensibly aimed to improve American port security. A late amendment to the bill meant that the Unlawful Internet Gambling Enforcement Act was simultaneously incorporated into the legislation. The principal thrust of this additional act is to restrict financial institutions from processing transactions to and from the now outlawed Internet gaming sites on behalf of their clients. Consequently, although online poker itself is not specifically illegal, players based in the America are effectively prevented from utilizing their online betting accounts which obviously reduces the incentive to play. Needless to say, both the online gaming companies and the vast army of online poker players are working towards overturning this legislation, their primary argument being that poker is a game of skill and not pure chance.

Above: The security and integrity of online casino operations is becoming increasingly trustworthy thanks to the fierce competition between companies offering the service. It is in their interests to make the financial dealings as simple and secure as possible. This includes offering players the option to restrict their involvement in games by means of responsible game settings.

Right: Collusion can be a problem in both real world and virtual poker rooms, and involves two or more players working together to gain an unfair advantage. However, online casino companies operate sophisticated security software that is designed to police collusive behaviour or fraudulent activity by monitoring playing patterns.

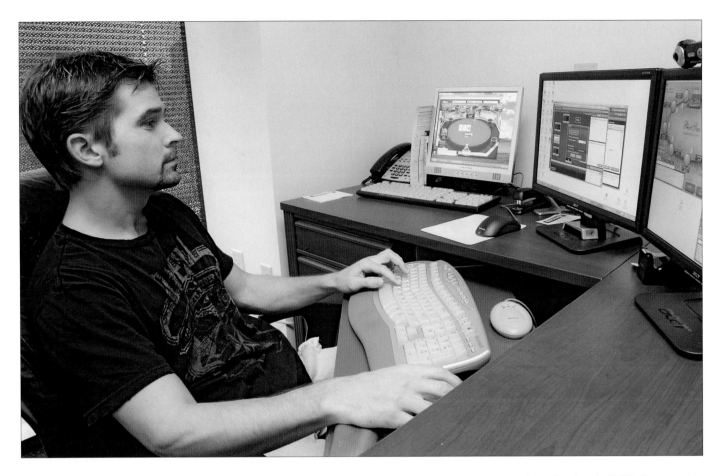

Above: Jeff Markley, vice president of Online Operations for Bluff Media, owner of America's largest poker magazine, peruses three online casino screens in his office following the successful passage of the Unlawful Internet Gaming Act in 2006. Within a week, gamblers in America had withdrawn thousands of dollars from their web accounts and access to online poker, casinos and sports-betting on some sites was blocked.

Regulations

Unsurprisingly, considering America's current responses to online gaming, very few countries are prepared to provide licences to online casinos and poker rooms, with most operations being concentrated in places such as Costa Rica, Gibraltar, Malta and countries dotted around the Caribbean. The UK, with one eye on the potential tax revenues that might accrue, is on the verge of legalizing the establishment of online gaming sites, which could instil more confidence in the industry among consumers.

Although it is true that reputable companies pay their host country a sizeable licensing fee and subject their operations to official scrutiny, the fact remains that the industry itself is mostly self-regulating. Several organizations monitor online gaming, of which the Interactive Gaming Council, Online Players' Association and Gambling Commission are perhaps most respected. In a competitive market, the vast majority of operators recognize that customer satisfaction is of paramount importance and promote the integrity of their businesses. Some rogue elements do still exist, and it is incumbent on the consumer to exercise a degree of caution when selecting an Internet site at which to play.

Online security

Although one cannot be assured of the security of online poker sites in view of the rapidly changing world of computer technology, the majority can be trusted to handle financial transactions and keep personal details confidential. The digital encryption methods are the same as those used by the world's financial institutions and it is in the interests of the operators to ensure that security is watertight.

The better sites monitor the virtual tables for signs of players cheating by colluding with each other during a game. Two or three players could gain a seat at the same table and communicate with each other about their respective hands remotely. High-stakes games are more likely to be targeted by cheats, but the better poker sites operate systems that identify suspect betting patterns. Players who suspect cheating can always alert the operator's customer support section. It may not compensate any immediate losses, but it will prompt the most reputable online poker rooms to investigate.

GETTING STARTED

The online poker market is immensely competitive, with literally hundreds of sites offering the chance for players to indulge their passion. Although launched in 2001, some three years after PlanetPoker became the first online poker site, PartyPoker has become the dominant force in the industry. A major advertising campaign in 2003 succeeded in elevating it to a position whereby it now commands almost half the total revenues generated from online poker. At peak times, there are over 20,000 people competing at this site alone, as is the case with PokerStars, which can boast similar figures for its tournaments, which are renowned for being some of the toughest to win. This is the site from which both Chris Moneymaker and Greg Raymer emerged to become WSOP world champions and, not surprisingly, it has a reputation for attracting solid and experienced players.

Other online poker rooms worthy of mention are PacificPoker, PokerRoom and UltimateBet, since these are also well regarded within the industry. Many of the sites are endorsed by poker professionals, while Doyle Brunson is just one player to exploit his reputation for integrity by creating his own online poker room.

Registration

Logging on to a preferred site is a straightforward process for anyone familiar with accessing the Internet. In order to play, however, it is necessary to register with the operator, which will involve submitting an email address, selecting a username and creating a password. An account number will be issued, although it is not always necessary to make an immediate cash deposit in order to be able to play, since there are usually play money tables in operation. Details of the account and access to the virtual poker tables can only be obtained by submitting the relevant username and password. It is not unusual for players to have accounts with several online poker rooms, so it is advisable to keep a separate record of the account numbers and passwords for each. The majority of sites require players to download the necessary software before being able to play, but several still offer the chance to play within a web browser.

Below: Four of the more established online gaming sites available today. There are over 140 similar sites catering for players seeking a game in the comfort of their own home. The astonishing growth in online poker is a 21st-century phenomenon with the first online card room PlanetPoker.com, opening for business just before the millennium.

Below: Poker is growing fast in Germany, and it is estimated that over 100,000 German players will log on to online gaming sites by the end of 2006. Deutsche Poker Tour is a free national online poker league whose members play on popular poker sites to gain points that will enable them to compete for the huge prizepool on offer at the end-of-season league championship.

Above: Armed with a low-grade personal computer (PC), a 56K modem and access to a telephone line, it is possible to engage in poker games with people from all over the world. The obvious benefit that online poker offers the novice is the chance to practise, without going to the trouble of finding a card room or organizing a game.

Navigating the virtual poker room

Rival sites differ cosmetically in terms of their graphics and presentation but access to the desired games and ancillary services is generally organized along very similar lines. Drop-down menus and clearly labelled tabs indicate the poker variations available, the stake levels that apply and the betting structures that are in operation. Distinguishing between cash games and tournaments is simple and there are a range of statistical details available for each table in operation including such key information as the average pot size and the number of hands dealt per hour. This can help a player to identify whether a game is tight or loose which is useful in formulating an initial strategy.

Once seated at a table, of course, a player must actively click on the relevant button to join a game at which point such elements as the deal and the payment of antes is automated. The options available to each player when a betting decision needs to be made are clearly displayed and only require the press of a button or a click of the mouse to check, bet or fold.

POKERBOTS
♦ ♣ ♥ ♠

All serious poker players are keen on having an edge over their opponents, and online players are no different. To this end, many are inclined to employ pokerbots, these being computer software programs that can access a game in progress and provide a player with a range of useful information. Pokerbots can read all the face-up cards and calculate pot odds as well as make recommendations on which hands to play and when to bet. In this regard, they can save a player time in making a decision, although it might be argued that this stunts the development of an individual's own ability to read a game. Some pokerbots can be programmed to play automatically, but their success rates are rather limited.

Modest returns at low-stakes games have been recorded, but, given the rigid strategies often employed by the pokerbots, this success is often attributed to the poor quality of the players that contest such games. Experienced players are better able to manipulate a hand when playing a predictable opponent, and, as yet, no pokerbot program is able to understand the subtleties of bluffing and checkraising to pose a serious threat.

ONLINE GAMES

Despite some variations from one card room to another, the mainstays of online poker are Texas Hold 'em, Omaha and seven-card stud, along with the split-pot games Omaha/8 and seven-card stud high/low. Draw poker is also available at some sites as is the Hold 'em derivative, crazy pineapple, a game in which players are dealt three cards rather than two, one of which must be discarded following the flop and the conclusion of the second betting round. Such is the scale of American influence on the game that the majority of sites trade in US dollars, irrespective of their registered location.

The betting structures operated are the staples of fixed-limit, pot-limit and no-limit, with the former recommended as the most likely to appeal to the beginner. Games for real money exist at levels ranging from a few cents up to hundreds of dollars and should easily match the means of anybody who wishes to play. Of course, the key difference when playing poker in a virtual card room compared to the live experience is that the pace of events is much quicker. Each hand may take less than a minute to complete and players rarely have the luxury of sitting back for more than 30 seconds to contemplate a decision.

Left: A leading Japanese online poker guide, featuring reviews of all major poker rooms, top lists, strategy advice for both beginners and advanced players as well as poker rules. It also offers daily freerolls and tournament schedules. The nation of 128 million is looking to lift its ban on casinos to increase tourist arrivals and revive its gaming industry. Japan's ruling party is holding talks with global gaming companies including Harrah's Entertainment Inc. to operate the nation's first casinos after 2010.

Right: Juega Poker Ya is one of Spain's leading online poker gaming sites offering freeroll and satellite tournaments. Thousands of budding Spanish poker players are queuing up to learn how to play in the hope of emulating the success of Spanish poker star Carlos Mortensen, World Poker Champion in 2001. Poker is similar to the popular Spanish gambling game Mus, another game of skill and psychology where players try to out wit their opponents.

Left: There are many online poker gaming sites in Russia, though Malta-based company Red Star Poker, which opened in June 2005, filled the crucial void of providing instruction and customer service in both Russian and English. Upon downloading the necessary gaming software, players may participate in satellite tournaments with international players.

Above: An online poker gaming site in Slovenia. Interestingly, casinos in Slovenia are attracting gamblers from Italy, where tight marketing restrictions and high tax rates have hampered growth in the industry. In 2004, over 87 per cent of all visits to Slovenian casinos were made by foreigners.

Above: An Israeli poker portal, in Hebrew. Gambling is currently illegal in Israel, but there are efforts to reverse that. The Israeli government is sitting on a proposal that would allow casinos to be built in Eilat, the country's principal holiday city. A formal decision has yet to be made, but many groups of investors are already vying for building contracts.

How many players?

In keeping with the standard tables in the card rooms and casinos of the world, online poker tables typically have space for nine or ten players. Texas Hold 'em and Omaha are the games most likely to accommodate the maximum per table, while seven-card stud games are usually limited to eight players. All these games, are also staged with lower limits on the number of participants, with heads-up contests widely available and many Texas Hold 'em tables limited to three, four or five players. The impact of having fewer competitors is that the blinds circulate the table quicker, of course, and this keeps players involved in the action. With the standard of the average winning hand also being reduced, such short-handed games tend to be loose betting affairs and appeal to those who perhaps do not have the patience or inclination to fold a succession of hands while watching others compete.

The rake

This is the fee charged by the online poker room for providing the facilities to play. To enter a US$10 tournament, for example, players are usually required to pay US$11, of which US$10 goes into the prize pool with the additional US$1 being claimed by the operator. A levy of ten per cent is typical for the lower-stakes games although it is often reduced in more expensive tournaments.

The fees that are charged in cash games differ quite considerably from site to site with levels varying from five to ten per cent of each pot at the lowest stake levels. A cap is often placed on the rake if a pot exceeds

PLAY-MONEY POKER
♦ ♣ ♥ ♠

Once registered to an online poker site, players will normally be credited with chips that may be used in play-money games only. These offer an ideal opportunity for novices to learn how to play at no expense and so represent a valuable educational resource. Experienced players may also find them useful as a means of warming up prior to sitting in on a real money game. Obviously, with nothing at stake, the games tend to be fairly loose affairs, but that does not diminish their potential for helping a player focus on the key facets of the game prior to playing for real.

a certain size but the poker room's cut could easily be a dollar or more for every hand. Since 60 hands per hour is a fairly common rate of play per table, the scale of the potential income to be accrued becomes apparent given the thousands of virtual tables simultaneously staging a game at any one time.

From a consumer's perspective it is obviously worth checking the rake charts that are published by the majority of reputable online poker rooms. A comparison between the different rates applicable at the preferred betting levels will certainly prove worthwhile for anyone considering playing for several hours a week. Even those who win consistently may be paying more for the privilege than need be the case.

CASH GAMES

One of the great advantages of online poker is the sheer wealth of information available to players who wish to engage in a cash game. Those with some experience of the medium will consider the statistics for each table at the betting level they favour, taking into account such information as the average pot size and, at Texas Hold 'em tables, how many players are seeing the flop, usually expressed in percentage terms. A loose table can be identified as one where at least half the players are regularly calling to see the flop, probably with some modest hands among them. Such a game would be a very attractive proposition for an experienced poker player who is able to exercise more discipline in selecting which hands to support. Games with a minimum bet of US$1 or more can normally be expected to attract reasonably good players, whereas the levels below this appeal more to those who treat their poker casually.

Understanding the likely quality of opposition is a key consideration, of course, with many online players content to compete without a solid appreciation of strategy and the nuances of a particular game. Identifying these players can certainly help, but unsophisticated opponents pose problems in that they are difficult to bluff, being unable to understand the implications behind a strong bet. Similarly, any calling stations or maniacs at the table who are content to play many hands cannot beat the odds in the long run but will, on occasions, strike it lucky by hitting the cards they need to win. Such players are hazardous, but not as daunting as those who sit patiently, folding hand after hand while waiting for the cards that will justify a large bet. Becoming involved in betting confrontations with tight, aggressive players should only be considered when holding an exceptionally good hand.

Stake levels

A minimum and maximum buy-in normally applies at whichever table one chooses to play, particularly in pot-limit and no-limit games, while in fixed-limit, poker players may be able to buy in for their entire bankroll. Ordinarily, the upper limit is one hundred times the minimum bet and it is recommended that players always buy in for the maximum permitted. Maintaining a chip stack that is well in excess of the average pot size at the table is essential to ward off pressure from the chip leaders and to ensure that, in the event of holding a winning hand, a player can capitalize on it to best advantage. Topping up one's chip stack where permitted is therefore advisable,

Left: There has been a huge upsurge in people playing poker online globally and the Eastern European nation, Croatia, is no exception. On land, the country boasts 12 casinos, of which four are located in Zagreb, the capital city. The largest casino in the country, Miro hotel and casino Minera in Plovanija, has 34 gaming tables and 250 video poker or other gaming machines.

Right: An online poker gaming website in Chinese. ESPN, an American cable TV network dedicated to broadcasting sports-related programming 24 hours a day is the major broadcaster of poker. The sports network now airs in China and has exposed 1.3 billion people to the game. The first to feel these benefits will be the online gaming sites.

Middle right: Sweden's leading portal about poker and related information. The site offers reviews of poker rooms, articles, rules, tournaments and a poker forum.

Right: Land-based casino gambling in France is highly restricted and if you want to play casino games in France your only choice is state-managed operations, but the nation's online casino business has been in full swing for many years.

although there is little point in continually doing so at a table where an opponent has amassed a chip lead of perhaps two or three times the maximum buy-in.

Similarly, players should be incredibly confident in their ability to consider joining a table where one opponent already has such an advantage. It is usually indicative of having played well for several hours, and confronting an in-form opponent with the means to make intimidating bets is inadvisable in the extreme.

Online poker tells

The ability to read opponents in order to assess the meaning behind any bet is an asset and, to this end, deciphering clues from a player's body language can often be helpful. However, distinctive physical mannerisms are quite obviously not visible when playing online, although there are still some clues available to the keen observer regarding opponents' styles and attitudes.

Messages in the chat box, if taken at face value, might prove a good indicator of an opponent's mood, given that many players could easily be tired, bored or even drunk. During a game there are some who take the maximum permitted time to make a decision, which could be the result of a poor connection, but could also indicate that the individual concerned is either a novice or is playing several tables simultaneously. If the latter is suspected, the opponent may be restricting play to aggressive support for premium starting hands at each table as that is a much easier strategy to manage. Any bet or raise from such an opponent would evidently merit respect under these circumstances. Similarly, an opponent who raises a bet almost instantaneously usually indicates possession of a good hand, the speed of the response suggesting maximum confidence. Conversely, an opponent who takes much more time than usual in playing one particular hand may be consciously trying to disguise its true value.

Online poker rooms do offer the facility for players to make notes about their opponents while games are in progress, and many offer a statistical breakdown of one's own play during any session. However, the speed of the games themselves and the tendency for virtual tables to experience a high turnover of players makes it difficult to read opponents. Taking note of new players joining the table and adjusting one's strategy accordingly is crucial to success at the online game.

ONLINE TOURNAMENTS

The inspiration provided by the spectacle of televised tournament poker is undoubtedly responsible for the popularity of the knockout game in online poker rooms. While trying to make a regular profit from cash games requires a long-term strategy and a consistently disciplined approach, the appeal of tournament poker is that a single victory could realize a dramatic profit for a few hours' work. In addition, because the entry fees are always stipulated, it is possible to know in advance the maximum loss that will be incurred if a player is knocked out before reaching the prize-money positions.

One other aspect of tournaments that makes them so appealing to the new generation of poker players is that luck has the potential to undermine the strategies of opponents who are regarded as more skilful. One bad beat and the loss of a substantial pot can seriously undermine a good player's attempts to win a tournament as easily as those of a novice. However, it must be remembered that the very best professionals regularly finish in the prize money in live tournaments so there is no reason to suppose that experienced online tournament players are not similarly successful, particularly in the high-stakes contests.

Tournament structures

The very nature of online poker permits a greater range of tournament styles and structures than might be found in a typical card room, such are the benefits of having a computer program in control of proceedings. The single-table sit 'n' go tournaments for between five and ten players are especially popular, since they rarely take more than an hour to complete at most. Indeed, if played as high-speed turbo tournaments, they may be resolved in less than half that time.

At the other end of the scale, the multi-table tournaments hosted by online poker rooms can take several hours to complete, making them more appealing to players with time on their hands. Texas Hold 'em is the preferred game for most online tournament players, although other popular variations are also played in tournament format using the standard range of betting structures.

Strategic considerations

In terms of actual tournament strategy, the basic advice is for players to be cautiously disciplined during the early stages while taking stock of opponents, only betting when in possession of a very good hand. All

Left: The computer age may soon be creeping into card rooms, and taking jobs from dealers. Here a game of Texas Hold 'em is being played on the new PokerPro dealer-free electronic poker tables at the Hollywood Park Casino in Inglewood, California. The electronic tables require no dealers, as the players select all their actions via the touch screen in front of them. The casino unveiled its e-poker room in October 2006, making it the first casino in California to feature e-poker tables which combine the speed and accuracy of online poker with the personal player interaction of traditional 'brick and mortar' casino poker.

Left and below: All Aussie Poker is an Australian online poker resource, offering a comprehensive range of poker-related services, whilst Mega poker is its Dutch equivalent. Type in 'online poker' to almost any local search engine in the world and and you will score a barrage of hits.

Below right: The convenience and anonymity associated with playing online poker has led to women representing roughly 40 per cent of the card-room clientele, compared to just 5 per cent in real life card rooms and casinos.

players start with the same number of chips, but this selective approach can help to conserve a player's resources while opponents knock each other out.

From the middle stages onwards, players need to be selectively more aggressive in order to withstand the increasing betting levels, this being easier for those in healthy chip positions, of course. Varying one's playing style to accommodate the changing fortunes of opponents is a requirement at this point, and those with the largest stacks are obviously in a position to take a few more risks with moderate hands without necessarily damaging their overall prospects.

By the time the tournament reaches its final stages, betting choices are often dictated by the size of a player's chip stack as much as by the cards themselves. Those in the lead will be pressurizing those with fewer chips and on the verge of elimination in order to move one step nearer the top prize. Understandably, it is this level of volatility at the business end of the event that makes tournament poker so exciting for regular participants.

PRIZES
♦ ♣ ♥ ♠

Prize money is normally distributed among the leading ten per cent of players in any tournament, though some events are organized on a 'winner takes all' basis. A single-table tournament of ten players will usually see the first three rewarded, the winner taking 50 per cent of the prize pool. A US$10 event will see the winner claiming US$50, the runner-up US$30 and third-place US$20. Multi-table events featuring 1,000 entrants could see the winner's share reduced to 25 per cent of the total prize pool, to accommodate payments for the top 100 finishers. Assuming a US$10 event once more, the first prize would still amount to US$2,500, which is an attractive sum for a modest outlay. However, beating up to 1,000 opponents in a hugely competitive environment is obviously a major achievement and not something that many poker players are regularly able to repeat.

CASINOS AND CLUBS

The recent popularity of playing online poker over the last decade has created an increased demand for the game in the world's foremost casinos, although many of the smaller establishments are still reluctant to provide poker facilities. From a purely commercial perspective, the cost of operating a poker table is rarely as profitable for the house as a range of other gambling games such as roulette, craps or the ubiquitous slot machines. In these, of course, players bet against the house rather than each other, assuring the casinos of a regular and predictable stream of income. However, despite the fact that the rake from a poker table may never match the revenue of a dozen slot machines that could easily take its place, consumer demand has helped prompt a change of approach. As a result, the opportunity to play the game in public has attracted many more poker players into the casinos of the world. For those new to the experience, this chapter highlights some of the key factors to bear in mind when playing poker in a commercial card room.

Right: In poker, the cards are shuffled prior to the deal of each hand. The players will normally shuffle and deal in home games and smaller clubs, while in casinos it is more likely that a dealer will be employed specifically to manage this aspect of the game. A professional dealer can help to speed up proceedings, leaving players free to concentrate on their poker strategies although this luxury comes at a price in the form of the casino rake, a fee often levied on each pot to cover the costs of the dealer and other facilities.

WHAT TO EXPECT

Players who are used to enjoying poker in home games against friends, particularly for modest stakes, are entitled to be intimidated when they first venture into a dedicated poker room. Of course, the setting will differ from one card room to another, with the glitz and glamour of the palatial hotel-casinos in Las Vegas not replicated in small, urban poker clubs. There may be five tables in operation or 50, but the fact remains that anyone who takes a seat in a commercial card room for the first time, to play poker against complete strangers, is likely to feel nervous.

The unfamiliar environment, the potential distractions and the need to keep stock of developments at the table can all conspire to disrupt a player's concentration. This, of course, can prove costly, so those considering a visit to a card room are well advised to familiarize themselves with the venue for a while before engaging in a game. There will always be members of staff on hand to answer any questions concerning the facilities on offer and the general rules that apply to specific games. Most poker commentators suggest that it is always a good idea to watch a game in progress for a while rather than take a seat immediately, should one be available. This helps acclimatize a player to the environment and offers the chance to gauge the quality of the opposition and the style of the games in progress.

Above: The Bellagio hotel and casino, inspired by the Lake Como resort of Bellagio in Italy and located on the Las Vegas Strip, was the most expensive hotel ever built when opened in 1998, having cost over US$1.6 billion. Many professional poker players prefer to play there, calling it their home base, due in part to the high table limits.

House rules

Every poker room will have a manager, cashiers and a set of rules governing the games, as well as points of general etiquette. Larger operations will, of course, employ several dealers and have staff on hand to deal with any disputes as they arise. Although a degree of consistency is common in card rooms operating in close proximity to each other, there are often variations governing the betting limits, the permitted buy-ins and the structures of the games. Few people are likely to play poker in a formal setting without having some experience of the game, but it is still incumbent upon the individual to be aware of the different regulations in operation.

It is also worth remembering that experienced players prefer a fairly swift pace to proceedings and, because of the rake and the potential for earning tips, dealers are inclined to meet this demand. Inexperienced players can soon become a nuisance to opponents and dealers alike if they continually struggle to follow events and delay the game by seeking continual guidance on what options are available to them. This underlines how harshly competitive the game can be when played in a commercial setting and confirms the need for proper preparation on the part of any prospective participant.

Left: Laser light show at the Las Vegas Golden Nugget casino-hotel, owned and operated by Landry's Restaurants. The world's largest gold nugget on display, the Hand of faith, is in the lobby. Weighing 876 troy ounces (27.2kg) and 46 centimetres (18 inches) in length, it was found near the Golden Triangle in Australia in 1980.

Right: The famous 'Welcome to Las Vegas' sign, located just to the south of the Las Vegas Strip. Betty Willis and Ted Rogich created the sign, characteristic of the Googie architecture movement popular at the time, for Clark County, Nevada. The back of the sign reads 'Drive Carefully and Come Back Soon'. When seen up close, the circles on which the letters of the word 'WELCOME' appear reveal themselves to be silver dollars.

Las Vegas

Poker's long association with Las Vegas has helped it develop a magnetic appeal that attracts players from all over the world. The choice of games and venues on offer is staggering, with over 50 dedicated card rooms catering for their needs. Many, such as the Bellagio, the Mirage and Caesar's Palace, are located in the plush casinos of the Las Vegas Strip, while Binion's Horseshoe, the former home of the WSOP, is in the downtown area, along with the Golden Nugget. Although each poker room has its own unique personality, there are aspects common to all, with relaxed dress codes the norm and, increasingly, a ban on smoking at the poker tables. Not surprisingly, many of the world's best poker players live and work in Las Vegas and anyone seriously considering a visit can expect fierce competition in whichever room they choose to play.

BINION'S, LAS VEGAS
♦ ♣ ♥ ♠

For many, this is the only place to play poker, such is the casino's famous association with the WSOP, instigated by the venue's original owner, Benny Binion. Originally known as Binion's Horseshoe, the casino was rebranded following a change of ownership, while the WSOP has moved to Harrah's Rio Casino, having outgrown its original home. Situated at 128 East Fremont, Binion's has 14 tables in a room regarded as spacious by casino standards, with the usual roster of Texas Hold 'em, seven-card stud and Omaha. Betting limits are among the lowest in town, with US$2/$4 fixed-limit Texas Hold 'em on offer, while the minimum buy-in for a no-limit game is US$100, the blinds being set at US$1 and US$2. No-limit Texas Hold 'em tournaments are organized daily, the buy-in being US$70 – plus US$20 for administration – although the cost rises to US$150 plus US$50 on Friday, Saturday and Sunday evenings. Basic lessons in how to play Texas Hold 'em are held at 11am each day.

Right: Binion's Horsehoe casino, located in the centre of Fremont Street, where two million light bulbs and 540,000 watts of sound transform the canopy into the world's largest animated light show every night. Although it is most famous for its gaming, the Horseshoe has other popular attractions, including the Poker Hall of Fame wall inside, which honours the greatest players in the history of poker.

THE CASINO RAKE

As mentioned earlier, while poker clubs do exist, many established international casinos have at times been reluctant to offer players the facilities required to pursue their preferred gambling interest. The resurgence of interest in the game has encouraged a change of heart in many cases, but the services provided by any commercial card room do come at a price, of course. This takes the form of the 'rake', sometimes referred to as the 'cut', the 'vigorish' or 'vig'. It is usually set at a minimum of three per cent, and could be as high as ten per cent of every pot contested, although there will usually be a cap on the rake once any pot exceeds a certain level.

Given that it is often customary for the winner of each pot to tip the dealer, it soon becomes evident how difficult it is to make money from the game. This is particularly the case at the lower-stake levels, where, even when capped, the rake can seem a relatively big slice of the smaller pots usually contested. Winning an average number of pots may not be enough to break even unless players limit themselves to playing hands that promise an early advantage. Exerting this discipline requires folding on most occasions, perhaps making for a gruelling session. However, it is the only way that any player can realistically hope to beat both the opposition and the house cut.

Above: A waitress serves poker players at Binion's Horseshoe casino. With food and drink constantly on offer during play, casinos do have ways other than gambling to extract money from visitors' pockets. The casino environment is geared towards cutting you off from the outside world and the level of concentration required to play well is difficult to sustain for long. It is advisable to regulate your time at the table and take regular breaks for refreshment.

Left: Among the signature attractions at Caesar's Palace hotel-casino, located on the Las Vegas Strip between the Bellagio and the Mirage, is the Colosseum theatre, where Céline Dion and Elton John are regular performers. It was specifically built for the show, *A New Day*, a spectacular produced by former Cirque du Soleil director Franco Dragone. Despite having some of the highest ticket prices for any show in the city, with seats as high as US$200 each, the show regularly sells out.

Right: To win when playing in poker games where the house takes a cut, a player must not only beat opponents, but also the financial drain of the rake. The rake represents a fee for the facilities, and it's also customary to tip the dealer when you win the pot. So even a winning session does not come without some expense.

Games and facilities

The poker variations on offer in casinos tend to reflect current trends, with Texas Hold 'em, seven-card stud and Omaha most prominent, although other games are generally available on request. The split-pot and low-only games such as Omaha/8, razz, lowball and seven-card stud/8 are also popular, although not as widely available. Larger establishments sometimes offer separate rates for a private room or table at which players may engage in whichever game they choose. Typically, hiring such a facility is usually conditional on it being in use for a minimum of, perhaps, six hours.

Aside from poker, of course, casinos offer many other gambling facilities that have proved the downfall of many successful poker players. Even the late Stu Ungar, three times a world champion, had a reputation for leaving a casino broke on occasions, despite having won substantial sums at the poker table. In terms of ancillary services, players will often find themselves waited on while playing poker, since staff will be on hand to take orders for drinks and perhaps even food. Play for long enough and there is a chance that complimentary refreshments will be offered, but this service is not universally available.

Above: One of several slot machine halls inside the Golden Nugget casino-hotel. Casinos operate to make money and they are generally very good at it. Given that the space occupied by one poker table could easily accommodate perhaps a dozen machines, simple economics have contributed to the game being marginalized by casinos in the past.

AVIATION CLUB DE FRANCE, PARIS
♦ ♣ ♥ ♠

Situated at 10, Avenue de Champs-Elysées, the Aviation Club de France in Paris is regarded as one of the most stylish casinos in the world. It was established in 1907 primarily to cater for baccarat players but is now readily associated with poker courtesy of the Grand Prix de Paris, a Texas Hold 'em tournament that ranks among the most prestigious in Europe and constitutes part of the World Poker Tour. The card room offers a wide range of cash games including Omaha, seven-card stud and their high-low variations, along with Texas Hold 'em. It also boasts its own hybrid of Hold 'em in which players are dealt four cards, one of which must be discarded before the flop while a second must be mucked before the turn card is revealed. Buying in to a game can cost from €30 to €10,000 and the betting structures, starting at €2/€4 for fixed-limit tables, vary according to the minimum buy-in but include fixed-, pot- and no-limit games. A daily €30 no-limit Hold 'em tournament is staged each afternoon and on Saturday evenings there is a similar event for which the buy-in is €200. In common with many of Europe's prominent casinos, the Aviation Club insists that its patrons dress smartly, declining to admit anyone wearing a t-shirt or trainers.

THE PLAYERS

While the number of regular players who attend a home game may vary, in a casino the likelihood is that cash game tables will have from seven to ten players at a time competing against each other. If this represents a greater number of opponents than an individual is used to facing, then it is worth remembering that a more conservative approach will be required to garner any success. This is particularly important when bearing in mind that some of these opponents may be very good players indeed, added to which the house rake is an ever-present obstacle to negotiate. The standard of opposition very much depends on the location of the poker room, the stake levels in operation and, perhaps, even the time of day chosen to play. Peak times tend to be during the evenings and at weekends, of course, when games are likely to represent far tougher propositions.

Pros, semi-pros and tourists

The nature of the opposition varies from one card room to another, so a little research is advisable when considering a visit to a commercial establishment. Online reviews of specific venues can help players identify those that may best suit their financial means and skills. This is certainly a useful tool for anyone thinking of playing in Las Vegas or Atlantic City, although not all locations are as saturated with poker rooms as these hotbeds of tourism.

Wherever a player's chosen card room is situated, the likelihood is that there will be a regular clientele for whom poker is a major source of income. Such professionals, given their experience, will normally play at the higher-stakes tables, but they can be found playing lower-stakes cash games too. They may be passing the time waiting for a seat at a bigger game to

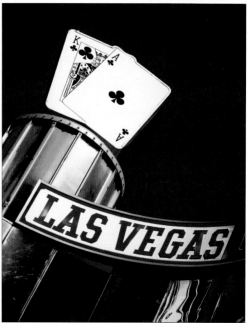

Above: Many of the largest hotel, casino and resort properties in the world are located on 'The Strip'– four miles of boulevard that has been designated an All-American Road. New casinos design their facades to attract walk-up customers and many of these entrances have become attractions themselves.

Left: Professional Danish poker player Mads Andersen, winner of the four-day EPT Scandinavian Open 2006, which saw him take home €341,000 in winnings. The Dane had to work hard for the money, with the final table lasting a record 10 hours. Before making his mark in the poker world, Andersen was a former World Backgammon Champion.

become available or, having endured a run of bad fortune, may be trying to restore their bankroll by capitalizing on the inexperience of casual players. Such tourists commonly make the mistake of playing a little too loosely in their eagerness to become involved in the action, perhaps replicating the style of play in their regular home games. By trying to force the issue in this fashion, inexperienced players make the task of the patient professionals and semi-professionals that much easier. The latter will know that by waiting for a top-quality hand before betting, they will almost certainly find a caller or two who is immediately at a disadvantage and so likely to lose the pot.

Anybody considering a poker holiday of some form, particularly to Las Vegas, should approach the experience with a realistic set of expectations. The prospect of an average player winning a fortune at the poker table is unlikely given the typical standard of competition. Indeed, conventional wisdom suggests that poker tourists should budget for losses at the table as they would for any other leisure entertainment. Anyone who breaks even over a few sessions while managing to combat the ravages of the rake can then be satisfied that they have skills of a competent player.

Above: Tourists enjoying the nightlife in Las Vegas, marketed as 'the entertainment capital of the world', also commonly known as 'sin city' due to the popularity of legalized gambling, availability of alcohol at any time, and various forms of adult entertainment. The city's image has made it a popular setting for films and television programmes.

Below: Increasing numbers of casinos offer table card games where there are alternative ways to play and win. Three card poker is an exciting stud poker game where players may bet against the dealer or bet on the value of their own three-card hand or bet both. Bonus payouts may be had for certain wagers against the dealer.

CONCORD CARD CASINO, VIENNA
♦ ♣ ♥ ♠

The Concord Card Casino, located on the Geiselbergstrasse in Vienna, has only been open since 1993 and is renowned for having the largest poker room in Europe. No-limit Texas Hold 'em, pot-limit Omaha and fixed-limit seven-card stud account for the bulk of the games played, with the casino acknowledging that many more young players are taking seats at its 30 poker tables. Fixed-limit Hold 'em is also on offer, with stakes ranging from €3/€6 up to €15/€30, while seven-card stud games begin at the €20/€40 level. Tournaments are organized each evening with buy-ins ranging from €4 to €200. The Concord stages several high-stakes tournaments during the year, the most prestigious being the Austrian Poker Championship, part of Vienna's Spring Poker Festival held in March, and the European Poker Masters, one element of the Austrian Classics held each October. Both competitions require a buy-in of €3,000. The Concord has no membership policy although it insists that players dress relatively smartly and refrain from wearing jeans and t-shirts.

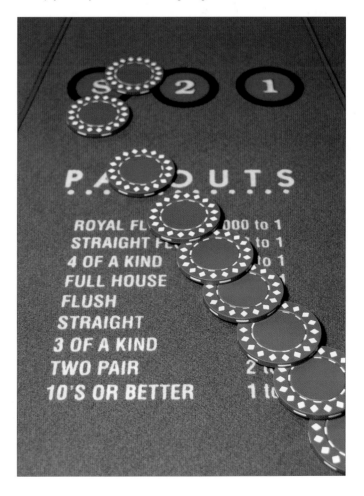

THE CASINO ENVIRONMENT

Casino profitability is dependent upon keeping customers comfortably entertained for as long as possible, since the longer they stay, the more likely it is that they will lose money. Windows and clocks are noticeable by their absence and, with air-conditioning systems that help maintain a constant temperature, the whole casino experience is geared towards separating clients from any connection with the outside world.

Poker players may benefit from preferential facilities in some establishments, but many poker rooms compete for space with other gambling attractions. Consequently, it is quite common for a busy room with plenty of tables in operation to generate a great volume of noise, which, along with the distractions emanating from other gaming tables, can test a player's powers of concentration. Technological developments have seen the larger, more prestigious poker rooms striving to improve their booking systems in an effort to help operations run more smoothly, but regular poker players can be tough customers to please.

Playing conditions

Anyone seriously contemplating a game of poker normally expects to spend several hours engaged in competition, even if moving from one table to another during a session. With this in mind, the conditions of play with regard to the poker room itself become more significant. The large oval tables could host ten players who are all sat in close proximity to each other, which, if the scene is replicated throughout the room, can make the experience slightly claustrophobic. If this in itself is not too intimidating, then confronting opponents wearing hats or sunglasses to obscure their facial expressions may seem slightly disconcerting. In terms of physical well-being, an occasional break from even the most comfortable seat will be needed and poker rooms with toilet facilities nearby always score highly with reviewers.

At the tables, competent dealers will ensure a steady pace to the game, with some venues even possessing automatic shuffling machines to help reduce the inevitable pause between hands. There will rarely be time for players to indulge in a weighty discussion on the outcome of a hand before the next is dealt, such inquests being of little interest to those who were not involved, in any case.

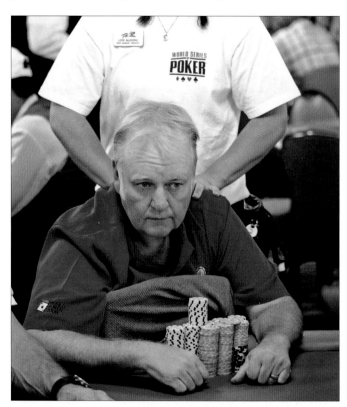

Above: American professional Russ Hamilton receiving a massage during the Hold 'em main event in the 2005 World Series of Poker. Hamilton, who started playing poker when he was seven years old, won the event in 1994, claiming a US$1 million prize. Since it was the 25th anniversary of the WSOP, he also won his weight in silver.

Above: Inside the Casino Barrière de Deauville in Normandy, France, during the French Open tournament of 2005. In the annals of James Bond memorabilia, it is said that Ian Fleming, the spy's creator, modelled the gambling salon of his novel *Casino Royale* on the baize tables and spinning roulette wheels in Deauville.

Distractions

Coming to terms with an unfamiliar environment, speed of play at the table and the quality of the opposition is a major challenge, given the other potential distractions in a card room. It can be difficult to ignore the general level of background noise arising from adjacent tables and the steady stream of players coming and going from the facility. Also, spectators may sometimes stop by to see how play is progressing, either because they are checking out the competition at a table for which they would like a seat or, perhaps, because they are friendly with one of the players competing in the game. If waiting staff are on hand to provide table service as well, the potential level of disruption to a player's concentration becomes apparent.

Coping with these factors is a test of character, of course, but if a player feels uncomfortable at any time, it is always best to take a break or change tables if possible. Anything that creates a degree of stress while playing is bound to have an impact on an individual's performance, which will inevitably detract from the experience of playing in a dedicated poker room.

TRUMP TAJ MAHAL, ATLANTIC CITY
♦ ♣ ♥ ♠

Recently voted 'best casino' by *Casino Player* magazine readers, the Trump Taj Mahal boasts Atlantic City's biggest poker room and has played host to the US Poker Championships for the past 10 years. Tables are dedicated to Texas Hold 'em, Omaha and seven-card stud, along with their high-low variants, and there are free daily lessons teaching newcomers. Stake levels begin at US$1/$3 for seven-card stud and US$2/$4 for pot-limit Texas Hold 'em, while there are no-limit Texas Hold 'em tournaments staged each day. The minimum buy-in is for US$38 plus US$12, although these games begin at midnight on weekdays, with the betting levels rising every 12 minutes. Opened in 1990 and built to rival anything on offer in Las Vegas, the Trump Taj Mahal is a major attraction for holidaymakers, as well as poker tourists, drawn to the east coast of America.

Above: The trademark sunglasses that professional poker player Greg Raymer wore when he won the 2004 World Series of Poker tournament. The holographic lizard eyes began as a joke during a big hand in the 2002 WSOP, but it seemed to have a desirable effect, distracting his opponent. Since then, Raymer has worn the glasses in all the major poker tournaments that he has played.

Right: A lit fountain shimmers at night in front of a large neon sign at the Trump Taj Mahal casino resort in Atlantic City. It is currently undergoing a US$250 million renovation and addition of a new hotel tower, on which work commenced in July 2006.

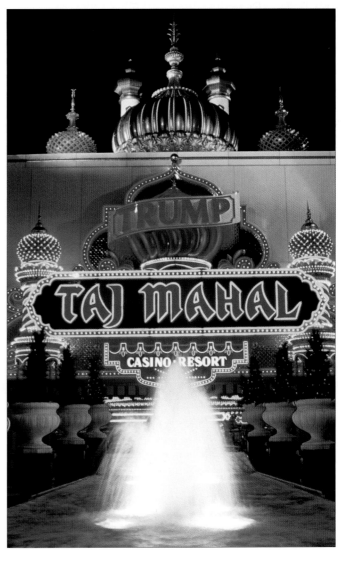

KEY ADVICE

Putting into practice the principles outlined so far is always going to be difficult the first time a player tackles casino poker. However, while it may take a while to adjust to the different conditions, there are several key factors worth remembering that can help alleviate any initial stress. Perhaps the most obvious is to choose a game at a comfortable stake level that is relative to the size of a player's bankroll. If successfully adopting a more cautious attitude, it is possible that a player could see the deal circulate the table several times before winning a hand. Having sufficient chips to cover the antes or blinds while, perhaps, losing the odd contested pot is therefore essential to enable a player to sustain interest throughout such a lean spell.

Should a game at the right level not be available, then it is better to play for lower stakes, rather than joining a game that is, in all conscience, beyond one's means. A profitable session against players of similar ability might provide the impetus to move up a grade, and this situation is certainly more likely to enhance a player's confidence than dropping down a level, having already lost a substantial chunk of one's bankroll. Understanding the routines of a chosen poker variation is also vital, of course, since playing an unfamiliar game is likely to prove a costly exercise in education without some prior knowledge of even the most basic strategies to adopt.

Above: Edgar Skjervold at the EPT Monte Carlo event in 2006. Skjervold, a 30-year-old financial analyst from Oslo, Norway, is part of a talented Norwegian group of players who have burst upon the poker scene in recent years. He shot to prominence after winning the World Championship of Online Poker in 2004, taking home US$424,945. No Internet-based competition of any kind in history has ever awarded such a large cash prize.

Above: A tired-looking actor Tobey Maguire reacting to losing during a game of Texas Hold 'em at the World Series of Poker in Las Vegas in 2005. Casinos are designed to shake cash from your pockets and can wear you down if you do not take regular breaks. Players who are really exhausted would do well to remember that the casino is probably open 24 hours a day and a game will always be happening somewhere tomorrow.

Budgeting time

Presented with an opportunity to play poker at any time, day or night, it is easy for players to fall into the trap of over-indulging their interest. Maintaining the levels of concentration required to play studiously and competently is a tall order for even the most accomplished professionals. Knowing when to walk away from the table is therefore as much a part of disciplined poker play as anything a player may need to exhibit while in competition. One lapse in concentration could undo plenty of good work earlier in the session, so regular breaks are also advisable when intending to play for several hours at a time.

This is particularly important if, having played well, an individual suffers a bad beat that wipes out any short-term gains already accrued. Controlling the anger or frustration experienced following an unlucky loss can test the mettle of almost any player, but only the very best are able to accept the result calmly and not allow it to prejudice their subsequent betting patterns. The crucial thing to

Right: Chips from the Grosvenor Victoria casino. A highlight of The Vic's poker calendar is the annual Grosvenor Grand Prix, an event which features a collection of big buy-in tournaments and attracts players from all over Europe to compete for millions of pounds in prize money.

Left: Among the largest and oldest of the casinos in the UK, The Vic as it is known, featured a classic upset during The Poker Classics, held there in April 2005, when the relatively unknown Andy Church placed first among nearly two hundred players, including many who are well known on the circuit.

avoid in such circumstances is the type of reckless play that signifies a player is 'on tilt' – this is characterized by betting more heavily on marginal hands to try and compensate for earlier perceived injustices. Should any player suspect that their game is deteriorating along these lines, it is well worth remembering that a fresh opportunity to play is rarely long in coming, such is the widespread access to poker now available.

GROSVENOR VICTORIA CASINO, LONDON
♦ ♣ ♥ ♠

London's Grosvenor Victoria Casino, often referred to as 'The Vic', is a popular haunt for many of the city's top poker players and it regularly stages high-stakes tournaments, some occasionally recorded for television. Its two card rooms offer 14 poker tables and there are daily no-limit Texas Hold 'em tournaments at stake levels ranging from £10 to £100, plus administration fees. Inexpensive rebuy tournaments for beginners are a feature of Friday nights and such games are an increasingly common part of the casino scene, such is the demand for the game in the UK. Anyone wishing to enter the Grosvenor Victoria will have to register for free membership by producing some form of personal identification. However, players are permitted to enter the premises promptly, having registered, rather than being forced to wait for 24 hours before sampling the action, as was the case until the UK removed this legal stipulation in 2005. Along with most of the country's casinos, a 'smart casual' dress code is *de rigeur*.

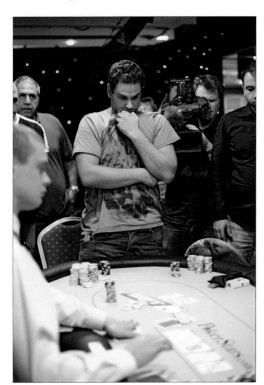

Above: English Roland 'the Sheep' de Wolfe deep in thought at the final table of the EPT event in Dublin in 2006. He went on to win the tournament and the top prize of €554,300 (US$737,208) in the no-limit Texas Hold 'em event.

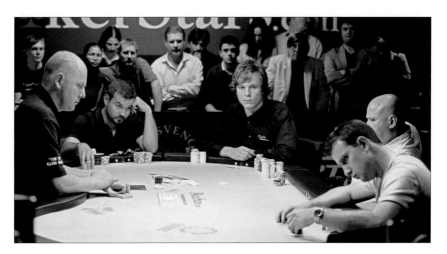

Above: The final table during the European Poker Tour's second season held in London in October 2005 at the Grosvenor Victoria Casino. American Noah Jefferson and Norwegian Jonas Helness watch as British player Mark Teltscher checks his cards. Teltscher went on to win the £3,000 (US$5,900) no-limit Hold 'em main event, taking home the £280,000 (US$552,000) first prize.

CASH GAMES AND TOURNAMENTS

As a gambling medium, poker has always been premised upon the idea of players vying with each other for sums of cash or some other meaningful currency. Since its early days, however, poker has developed into a wide range of different games with a variety of betting structures to match. Up until the 1970s, poker remained conceptually a cash game, with players buying in for a stipulated maximum or minimum sum prior to a session. But the success of the WSOP and the exposure of poker on television have increased the popularity of tournament poker, which has also been given a phenomenal boost by the advent of online gambling sites. This has led to distinctive differences in the strategies and approaches to be adopted when playing cash game poker as opposed to a tournament. The purpose of this chapter is to identify some of those differences and outline the key facets of both forms of the game.

Right: A player rakes in the chips at the conclusion of a hand. Whether playing a cash game or a tournament, winning a hand and claiming the pot is every player's objective as the cards are being dealt. Those new to the game often mistakenly believe that winning at poker is predicated upon winning a majority of hands played during a session. Experienced players know, however, that the key to long-term success lies in winning the few hands that generate big pots. This holds true for both cash games and poker tournaments even if strategies applied in one form of the game may not always be advisable in the other.

CASH GAMES

Cash games, or ring games if preferred, are the mainstay of poker and involve players gambling with the money at their disposal, usually in the form of chips obtained from the acting cashier. The stake levels and betting limits of the various games differ, of course, and players will naturally gravitate towards those that suit them best.

Typically, in a formal card room, there will be a minimum buy-in required of perhaps as little as five times the maximum bet, offering the scope for playing at minimal cost. However, most experts recommend that players should not consider sitting in on any game with less than forty times the maximum bet. This is premised on the assumption that any fulfilling poker session will most probably last for several hours during which time a sustained run of poor cards or bad beats is almost inevitable.

In games where a maximum buy-in also applies, players may be allowed to rebuy chips during a pause in play to maintain their stacks at that level. Taking advantage of this possibility is also advised as a very positive strategy for two reasons. First, under table-stakes rules, players can only bet with the chips currently on the table, with any rebuys to be conducted at the conclusion of the hand. Betting all-in when holding the nuts is much more profitable with a large stack than with a small one, should a big pot develop, therefore it makes sense to keep as many chips as possible available for such an eventuality. This obviously involves avoiding games in which the buy-in could immediately absorb a player's entire bankroll. The second reason for doing so is simply to maintain a credible defence against opponents who bet aggressively to intimidate those short on chips. Without the

Above: Actor Lou Diamond Phillips playing poker at the Celebrity World Poker Tour held at the Commerce Casino in Los Angeles, USA. A popular spectator sport, celebrity poker has many actors among its leading lights. The cash winnings are often donated to charity.

Left: Rhett Butler (Clark Gable) keeps a cool head while playing poker in the film of *Gone with the Wind*. In real life too, containing one's emotions is an essential part of playing the game well.

Left: Jamie Gold of Malibu, California, becomes the new World Series of Poker champion, winning US$12 million in Las Vegas, Nevada, 11 August 2006. The prize of US$12 million is the largest ever won in television or sport. The top 12 players competing in this tournament became millionaires.

Below: When playing cash games, you need to decide what sort of bankroll you are willing to commit to the game. It is not advisable to play in games that are either too big or too small for your bankroll and comfort. If you do so, your emotions may well get in the way of your ability to think logically.

resources to make the occasional re-raise, players run the risk of being anted away in the face of aggressive betting while they are waiting for a competitive hand. It is difficult to be successful if, when such as hand is held, a player does not have the resources to capitalize upon it to the fullest extent.

The long-term strategy

Although poker is rooted in competition, the risks that must be taken in order to win will very often lead to defeat. This applies during every hand of every session, which means that players must very quickly come to terms with losing and how it can affect their decisions. Having the discipline to control one's emotional reactions while playing poker is an asset, since it is all too easy to tilt, following a succession of losing hands. By allowing frustration or anger to guide one's play, it is likely that any losses will be compounded by poor betting decisions. Not every session will prove profitable and being able to walk away from the table while losing is a test of character that confronts every poker player.

Such a prospect is easier to accept when each individual session is considered merely one of countless others to be played during a lifetime. By setting realistic targets and keeping a record of performances, regular players who hope to improve their game, and perhaps even make it profitable, are better able to put losing sessions into perspective.

THE BANKROLL
♦ ♣ ♥ ♠

Managing the bankroll is of the utmost importance for a poker player, this being the cash specifically reserved for playing the game. Very few poker players are sponsored and the majority of full-time professionals are entirely reliant upon their ability to win in order to earn an income. Should their bankroll become exhausted, they have no immediate means of buying in to another game, which is one of the reasons why the best players are ruthless and clinical in their approach; they cannot afford to adopt any other attitude. Most players, however, will simply allocate a proportion of their income to poker in much the same way as they would for any other leisure interest. For the amateur, the test of discipline comes in treating the bankroll in the same way as a professional, since that is the surest way of promoting a competitive instinct.

ADOPTING THE RIGHT APPROACH

The reasons for playing poker are as many and varied as the people who enjoy the game, although purists insist that players should always strive to be as tough, ruthless and competitive as possible in order to do themselves justice. Each individual may have contrasting motives for playing, but all should consider some basic questions concerning how long they may wish to play, the nature of the opposition, and the potential cost involved. Only when these questions are satisfactorily answered can they hope to feel at ease and ready to play their best. Similarly, approaching the game in a positive frame of mind is obviously advantageous, with players who are tired, jaded or otherwise distracted by external pressures unlikely to exploit their true ability.

Home games

Regular games conducted at home between friends or colleagues have the potential to be as harshly competitive as any casino session involving poker's high-rollers. On the whole, though, such games are typically social events played for sums that are rarely large enough to endanger long-lasting friendships. Food, drink and conversation are as much a part of such events as playing cards, and this should be taken into account when devising even the vaguest of strategies.

Winning may not be the most pressing concern for the amateur player but nobody deliberately sets out to lose. Observing opponents to gather an appreciation of their playing styles and levels of ability remains an important skill. This is particularly true when invited to play in a regular home game for the first time, since even good friends may reveal personal characteristics in their poker that had previously never surfaced during the relationship.

Clubs and casinos

Buying in to a table operated by a club or casino can be a daunting experience for the novice player who is better acquainted with the home game. Although the stake levels may offer clues regarding the ability of the opposition, engaging in competition with strangers still requires a degree of self-confidence in one's own skill. Choosing the correct level at which to play is crucial, of course, and a disciplined approach to the time that is to be spent playing during a session is also important. Also, in formal card rooms there is always the rake to consider, this being the fee levied by the house for operating the game. The fee could be charged on an hourly basis, either per table or per player, or it could simply be that the dealer takes a few

Above: The home game is where poker maintains its hold on the public imagination as this is where most poker is played. Using proper poker chips brings credibility to the game. Apart from being easier to use than cash, they help speed up the action.

Right: Extreme Poker is an initiative that is taking the game to exhilarating frontiers, no matter how strange. Poker professional Rob Varkonyi (far left) competes against other players during the second Extreme Poker tournament, held atop the vast ice fields of the Arctic Sea in Kemi, Finland, in March 2006.

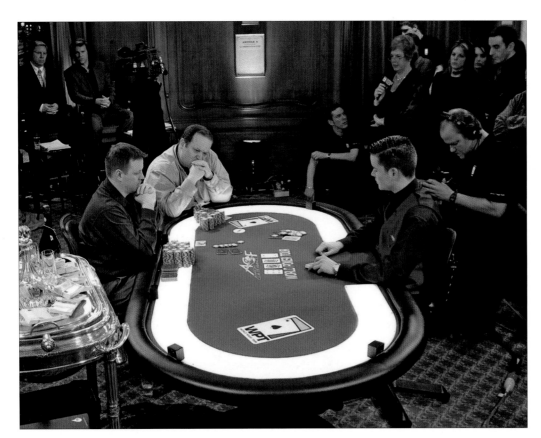

Left: Swede Christer Johansson (far left), ultimate winner of the World Poker Tour (WPT) first season Grand Prix de Paris event in 2003, playing heads-up at the final table with Frenchman Claude Cohen (centre), considered by many to be France's top player. Christer took home the €500,000 (US$659,450) first prize. Timing in poker is of huge importance and never more so than when competing at the highest level. To be successful in a competitive arena, being able to adjust your style of play and frequently change gear are invaluable skills.

chips from every winning pot up to a maximum of perhaps 10 per cent. With a cut from each pot going to the house and the winner of each reasonable pot customarily tipping the dealer, the pace of the game will also be quicker than in home games, it being in the dealer's interests to ensure that is the case. The combination of all these factors underlines, once more, the need for a realistic assessment of one's ability when deciding to play in public.

Quality of opponents

Players can expect to encounter opponents of much higher quality in commercial card rooms than they would in their home games. Leaving aside the tournament-level professionals, many other players manage to grind out a living from poker, defying the rake and their opponents in order to do it. For these players and the semi-professionals who supplement their regular income with profitable stints at the table, poker is simply a job requiring a high degree of application. Those they prey upon are the tourists, occasional poker players whose bankrolls, perhaps, exceed their abilities but who enjoy the chance to pit their wits against the best. Although it is a much more impersonal experience, the same considerations still apply for those who play online.

KEEPING COUNT

♦ ♣ ♥ ♠

So much advice concerning sound poker play emphasizes the benefits of analysing performance, as well as exercising discipline and patience. These virtues are also important for the serious player who wishes to improve with experience. Keeping a mental record of one's play in certain scenarios is an asset when studying the game away from the table. Players should also keep accurate financial records of their poker. Ultimately, money is simply a means of keeping score, with a good poker player being one who, year after year, regularly makes a profit. Only by being honest with themselves and making an accurate note of poker income and expenditure can players expect to be objective about their overall performance.

Left: It can be argued that the televising of poker tournaments has already given poker playing a whole new air of respectability, which is sure to attract a lot of people to tip their hand at it.

TOURNAMENT PLAY

Inspired by television coverage of tournament poker and the potential prize money on offer for winning, many more players are developing a taste for this form of the game. Whereas a commercial cash game in a 24-hour club or casino may, in theory, continue indefinitely as players come and go from the table, a tournament is structured to ensure a definitive winner at the end of the event. To this end, the antes and blinds in tournaments progressively increase, whereas in cash poker, they remain at a constant level as dictated by the terms of the game. Each betting level may apply for a matter of minutes or a matter of hours, depending on the nature and scale of the tournament, but the principle is always the same, with the objective for each player, of course, being to win all the chips in play.

Knockout poker

The major difference between cash games and tournaments is, of course, the knockout element that sees players eliminated when they run out of chips. To last the distance, players are compelled to engage in betting confrontations, which means they have to implement different strategies and contrasting styles of play at the various stages of the tournament.

In a cash game, tight players can usually allow the deal to circulate the table a couple of times while waiting for a playable hand, without the antes seriously damaging their chip stacks. Although commendable as a general long-term playing strategy, the nature of knockout poker precludes maintaining this patient approach throughout a tournament. During the early stages, when survival is of primary concern, patience is certainly required, but, as the antes increase and opponents acquire more chips, players must bet forcefully and be prepared to take greater risks.

Above: American Joe Bartholdi, winner of the 2006 WPT no-limit Hold 'em US$25,000 buy-in championship sits amid bundles of cash after winning US$3.7 million – the biggest pot ever in the tournament's history up to that point. Bartholdi outlasted a field of 605 players to claim the first place prize. The victory came after years of mixed fortunes due to experiencing difficulty maintaining a stable bankroll.

Left: An enormous poster for Full Tilt Poker, found outside the game room at the 2005 WSOP. The online gaming site is well known for having a huge team of poker professionals on its advertising team (Phil Ivey, Chris 'Jesus' Ferguson, Howard Lederer, Mike Matusow, to name but a few). Exposure aside, the site has excellent reviews for its software: its player-friendly website was conceived and designed by professional players. Full Tilt's advertising campaigns have taken promotion of the game to a new level.

Entry fees and prize structures

For tournaments, entry fees vary dramatically, with the events held at the WSOP, for example, generally costing US$500 and upwards, while the World Championship game itself requires a buy-in of US$10,000. At the lower end of the scale, casinos and clubs stage tournaments for much smaller entry fees and such games are also a very popular element of online poker. There are even freeroll tournaments that require no entry fee but usually result in the winner being offered a seat in a more prestigious competition. Satellite tournaments are similar in nature, with players paying a small fee for the chance to win a place in the next round of the main event.

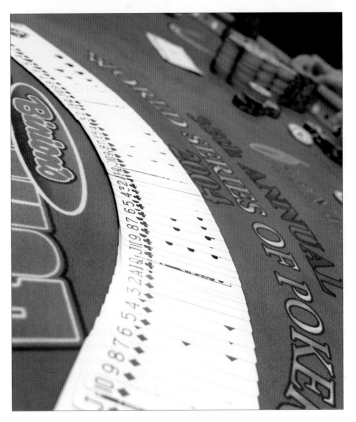

The great benefit of playing tournament poker compared to cash games is that players can be certain at the outset of the maximum they stand to lose. In order to win, however, it is possible they may have to outlast several hundred opponents, which is obviously a major challenge. The prize money is usually allocated to those who finish in the top ten per cent of entrants, but the lion's share of the cash tends to be reserved for the top three or four per cent, the winner perhaps claiming between a quarter and a half of the entire prize pool.

Types of tournament

Most of the popular variations are played in tournament fashion and all can be conducted as fixed-pot or no-limit contests. The number of competitors may range from the 8,000-strong entry for the WSOP World Championship, the most celebrated of all multi-table tournaments, to a private heads-up contest between just two players. Single-table tournaments exist that offer players a better chance of victory for a much smaller top prize, of course, and many of these are known as sit 'n' go events. Players simply pay the required fee and, when all seats are taken, the tournament immediately begins. These differ from the regular diarized competitions for which players may enter some time in advance.

One other key factor for players to bear in mind is the distinction between freeze-out and rebuy tournaments. In the former, all players start with the same number of chips for their fixed fee and play until they either lose them all or win the tournament. Subject to certain conditions, players may purchase more chips during a rebuy tournament, with the opportunity to do this typically restricted to the first hour or two of the event. After that, the tournament continues as a freeze-out competition.

Above left: Eventual winner of the WSOP 2006 championship, Jamie Gold (centre), focuses on a hand as the players compete to be in the final nine. It stands to reason that at this stage, players must be observant in order to pick up clues from the table. The prospect of reaching the final table beckons, and with it a share of the prize pool, so players may tighten up their play to protect their chip position.

Left: Pack of cards on display at the WSOP championship in 2004. Like any major sporting event, the WSOP has corporate sponsors which pay fees to market themselves as an official sponsor or licensee and exclusively use the WSOP insignia and cross-promote with their events. In addition to Harrah's properties and cable TV networks dedicated to sports broadcasting, the major sponsors have included Miller Brewing, Pepsi, GlaxoSmithKline/Bayer and Nintendo.

Tournament Strategy

A single-table event with rapidly increasing betting levels may be over in a matter of minutes, while most multi-table tournaments comprising thirty or more entrants could easily last for several hours. The likely duration of the tournament will therefore have a bearing on strategy, as only those who finish in the top ten per cent typically win a share of the prize pool.

During the early stages, survival is very much the primary concern and players are advised to adopt a tight and cautious approach while they evaluate the opposition. Judgement of starting hands is crucial and, whichever poker variation is being played, avoiding unnecessary and potentially costly confrontations early on in the tournament is generally advisable. There will always be those who prefer to gamble from the outset, in an attempt to gain an early advantage, but playing a conservative game while reckless opponents knock each other out is arguably a better long-term strategy.

Having evaded an early exit, however, players can still expect the pressure to build as the tournament develops. The regular increases in the minimum betting level ensure this as players find themselves having to contest pots with hands they might ordinarily fold. Those who are short of chips can expect to see large and intimidating bets emanating from the chip leaders as the proximity of the prize-money places draws near.

Distinguishing features

Recognizing distinctive betting patterns among opponents is always important at the poker table. This is no less true in a tournament and is an asset at a single-table event in which players only vacate their seats when they are eliminated. Distinguishing the cautious strategists from the loose gamblers is relatively straightforward under these circumstances.

Multi-table tournaments present a different challenge, however, since players will be moved between tables, to equalize numbers as others are

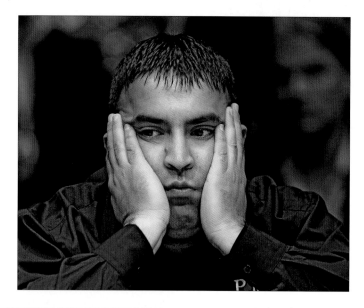

Above: British player Arshad Hussain, at the EPT 2006 grand final held in Monte Carlo. The dramatic final stages of the tournament ended with Hussain in a heads-up showdown against American political science student Jeff Williams, who went on to win the big event taking home €900,000 (US$1,078,000). Arshad had spent nothing to reach Monte Carlo after winning an online satellite tournament and took home €492,000 (US$592,607) for his second place.

Left: Players try their luck during the early stages of the WSOP 2006 held at the Rio hotel and casino, in Las Vegas. The enormous scale of the tournament can be intimidating for amateur players, and ten- or eleven-handed games mean that space at tables is tight.

eliminated and tables are taken out of action. Having acquired a healthy chip lead at one table and profited from the opportunity to intimidate the short stacks, a player could be moved to another table where an opponent or two may have many more chips. If this is the case, a player once again needs to take stock of the opposition and their betting styles to discover whether the leaders have been skilfully shrewd or simply lucky. Of course, as the tournament progresses towards the final table and the antes or blinds increase, betting patterns tend to be dictated by the chips at a player's disposal more than any other factor.

Monitoring chip stacks

The need to keep abreast of developments elsewhere is an element of multi-table tournament play that is not replicated in cash games. The technology behind online tournaments facilitates hand-by-hand updates, allowing contestants to gauge their progress against opponents at other tables. Outside the world of the virtual casino, however, players may have to take the occasional break from their own game in order to regroup their thoughts and check the progress of opponents at other tables.

In a freeze-out contest, the total number of chips in play is constant, so calculating the current average is a straightforward matter of dividing the chip total by the number of players remaining. Maintaining an

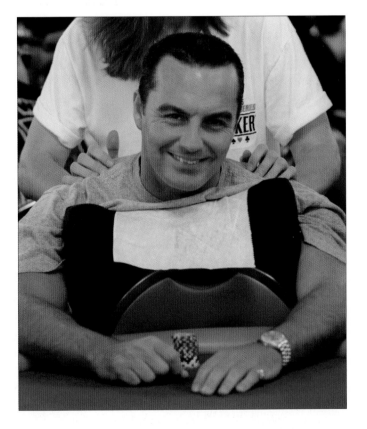

above-average chip stack during the earlier stages of a tournament can provide the foundation for more attacking play as short-stacked opponents are threatened by the prospect of elimination. However, it is worth remembering that from the middle stages onwards, the average stack may be some way short of the chip leader if one player has managed to attain a dominant lead.

HOW TO WIN

The greater the number of competitors, the more difficult any tournament is to win, of course, and it is true that players may have to rely on good fortune at key moments to a greater extent than when contesting a cash game. Armed with a sound strategy and a consistent approach in the selection of which hands to support, players are more likely to finish ahead on a regular basis if restricting their poker to the cash game format.

Tournament poker, however, calls for more risks to be taken in order both to survive and to prosper. The size of a player's chip stack will dictate the frequency and scale of those risks, with players who are down to ten times the minimum bet or less faced with the prospect that every hand could be their last. Those in good shape have more options from which to choose, since they can contest a few more multi-handed pots with low-ranking cards if opponents choose not to raise the betting. Alternatively, there is always the option to sit back for a while and wait patiently while opponents jostle for position by eliminating each other. Anyone who has improved on their starting stack by judiciously sticking to a tight game plan is also in a better position to bluff from the middle stages onwards as the cost of participating in a hand inevitably increases. Opponents will be wary of calling such a solid player and this provides the opportunity to pick up some valuable chips from some weakly contested pots.

Stay alert

The key to absorbing all the information available while playing poker is concentration, whatever form of the game is being played. In tournaments, taking stock of the opposition, their playing styles and the fluctuations in stack sizes requires a high degree of mental application. Accomplishing this as well as monitoring events at the surrounding tables demands that competitors stay alert. As the average chip count increases, for example, players should be acutely aware that they need to win a few pots to stay ahead of the game. The danger with playing too tightly and falling well behind is that a player may eventually face betting all-in with such limited resources that even winning the hand may be of little benefit. Being alert to the possibility of this happening and adjusting one's play accordingly can therefore prevent a player from having to implement increasingly desperate strategies.

Above: Victoria Cohen, well-known British newspaper columnist, author and TV presenter beat 397 others to win £500,000 (US$976,200) in the sell-out EPT event in London in 2006.

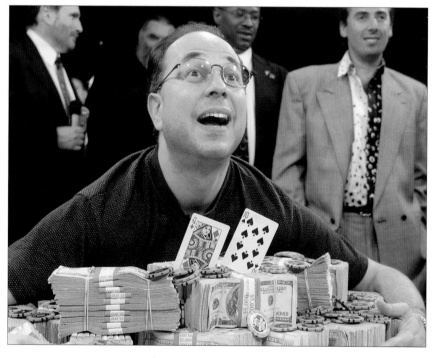

Above: Former investment banker Rob Varkonyi looks on in amazement after winning the WSOP in 2002. The American became an instant celebrity and professional poker player following his surprise victory. Phil Hellmuth said at the time that the odds against Varkonyi winning were so high that he would shave his head if he won.

Above: Norwegian Bjorn-Erik Glenne was crowned winner of the European Poker Tour event in Barcelona in 2006, beating 480 players to claim the €691,000 prize (US$875,000). The former marketing manager is the first Norwegian to win an EPT event. Glenne is also a high-ranking chess player and enjoys substantial success online.

Left: Chris Moneymaker at the final table of the 2003 WSOP. He earned his way into the championship event by playing in an online poker tournament at a cost of US$40 and went on to win the first prize of US$2.5 million, despite the fact it was his first experience of a 'live' poker tournament.

From the chip leader's perspective, choosing the right time to pressurize a short-stacked opponent is no less challenging. While intimidating the opposition with large bets is a viable option, it is still best to do so when in possession of a strong hand. Inducing all-in calls or raises from opponents short on chips can easily backfire if betting with a marginal hand, since being vulnerable does not preclude them from having excellent cards. Similarly, calling a short-stacked opponent's all-in bet is easier to justify when holding a decent hand, there being little profit from continually calling in such situations simply because one has the chips to spare.

Change gear
The ability to change gear by varying one's betting patterns and general approach is required in both cash games and tournaments. In the former, adopting a contrasting style to that prevalent among the opposition can be beneficial, with tight play best at a table of loose players, and more expansive play possible when the opposition is ultra-conservative.

Responding in a similar way during a tournament is a good policy in the early stages, but the need to change gear is dictated by the increasing betting levels and the unavoidable impact they have on each competitor's play. Acquiring chips to withstand the ravages of the antes and blinds means players will often have to contemplate betting with a poor hand. Taking a positive stance and betting aggressively in this situation is generally a better policy than passively calling and hoping for the best. Having to adopt this more forceful approach on occasions is probably the greatest distinguishing factor between tournaments and cash games, where a consistently patient strategy can prove rewarding. As a result, individuals who regularly play tournament poker should adjust their thinking accordingly when reverting to a cash game.

GLOSSARY

A

Ace in the hole A slang expression referring to the ace playing card a player has as a hole card (or face-down card) in a game of stud poker.

Aces up The term used to indicate that a player possesses a pair of aces coupled with a pair of lower rank.

Action The betting activity at the poker table.

Add-on A purchase of more chips (optional) at the end of the rebuy period in a tournament.

All-in Wagering all one's remaining chips in a single bet.

Ante A compulsory bet made by one or more players before the deal.

Ante-up Put one's ante in the pot.

B

Back-door flush Securing a flush against the odds when the turn and river cards fall favourably in community card games like Texas Hold 'em and Omaha.

Back-door straight Securing a straight in the same manner as above.

Bad beat This occurs when a strong hand is beaten by an inferior hand that improves against the odds.

Bankroll Stake money. It can refer to a player's stake during a single session or to the total amount allocated solely for the purpose of playing poker over an extended period.

Bet The action of putting chips in the pot.

Betting intervals The occasions during play when bets are permitted.

Bicycle The lowest possible straight comprising A, 2, 3, 4, 5.

Big slick Slang term for hole cards of A, K when dealt in Texas Hold 'em.

Blind Compulsory bet, or ante, made in games such as Texas Hold 'em and Omaha. Usually, the player to the immediate left of the dealer bets the small blind and the next player to act bets the big blind, generally set at twice the level of the small.

Bluff The act of deception: making a strong bet to disguise a weak hand.

Board card The visible, face-up cards in play during stud poker, and the community cards revealed during Texas Hold 'em and Omaha.

Boat Another term for a full house.

Bring-in The forced bet made in the first round of betting by the player who is dealt the lowest card showing.

Bug A single wild card in play, typically the joker.

Bump To raise the betting in the pot.

Burn The discarding of the top card from the deck by the dealer, in order to guard against cheating.

Buy-in The fee required to sit in at a poker game.

C

Call Matching a bet already made to maintain interest in the hand.

Caller A player who makes a call bet.

Call the blind Matching the bet amount of the blinds. These are bets made by the two players sitting directly to the dealer's left to start the action on the first round of betting.

Card sharp A person who cheats at cards.

Calling station A passive and loose player who does not raise much and who repeatedly calls other players' bets, irrespective of his chances of winning.

Cards speak The means of adjudicating a decision at the showdown. In wild card games it prevent players from wrongly declaring the value of their hand.

Cash game The mainstay of poker games in casinos and online, involving players competing against each other, typically for several hours, in games with constant betting structures.

Cash in Exchanging chips for cash at the end of a session.

Chasing hand Hands that need two cards to realize their potential.

Check The act of deferring a betting decision while remaining in the hand. A player can only check if no bet has yet been made during the betting round.

Checkraise This describes the tactic of checking in a betting round and then raising a subsequent bet made by an opponent.

Chips Coloured counters used to represent cash sums at the poker table. Each colour represents a different denomination.

Coffeehousing Making abusive or critical comments regarding an opponent's hand while contesting a hand.

Community cards Cards dealt during a game that are common to all players.

Cut To divide the deck of cards after the shuffle, usually the responsibility of the player to the dealer's right.

D

Dealer's choice A style of play, popular in home games, whereby each successive dealer nominates which poker variation will apply for the hand they deal.

Declare Applicable to high-low games, this is the means by which players indicate whether they are aiming for the high hand, the low hand or both.

Deuce Slang term used to describe any of the four twos in the deck.

Door card The first exposed card in a player's hand in stud games.

Down the river Another name for the game of seven-card stud.

Draw The exchange of cards during a draw poker game. The word also applies generally to the need for a player to hit specific cards to secure a viable hand.

Drawing dead To be unable to beat an existing hand in play despite having more cards to come.

Drawing hand A hand that needs one more relevant card on the turn or river to improve sufficiently past a leading hand to win.

F

Family pot A pot contested by all, or nearly all, the players in the game.

Fifth street Simply the fifth card dealt in stud poker games, or the fifth card dealt to the board in community card games.

Fish Poor players.

Fixed-limit A betting structure that stipulates a fixed amount to be bet during each round. For example in a US$5/$10 fixed-limit game of Texas Hold 'em, bets and raises during the first two betting rounds must be in US$5 increments. During the final two rounds bets and raises are in US$10 increments.

Floorman A casino or card room employee who officiates over proceedings and arbitrates in any disputes.

Flop The first three community cards revealed, simultaneously, in Texas Hold 'em and similar games.

Flush A poker hand of five cards of the same suit not in sequential order.

Fold To discard one's cards and take no further part in a particular hand. Also called passing or mucking one's hand.

Forced bet An obligatory bet at a fixed amount.

Four of a kind Four cards of the same rank (number) supplemented by an additional card.

Fourth street The fourth card dealt in stud poker games, or the fourth community card dealt to the board.

Free card A card seen by players for no extra cost, usually occurring after a betting round in which all players checked.

Freeze-out A style of tournament in which all players begin with an equal amount in chips which cannot be replenished during the game.

Freeroll A chance to win something at no risk or cost.

Full-handed game A poker game that involves nine or ten players.

Full house A hand comprising three cards of one rank and two of another.

G

Geese Poor players.

Gut straight draw When the middle card of a straight sequence is needed to make the hand: a hand of 6, 7, 9, 10 needs an 8 to secure the straight.

H

Hand Each successive game dealt during a poker session, typically lasting just a few minutes. The term also describes the cards each individual player holds during each of these games.

Heads-up A confrontation between two players, typically the last two players left competing at a tournament table.

Hidden pair Two cards of the same rank dealt face down in a player's starting hand.

High card Simply the highest card counting in a player's hand when no pair or better is obtained.

High hand The best hand in any round of poker.

High-low A term used for split pot poker games, where the total stakes bet during the playing of each hand are divided equally between the highest and lowest hands still standing at the time of the showdown.

High-roller A gambler who plays for large stakes. Extreme high rollers are also referred to as 'whales'.

Holdout machine A device designed to help a cheater conceal cards and then reintroduce them to the game at a later point, i.e., to hold them out.

Hole cards The cards dealt face down to each player and remaining unseen by opponents for the duration of the hand, up to the point of any showdown.

I

Ignorant end The lower end of a straight in community card games.

Inside straight draw The situation faced when needing the second or fourth card in a sequence to make a straight, for example, when holding 8, 10, J, Q and requiring a 9 to complete the hand.

J

Jackpots A prize fund awarded to a player who meets a set of predetermined requirements. Some casinos will give a jackpot to someone who gets four of a kind or higher and loses. The game 'jackpots' refers to a form of draw poker in which a player needs to have at least a pair of jacks to open the betting.

K

Kicker The highest value card in a player's hand apart from a stronger holding. Should a player hold 9, 9, A, K, 7 – a pair of nines – then the kicker is the A. The kicker is significant in a situation where two players have the same value pair, or even two pairs. For example a hand of 9, 9, Q, 10, 2 loses to the earlier example because the Q kicker is outranked by the A.

L

Lock hand A hand that cannot lose.

Loose player Someone who contests many pots, often betting against the odds.

M

Main pot A pot contested by interested parties to the point when a player is all-in. Any further betting, excluding the all-in player, is entered in a side pot. It is possible to have several side pots in play during a hand.

Maniac A loose and unpredictable player.

Misdeal To make an error when dealing a hand.

Muck The pile of discarded cards that accrues during the play of a hand.

N

Naked bluff A bet made by players in the knowledge that their hand cannot win unless all other players fold.

No-limit The betting structure, often used in knockout tournaments, that allows players to bet all their chips at any time during the game when it is their turn to act.

Nut flush The 'nuts' represents the best possible hand, so the nut flush is the best possible flush obtainable.

Nut full house The best full house available.

Nuts The best hand available from the cards in play.

O

Offsuit Term to describe hole cards of differing suits, most often applicable in Texas Hold 'em.

On the come A situation occurring when a player draws cards to a hand with potential rather than one that is already made.

Open-ended straight Four cards in a sequence requiring a high or low card to complete the five-card straight. For example when holding 8, 9, 10, J either a 7 or a Q will make the hand.

Openers A minimum hand required in some poker variations in order to open the betting: a pair of Js in some draw poker games, for instance.

Out A card required to transform a losing hand into a winner.

Overcard A card higher than any card on the board. For example a player with A, Q as hole cards when the flop is J, 7, 3, has two overcards.

P

Pass To fold a hand.

Pat hand In draw poker, a hand dealt to a player who then opts not to exchange any cards at the draw, suggesting it is already strong.

Pigeons Poor players.

Play the board When a player's best poker hand comprises the five community cards on the board in Texas Hold 'em or Omaha.

Pocket card The two cards dealt to you at the beginning of a Hold 'em hand that no one else is entitled to see.

Pocket pair Two cards of the same rank in a starting hand.

Pocket rockets A pair of aces in the hole.

Poker face An expressionless facial appearance revealing no thoughts or emotions. Every player should have one.

Post the blinds When you post a bet, you place your chips in the pot. The blinds are compulsory bet(s) made by the two players sitting directly to the dealer's left before any cards are dealt, which will start the action on the first round of betting.

Pot The collective total of chips staked during each individual hand for which players compete.

Pot-limit A betting structure in which the maximum bet can be no higher than the total currently in the pot.

Pot odds The amount of money in the pot compared to the amount you must put in the pot to continue playing. If there is US$60 in the pot and a player bets US$6, to raise the pot total to US$66, it costs a player US$6 to call, making the pot odds 11:1.

Pre-flop raise A raise made before the first three community cards are revealed in Texas Hold 'em and similar games.

Q

Quads Four cards of the same rank. Four of a kind.

Quitting time An agreed-upon time to end a poker game (curfew).

R

Rag A worthless card or hand.

Raise To increase the betting level, usually by calling the previous bet and then wagering at least the same amount again.

Rake The fee charged by a club or casino for staging a poker game. Typically it involves a small deduction being made from each pot.

Razz Seven-card stud game in which the lowest hand claims the pot.

Read To assess the strength of an opponent's hand.

Rebuy tournament A style of tournament in which all players are permitted to buy additional chips after the game has started.

Ring game A 'live' cash game that is not a tournament.

River The final card dealt in some poker games.

Rock A tight, cautious player who only plays premium hands.

Rolled-up trip Three cards of the same rank held by a player after the deal in seven-card stud.

Rounder A person who travels the country to earn a living through gambling.

Royal flush The highest ranking poker hand consisting of 10, J, Q, K, A all of one suit.

Run Another term for a straight.

Rush Experienced when cards fall favourably enough for a player to win several pots in a short space of time.

S

Sandbagging The practice of slow-playing a strong hand, perhaps by checkraising, in order to trap opponents into betting.

Satellite tournament A mini-tournament to gain an entry into a larger tournament.

See To call a bet.

Semi-bluff A bet made in support of a weak hand that still retains the possibility of becoming an outright winner.

Set Another term for three of a kind.

Seventh street The seventh card dealt in poker games, most commonly seven-card stud.

Shark A good, crafty player often posing as a fish early in the game.

Sheep Poor players.

Short-handed game A poker game that involves only a few players.

Showdown The moment when players remaining in the hand reveal their cards to determine the winner at the conclusion of all betting.

Side bet Any bet made outside the pot.

Side pot Chips bet by players competing separately from the main pot, usually after another player has made an all-in bet.

Sixth street The sixth card dealt in seven-card stud, prefacing the fourth round of betting.

Slow-play To bet lightly, or check, in order to disguise a strong hand and encourage opponents to remain in the pot.

Split pair Two cards of the same face or number value, one dealt face down and one face up in a player's starting hand.

Split-pot A pot shared by players who, at the showdown, reveal hands of equal value. Also describes high-low games in which the spoils are divided between the highest and lowest ranking hands.

Spread-limit A betting structure featuring a lower and upper limit. Players may bet any amount within these limits during the game.

Stake The amount of a player's buy-in, or the amount of money they are willing to play with in a given session.

Stand pat To not draw any cards in a draw game.

Steal A bluffing bet that succeeds in causing opponents to fold..

Straight Five cards of differing suits in a sequence, for example, 5, 6, 7, 8, 9. Also called a run.

Straight flush Five cards of the same suit in a sequence.

String bet Placing chips in the pot as if to call before announcing a raise. The delay in stating the true nature of the bet helps the perpetrator gather extra information from opponents' reactions and is considered to be unacceptable.

Sucker A very poor player. Also, an innocent victim in a crooked game.

T

Table stakes A style of game in which players may only bet the chips available to them during a hand. If additional chips are needed to continue in the game, these may be bought between the playing of hands, not during.

Tap-out To bet all one's chips.

Tapped-out To be out of chips and in Tap city.

Tell An involuntary mannerism that may reveal the strength of a player's hand.

Third street Simply the third card dealt in stud poker games.

Three of a kind Three cards of the same number or value. Also called trips.

Tight player Someone who plays cautiously and only with strong hands.

Tilt Players are described as 'on tilt' when they lose control of their emotions and bet irrationally and without discipline.

Toke A tip for the card room dealer.

Touching cards Two cards that are consecutive in rank: a J, 10 for example.

Trey Any 3 in the deck.

Trips Three cards of the same value, abbreviated from triplets.

Turn The fourth community card dealt in Texas Hold 'em and Omaha.

Two pairs A hand consisting of two different pairs.

U

Underdog The least likely hand to win the pot, often shortened to 'dog'.

Under the gun Being the first person to act, being in the earliest position.

Up card A card that is dealt face up.

W

Wheel The lowest possible straight: A, 2, 3, 4, 5. Also called a bicycle.

Wild card Any nominated card, or the joker perhaps, that can be used by players to represent any other card in the deck.

Widow A card or cards common to all hands.

BIBLIOGRAPHY

Alvarez, Al, *The Biggest Game in Town* (Houghton Mifflin, Boston, 1983)

Bellin, Andy, *Poker Nation: A High-Stakes, Low-Life Adventure into the Heart of Gambling* (Yellow Jersey Press, London, 2003)

Brunson, Doyle, *Doyle Brunson's Super System: A Course in Power Poker* (B & G Publishing, Las Vegas, 1978)

Dalla, Nolan, and Alson, Peter, *The Man Behind the Shades: The Rise and Fall of Stuey 'The Kid' Ungar, Poker's Greatest Player* (Phoenix, London, 2006)

Fletcher, Iain, *The Rough Guide to Poker* (Rough Guides Ltd, London, 2005)

Hellmuth Jr, Phil, *Play Poker Like the Pros* (HarperCollins, New York, 2003)

Marcus, Richard, *The Great Casino Heist* (Constable & Robinson Ltd, London, 2005)

McEoy, Tom, *Tournament Poker* (Cardoza, New York, 1995)

McNally, Brian, *How to Play Poker and Win* (Macmillan, London, 2000)

Scarne, John, *Scarne's Guide to Modern Poker* (Pocket Books, New York, 1980)

Sklansky, David, *Hold 'em Poker* (Two Plus Two Publishing LLC, Henderson, 1978)

Steiner, Peter O., *Thursday-Night Poker: How to Understand, Enjoy – and Win* (Random House, New York, 1996)

Wilson, Des, *Swimming with the Devilfish…under the surface of professional poker* (Macmillan, London, 2006)

Wolpin, Stewart, *The Rules of Neighbourhood Poker According to Hoyle* (New Chapter Press, New York, 1990)

Yarnold, Stuart, *Online Poker in Easy Steps* (Computer Step, Southam, 2005)

Magazines & Periodicals

Inside Edge (Dennis Publishing, London)

Poker Player (Dennis Publishing, London)

WPT Poker: The Official World Poker Tour Magazine (Future Publishing, Bath)

Some Useful Poker Websites

www.askmen.com

www.blindbetpoker.com

www.doylesroom.com

www.homepoker.com

www.launchpoker.com

www.pagat.com

www.playwinningpoker.com

www.poker.com

www.pokernews.com

www.pokerplayernewspaper.com

www.pokersourceonline.com

www.pokertips.org

www.pokertop10.com

www.thehendonmob.com

www.usplayingcard.com

www.worldcasinodirectory.com

AUTHOR ACKNOWLEDGEMENTS

In order to bring this publication to fruition I have had to call upon the support of many people and I would like to take this opportunity to thank them personally for their help and advice. Firstly, I wish to recognize the hardworking contribution of the editorial team at Bridgewater Books, particularly Polita Caaveiro and Sarah Doughty, whose guidance has been of immense benefit. Also, I am indebted to Paul Turner at Broadcasting Dataservices Ltd for his support in helping me to find and manage the time needed to complete the project, and I thank him for his interest and encouragement during the months spent researching and writing the text. Thanks also to Adam, Chris, Warren, Roy, Maureen and Joasia for their help at a crucial time in the summer of 2006. Finally, I must also thank my wonderfully understanding partner, Gosia Pilak, for once again proving so patiently supportive while I spent vast quantities of time flirting with the demanding mistress that is the game of poker. Dziekuje bardzo, kochanie.

PICTURE CREDITS

The Publisher would like to thank the following for kindly supplying photographs for this book: **Akg images** 14 (br), 49 (tr); **Alamy** 57 (t, b) 204 (b); **Bridgewater Book company** 11 (b); **Corbis** 10 (cr, b), 12 (bl, br), 13 (t, cr), 14 (bl), 15 (tr), 16 (bl) 17 (tr) 18 (cl, b), 19 (cr, b), 20 (cr), 22 (bl), 23 (cl, b), 25 (tr), 27 (tl, tr), 36 (bl, br), 37 (bl), 38 (br), 39 (tl), 40 (bl), 44 (b), 48 (cl), 54 (bl, br), 55 (tl), 56 (bl) 58 (tr, bl). 61 (cr), 67 (tl, tr), 68 (br), 69 (bl), 82 (br), 83 (tl, cl), 90 (b), 91 (cr), 92, 97 (t), 103 (b), 105, 108, 109, 169 (bl), 182, 195 (bl), 203, 206, 216 (br), 229, 230 (b), 231 (t), 232 (br), 233 (t), 234 (bl), 235 (br), 240 (bl, br), 241 (tl), 244 (cr) 245 (cl); **Empics** 17 (bl), 29 (tr), 31 (tl), 33 (tl main), 34 (bl), 47 (tr), 80 (tr) 83 (tr), 84 (bl),147, 217, 246 (bl), 236 (tr), 242 (br); **Getty** 15 (tl), 22 (cr), 48 (br), 142, 219 (tl), 224, 247 (tl); 85 (bl, br); **Golden Nugget casino** 228 (bl), 231 (bl); **iStock photography** 35 (tr), 52, 59 (cr, b), 60 (bl, br), 64 (br), 65, 66, 69 (tc), 71 (br), 74, 80 (b), 93 (tl, br), 97 (b), 102 (bl, br), 116, 118, 121, 127, 138, 139, 170, 172, 175, 177, 185, 189, 229 (t), 242 (bl); **The Kobal collection** 40 (br), Warner Bros 41 (tr), United artists 41 (b), Warner Bros 42 (bl), Universal (41 br), Warner Bros 43 (t), Columbia/Persky-Bright/Reno 43 (cr), MGM/Filmways 44 (cr), Miramax/John Clifford 45 (cl), Miramax/ John Clifford 45 (b), MGM/Filmways 103 (tr), Warner Bros 184; Mary Evans picture library: 96 (t); **Photo library** 225 (cr), 233 (br); **Photos.com** 55 (tr), 56 (tr), 187; **Pokerimages.com** 16 (br), 20 (tl), 21 (t), 24, 25 (b), 26 (bl), 28 (bl, br), 30 (bl), 31 (tr), 32 (bl, br), 33 (tr, tcr), 34 (br), 35 (b), 37 (t, br), 46 (cr, bl), 47 (tl), 49 (tl), 64 (cl), 70 (cr, bl), 71 (tl), 76, 80 (cr), 81 (tl), 82 (bl), 84 (br), 85 (tr), 91 (br), 168, 169 (tr), 195 (tr), 197, 228 (t), 230 (tr), 232 (bl), 234, (br), 235 (bl), 236 (b), 237 (tl, tr, bl, br), 241 (tr), 243 (br), 244 (bl), 246 (cr), 248 (bl, br), 249 (tl, tr); **Top foto** 26 (tr), 29 (tl), 30 (cr), 38 (bl), 69 (cr), 87;

www.pokerroom.com 216, 217; www.pacificpoker.com 218; www.partypoker.com: 218; www.pokerstars.com: 218; www.deutschepokertour.com 219; www.pokerguide.jp 220; www.juegapokerya.com 220; www.redstarpoker.com 220; www.slo-poker.com 221; www.poker.org.il 221; www.poker.com.hr 222; www.ecardroom.cn 222; www.poker24.pl 223; www.spelapoker.se 223; www.poker.fr 223; www.allaussiepoker.com 225; www.megapoker.nl 225;

All other photos by **Andrew Perris** 1, 2, 7, 8-9, 50-51, 61 (tl), 68 (bl), 72-73, 94-95, 101, 107, 111, 117, 130-131, 133, 137, 141, 143, 145, 148, 150, 151, 152, 156, 158, 159, 160, 161, 162, 163, 179, 181, 192, 204 (t), 205, 207, 209, 211, 214-215, 226-227, 238-239, 253, 254 (tc, br), 255.

Every effort has been made to obtain permission to reproduce copyright material, but there may be cases where we have been unable to trace a copyright holder. The publisher will be happy to correct any omissions in future printings.

INDEX

ODDS TABLES

Having an understanding of the odds and probabilities in poker is essential for anyone wishing to be successful at the game. It will give you a definite advantage over your opponents and help you work out your strategy for the rest of the game. Use the odds tables given here to decide on your play. For a detailed analysis of odds and probabilities turn to pages 74 to 77 of this book.

TEXAS HOLD 'EM: Odds Against Receiving Specific Starting Hands

Pair of Aces	220 to 1
Pair of Aces or Kings	119 to 1
Pair of Tens or better	43 to 1
Any Pair	16 to 1
Ace King suited	331 to 1
Ace King offsuit	110 to 1
Any two suited cards	3.25 to 1
Any hand with a pair or an Ace	4 to 1

SEVEN-CARD STUD: Odds Against Receiving Specific Starting Hands

Three Aces	5,524 to 1
Three Queens or better	1, 841 to 1
Three Tens or better	1,104 to 1
Any three of a kind (Trips)	424 to 1
Pair of Aces	76 to 1
Pair of Queens or better	25 to 1
Pair of Tens or better	14 to 1
Three cards to a straight flush	85 to 1
Three cards to a flush	24 to 1
Three cards to a straight	5 to 1

DRAW POKER: Odds Against Improvement Following the Draw

Player Holds	Result	
One pair – draws three cards	Any improvement	5 to 2
	Two Pairs	5 to 1
	Three of a Kind (Trips)	8 to 1
	Full House	97 to 1
	Four of a Kind (Quads)	360 to 1
One pair plus a kicker – draws two cards	Any improvement	3 to 1
	Two Pairs	5 to
	Trips	12 to 1
	Full House	120 to 1
Two pairs – draws one card	Full House	11 to 1
Trips – draws two cards	Any improvement	9 to 1
	Full House	15 to 1
	Quads	23 to 1
Trips plus a kicker – draws one card	Any improvement	11 to 1
	Full House	15 to 1
	Quads	46 to 1
Open-ended straight draw – draws one card	Improvement to Straight	5 to 1
Inside straight draw – draws one card	Improvement to Straight	11 to 1
Four-card flush – draws one card	Improvement to Flush	4 to 1
Open-ended four-card straight flush – draws one card	Improvement to Straight Flush	23 to 1

TEXAS HOLD 'EM: On the Flop

Player holds	Result	
A Pair	Quads	407 to 1
	Full House	136 to 1
	Trips	7.5 to 1
Two unpaired cards	Full House	1087 to 1
	Trips	73 to 1
	Two Pairs (using both hole cards)	48 to 1
	Any Two Pairs	24 to 1
	Pair	2 to 1
Two suited cards	Flush completed	118 to 1
	Four-card Flush	7.5 to 1
	Three-card Flush	1.4 to 1